Fading Out Black and White

Fading Out Black and White

Racial Ambiguity in American Culture

Lisa Simone Kingstone

ROWMAN & LITTLEFIELD
INTERNATIONAL

Lanham • Boulder • New York • London

Published by Rowman & Littlefield International, Ltd.
Unit A, Whitacre Mews, 26-34 Stannary Street, London SE11 4AB
www.rowmaninternational.com

Rowman & Littlefield International, Ltd. is an affiliate of
Rowman & Littlefield
4501 Forbes Boulevard, Suite 200, Lanham, Maryland 20706, USA
With additional offices in Boulder, New York, Toronto (Canada), and Plymouth (UK)
www.rowman.com

British Library Cataloguing in Publication Data
A catalogue record for this book is available from the British Library

ISBN: HB 978-1-78660-254-1
   PB 978-1-78660-255-8

Library of Congress Cataloging-in-Publication Data

Names: Kingstone, Lisa Simone, author.
Title: Fading out black and white : racial ambiguity in American culture / Lisa Simone
   Kingstone.
Description: Lanham : Rowman & Littlefield International, [2018] | Includes
   bibliographical references and index.
Identifiers: LCCN 2018021751 (print) | LCCN 2018032779 (ebook)
   | ISBN 9781786602565 (Electronic) | ISBN 9781786602541 (cloth : alk. paper)
   | ISBN 9781786602558 (pbk. : alk. paper)
Subjects: LCSH: Blacks—Race identity—United States. | Whites—Race identity—
   United States. | Race awareness—United States. | Racism—United States.
Classification: LCC E185.625 (ebook) | LCC E185.625.K567 2018 (print) | DDC
   305.800973—dc23
LC record available at https://lccn.loc.gov/2018021751

∞™ The paper used in this publication meets the minimum requirements of American
National Standard for Information Sciences—Permanence of Paper for Printed Library
Materials, ANSI/NISO Z39.48-1992.

Printed in the United States of America

for the clove

and for my mother Lauraine

Contents

List of Figures

Acknowledgments

I had vital assistance from many in making this book and it is a pleasure to thank them here. Martina O'Sullivan at Palgrave Macmillan first discussed the idea with me, and Holly Tyler, Dymphna Evans, Melissa McClellan, and Natalie Linh Bolderston at Rowman & Littlefield helped guide me through my first book. I am indebted to the unstoppable Zoie Babakitis, who coordinated participants in focus groups and got all the paperwork done without a hitch. My co-facilitators Andrea Adomako and Linda Luu made participants feel at home and open to sharing. Allan Frei at Hunter College and Reverend Bertram Johnson and Daniel Conover at Riverside Church provided space for the focus groups and access to the communities. Reverend Michael Livingston, Reverend Bertram Johnson, and Reverend Lynn Harper at Riverside Church gave their gracious support. Richard Wilson advised on focus groups, helping me remember to be quiet and listen and let the group form its own dynamic. Being taped while you talk about race in a group isn't easy, yet the communities at Hunter, Riverside Church, and a few people from the surrounding neighborhoods shared their humor, tears, anger, and bafflement on this thing we call race. All that was murky and opaque became a little more clear with their help.

The Department of International Development at King's provided research funding and a chance to design a course and teach on this subject to both undergraduate and graduate students. King's Cultural Institute awarded an early grant, and Paul Goodwin brought to light our project, African Diaspora Artists in the 21st Century, where we explored the notion of "blackness" in a workshop with UK artists, curators, and academics. Celeste-Marie Bernier in her guest lecture "Representing Slavery" got me interested in the visual aspects of reading race in photography, and welcomed me into her workshop at Oxford. She has been a crucial mentor and friend. Gus

Casely-Hayford offered his stellar guidance on our grant application and countless conversations that helped me bring my ideas into sharper resolution. I am grateful to Dan Matlin for his provocative questions in our "Race" reading group at King's and his incisive notes on my introduction. Anita Foeman met with me to discuss her work on Ancestry DNA and family narratives and gave crucial suggestions on the focus group chapter. Kristal Brent Zook's important work on the black sitcom guided me as did her notes on the *Black-ish* chapter. George Lewis helped me fine-tune my chapter on Barack Obama. Debbie Garrett shared her knowledge of black dolls. Debbie Newman-Carrasco, Kenyatta Jones, Robert Best, Stacey Mcbride-Irby all granted vital interviews. Rachel Dolezal granted permission to use her art and opened up to me in interviews and emails.

Andrea Adomako gave stellar feedback and valuable perspective on the entire manuscript. The unbelievably efficient Shannon Keough helped prepare the manuscript and gain permissions for the illustrations. Fredrika Akander and Lara Kingstone hunted down articles and books in London's voluminous libraries. Students at King's in my course, Race, Privilege and Identity, shared the complex building of their own racial identities in their thoughtful essays. They bring the scope of the world into my classroom not only with the variety of countries they represent, but with the infinite ways they express their own mix of ethnic, religious, cultural, and racial identities.

For their support on anything and everything, I thank my parent coalition: Lauraine Jaeger and Herb Gardner, Peter and Ann Braunstein, Hadassa and Danny Kingstone, Walter Gold, and the memory of Mary Belle Douglass.

I thank my children, Ben and Lara, my own millennials, who are nudging the world toward change in their own work and communities. They show me what openness and adaptation look like.

I am grateful to my mother Lauraine for providing invaluable generous support during some of the challenges of the last few years. She truly believes every problem has a solution—nihilism has no place in her universe. Looking at race in the United States can at times seem bleak and hopeless, but her optimism dictates that change does happen, even if slowly.

Finally, I thank my husband Peter for suggesting to me that this could be a book and offering, as always, his laser sharp observations and gift of clarity. He took time in the last weeks of his sabbatical to read the entire manuscript. I am grateful to him for sharing his wisdom and his life with me. There is no better partner I could dream up, and this book would not have been possible without him.

Preface

When I, a white woman in my early twenties, announced to an older black woman that I wanted to specialize in African American literature for my graduate studies, she answered, "leave that to the black folks." I had great love and respect for her, and so instead I got my PhD in American Literature specializing in modernism, but I was still drawn to questions of race. I ended up teaching Southern Gothic, which really is a trauma narrative written mostly by whites used to discuss the horror and sometimes surreal quality of racialized life in the South. White identity is deeply dependent on black identity. As Baldwin wrote, "you cannot lynch me and keep me in ghettos without becoming something monstrous yourselves."[1] As Morrison shows in her book *Playing in the Dark*,[2] American identity is formed against a black other or shadow. This shadow, a creation of the white imagination, then haunted the people who created it.

Despite their inextricable link to blackness, white people studying race are often seen as exploitative. As a black man in one of my focus groups said, "black people are still experimental; they're like lab rats to white America."[3] He then cited many instances where whites got financial reward for writing about blacks when blacks themselves weren't taken as credible sources. But a white person studying race is threatening for other reasons too—it disrupts the boundaries of black and white. A white woman in one of my focus groups stated that when white people are interested in race and say, " 'We have race! We have baggage, we have a history. It's not just other people who have race!' it gets dismissed as white guilt." As she put it, "people seem to be saying 'Come back, come on back' as they tug you back to more mainstream whiteness.'"[4] I occasionally get the question from students, why would I want to teach about race when I'm white, as if race is the subject for black people, and all the other subjects are fair game for white people. Although I'll never truly understand what it feels like to be black, I do know what it feels like to live in a place where the burden of race hangs over most interactions.

I was born in 1963 and grew up in Berkeley, California. When I was old enough for school, I was part of the first group that went through busing from kindergarten through high school. This was an attempt to enforce integration, which threw together drastically different social groups (wealthy white people from the Berkeley hills and poor black people from the Berkeley flats) and resulted in chaos and violence. I couldn't *not* think about race.

When in June 2015 Rachel Dolezal, a perceived black woman, was outed as white by her white parents, I was shocked by the intensity of the public response. The rage, mockery, and rush to judgment by both blacks and whites were so intense. It reminded me of the discussions about black people and white people during the Black Power movement where there was a flip of the switch: white was good, black was bad. Now black was good, white was bad. Today, new kinds of messages are being included in the college class curriculum, ones that see race as constructed, created for the purpose of exploitation, rather than part of nature. Here was Dolezal treating race as a construction, disregarding the white she was born into, and stepping where she would into black. Yet when she dared to test these boundaries, blacks and whites held up the barricade of the color line once again. I wondered what changes had been made in how people think of these binaries today. Had we really moved forward in blurring these boundaries? The force of the response made me think perhaps not much.

To answer that question, I wanted to look at the changing cultural narratives around race. To get a cross-section of different kinds of representation, I chose the media and public response to Dolezal as well as to Barack Obama's election; the sitcom *Black-ish*; the new product of racially ambiguous dolls. What do our reactions and changing representations of black and white say about either our shifting perceptions or the firmness of racial categories? I also sought out the voices of a variety of people in my focus groups where I gathered black, white, and mixed-race people in New York City to answer the questions: When did you first become aware of race? What makes someone black? Can a white woman become a black one?

I am studying a paradigm I have been fed since birth for being raised in the state of California (home of the Black Panther party, The Third World Liberation Front,[5] but also the beating of Rodney King, the O. J. Simpson trial, and the Watts riots). And this state is part of a nation that was founded on race. I am trying to dismantle it for myself and separate the fabric of how it was built to better understand my country and my own identity. I am not speaking for anyone but myself or claiming to know the truth about these questions, but I am interested in how our cultural narratives are shifting over time, and I hope I can contribute to this vast conversation.

NOTES

1. Peck, Raoul, *I Am Not Your Negro.*
2. Morrison, Toni, *Playing in the Dark: Whiteness and the Literary Imagination.*
3. 2B Focus Group.
4. 2B Focus Group.
5. A group formed in 1968, the first to create black and ethnic studies in response to a Eurocentric curriculum—the inception of the idea to "decolonize" education.

Introduction

America's most crucial founding concept is not that we are all created equal, but rather that we are all *not* created equal. The notion that we are innately different races defined by biology and history is often called the black/white binary.[1] Inherent in this idea is that the blood and nature of black and white people are different; sometimes called biological essentialism, this belief holds that we are in opposition to each other in our natures. This defining concept was created to enable slavery to flourish, but was then reinforced in Jim Crow, a system of apartheid for black and white Americans in all aspects of daily life. This was in part made possible by refueling the idea of black inferiority through visual and verbal propaganda narratives (plays, literature, radio, film, and television). These stories showed that black people were inferior in intelligence, morality, beauty, and potential, and that their unjust treatment was justified and even noble. Part of our cultural myth is that we are a country known for being an exemplary democracy, one that welcomes in immigrants as made iconic in Emma Lazarus's poem "The New Colossus" inscribed on the Statue of Liberty: "Give me your struggling masses, yearning to be free."[2] Our pride in our Declaration of Independence that "all men are created equal" and have a right to "Life, Liberty and the pursuit of Happiness," and our constitution that gives equal protection under the law make many feel the country is exceptional. Freedom and equality is what many Americans still associate with America, and many have an optimism about living up to these ideals one day.

Many Americans' response to the paradox between our founding creed and our racial injustice had been denial and a reinforcing of the creed through patriotism. Today, we see the cracking of that shield of patriotism in political movements like #taketheknee where NFL player Colin Kaepernick refused to stand during the national anthem, which claims America to be "land of the

1

free and home of the brave." Kaepernick wouldn't acknowledge that myth when the country continues to oppress black people and people of color;[3] many team members in the NFL (both black and white) are following his lead; and other college and high school sports teams have followed.

It is these changes in binary thinking and Americans' awareness of its loosening hold on identity that I wish to address here. The title of this book, *Fading Out Black and White,* refers to how we are at a time where the concept of the black/white binary is less robust. This is possible because of a new generation that sees identity as fluid rather than fixed and self-determined rather than ascribed. The subtitle *Racial Ambiguity in American Culture* refers both to a growing percentage of hard to categorize people which has changed the set determination of black and white to a more pluralistic approach. However, it also points to a new ambiguity in our *narratives* about what makes someone black and what makes someone white. People are scrutinizing the notion of race and questioning their racial identity and authenticity themselves; they are less accepting to have it determined from the outside. People are aware of their own performances of race and ethnicity and less clear on who is now the arbiter of authenticity.

This book addresses the fact that we are at a tipping point in thinking about the racial binary for a complex intersection of reasons. Our demographic is changing and white is no longer the majority; we have an awareness of race as a social construction; we are conscious of the amount of destruction this racial binary has done through a deluge of new scholarship that clearly documents the structure that holds this binary in place; white people are becoming aware of their own privilege in the racial system through changes in core curriculum and scholarship;[4] DNA testing has debunked the notion of pure racial categories; and our understanding of gender is beginning to be seen as a continuum, not a binary of male and female, as trans people are finding some acceptance. This array of factors is coming together to chip away our founding notions of black and white and is helping us move to a place where we do not see identity strictly in terms of this racial power relationship. This book looks at the cutting edge of change in certain parts of the country to gain insight into how we are reacting to this time of destabilized black/white binary. It explores how moving past these racist ideologies, we unsettle the founding notions of American identity in race. Using sociology, cultural analysis, and literary analysis, I gauge how the new margins of race are manifested, recalibrated, and recalculated through the filter of culture. Racism is part of culture and culture is learned for the most part in media. I am particularly interested in how racial narratives are sustained and negotiated in places like television, political campaigns, and the decision making process in commodities like raced dolls. When the narrative changes, the rest follows. The death of some stories and the birth of others means that the culture is evolving.

Early theorists anticipated this moment in America where the numbers of mixed-race and nonwhite citizens would outnumber white ones. What wasn't predicted is how our thinking would change to allow us to see the racial story differently. No one could have imagined how the internet has created an information democracy; how DNA testing has shown us to be from one place, one family; how gender is being dismantled, letting us see an identity that is without reference to binaries. However, these forecasters differed in how they interpreted the nature of this moment; one group saw it as utopian and the other as dystopian. This chapter looks at these two groups, the naysayers and the yaysayers on mixed-race America, from early incarnations to how these voices are manifested today in groups such as the AltRight, Social Justice Warriors, and the Politically Correct. But first, I'll outline the factors allowing this shift to happen.

Our racial despotism has been particularly shaken because we are at a critical moment demographically where it is estimated that by 2044, nonwhite multiracial indeterminate faces will soon outnumber the white majority. The new Census Bureau now estimates that babies of color outnumber non-Hispanic white babies age one or younger. On July 1, 2015, the population of racial or ethnic minority babies was 50.2 percent.[5] With the birth of the multicultural movement in the 1980s and the census allowing multiple boxes to be checked for race in 2000, we are moving away from a system predicated on the one-drop rule (or the belief that any fraction of black ancestry makes you black) into a new phase that has created a borderland in between.[6] This change is partly due to the rise in interracial families, transracial adoptions, immigration, and multiracial children. Robert P. Jones begins his *The End of White Christian America* with an obituary for White Christian America (WCA) and then proceeds to show how this dominant group's reign has finally ended—the evidence is in things like gay marriage, Barack Obama's presidency, and the huge disaffiliation from white churches that used to be the main organizing institution in American life for white citizens in the majority. He shows this through the change in architecture (the declining amount of churches, but also the layout of the cityscape), the change in church-linked institutions (e.g., the Boy Scouts, the Masonic Lodge, restricted country clubs). He then uses his Public Religion Research Institute's[7] public opinion polls to decimate the idea that this group, WCA, is still in control.

This demographic change is also altering our belief systems and making us more flexible about demarcating race. Kristen Pauker[8] in her Intergroup Social Perception Lab looks at the malleability in how people see each other across context and time. She has found that as a result of a multiracial population, people become less rigid in ascribing identities to others. Her study on

Hawaii, a state with a quarter of its population identified as multiracial, finds that white people who move to Hawaii become more relaxed in their defining of racial category. The prevalence of multiracial people in the United States is having the same effect. The Pew Research Center estimated multiracials at 7 percent and predicts they will grow to 20 percent by 2050.[9] Although black and white were concepts invented by white people in power, now a new group sometimes called Generation Mix is determining identity for themselves.

In addition to our racial makeup changing, DNA testing has exposed the myth of racial purity. Professor Luigi Luca Cavelli-Sforza at Stanford tested thousands of people's cells to reconstruct through DNA the path of human evolution.[10] The results point to a common ancestry in Africa and also a similarity of 99.9 percent in all people's DNA, showing us that phenotypic traits that people associate with race make up only 1 percent of a person's DNA, but also that differences between people of a particular race are larger than between people of different races. New popular DNA testing kits such as 23andMe allow people to see the mix of ancestry (race) in themselves in detailed maps and charts. The idea of racial purity is debunked in a vial of spit. It also has shown that phenotypic traits don't always match DNA. There can be genetic markers that don't express and others that dominate, so it is not just what you inherit but how that inheritance manifests itself in facial and bodily features that could be identified as raced that again complicates the idea of race being visible.

Anita Foeman and Bessie Lawton[11] in their DNA discussion project show it's hard to hold on to racist narratives about others when you share similar DNA. In their classes, they have tested 450 people whom they interview about their racial identity before and after being tested. People are often surprised by their results, forcing them to adapt to their new narrative, which makes them see themselves and classmates in a new light as well. As she puts it, "we are all real relatives."[12]

Equally important for the change in the black/white binary in the last few decades was the debunking of the myth that race is biological or in the body. In 1998, the American Anthropological Association formally acknowledged "present-day inequalities between so-called 'racial' groups are not consequences of their biological inheritance but products of historical and contemporary social, economic, educational, and political circumstances."[13] These ideas were foregrounded by the work of W. E. B. Du Bois in his concept of double consciousness. In *The Souls of Black Folk* (1903), he describes the phenomenon that most black Americans felt a split identity between what they felt themselves to be and how they were framed by the white racist narrative. In *Racial Formation*, Howard Winant and Michael Omi break down and reveal the way racial narratives are performed. It is the constant building and rebuilding of race in the structure of our daily life that keeps racial tropes alive. As they put it:

> Racial projects are efforts to shape the ways in which human identities and social structures are racially signified, and the reciprocal ways that racial meaning becomes embedded in social structures. . . . Racial formation is thus a vast summation of signifying actions and social structures, past and present, that have combined and clashed in the creation of the enormous complex of relationships and identities that is labeled race.[14]

By calling race constructed, they are in no way dismissing the reality of systemic racism; they are simply showing how, rather than biologically determined, race is something constantly being built through our institutions and social structures and remains fluid rather than fixed.

The other large change is a new generation of millennials who have been raised in an environment where they were made aware of white privilege and systemic racism as no other group before them. Joe Feagin explains the connection of slavery to white wealth:

> Social science research is clear that white-black inequalities today are substantially the result of a majority of whites socially inheriting unjust enrichments (money, land, home equities, social capital, etc.) from numerous previous white generations—the majority of whom benefited from the racialized slavery system and/or the de jure (Jim Crow) and de facto overt racial oppression that followed slavery for nearly a century, indeed until the late 1960s.[15]

These millennials have come to understand white privilege through curricula that include courses with titles such as Race, Gender, and Class; Abolition of Whiteness; Equality, Diversity, and Inclusion. They have seen the infrastructure of systemic racism exposed in our legal, religious, medical, and education systems, documented by mainstream scholars such as Michelle Alexander in *The New Jim Crow: Mass Incarceration in the Age of Colorblindness*[16] or Ava DuVernay's documentary *13th* on how the Thirteenth Amendment is being used today to criminalize black youth and restrict their rights,[17] among countless others.[18] They begin to see what was invisible before, the automatic asset of whiteness in all factors of life, what Peggy McIntosh refers to as an invisible knapsack.[19] A woman in one of my focus groups stood out as having a deeper understanding of the distorted worldview she carried about race and her waking up to her white identity:

> I think whiteness is sort of just the air I breathed and so it felt like that's the baseline normal. So, no one had a conversation with me. I guess when you're in a dominant group no one has to have the conversation that you have to represent

or be something other than just who you are, which is wonderful. And, so I see it now as very damaging, just to grow up like that's the air you breathe and that's normal. And, coming in, as I think back through like what it means to be raised white, and I had these flashes of the Rodney King. That's a visual in my mind, seeing those tapes, and then how we interpreted it. My father was a police officer and it was interpreted completely on the side of the police. What you're really seeing . . . I can remember the kicking and the beating, those police officers had reasons and that's with being raised white.[20]

For many white people, along with this has come shame and an interest in disassociating with whiteness. In contrast to generations before them that yearned to check the white box on the census, these students look for reasons to mark Other. As Kenyatta Forbes explains, "being called a racist is the deepest wound for a white person in America, it cuts to the core, then you get associated with the history of America (the lynchings, Jim Crow, slavery). If you get called this thing, people of noncolor will do anything that is necessary not to be put in that box even to not identify as white."[21] Whiteness that was previously associated with beauty, intelligence, and general superiority has become negatively symbolized. Nell Irvin Painter describes this new view of whiteness as "on a toggle switch between 'bland nothingness' and 'racist hatred.'"[22]

This disintegration of the categories of black and white is in part because of new intellectual and social possibilities from widespread use of the internet. Millennials have been influenced by the web to expand and explore identities as well as expose themselves more to difference. These digital natives' exposure from early on to others makes them unique. Rochelle Newman-Carrasco talks about how, in their classrooms, they are exposed to friendships with diverse students, while at home on the web they are intersecting with a range of people that used to be homogeneous and allowed one to "stick with [their] own." This new technology has "smashed us up against each other." She sees the hashtag as a symbol of this intersection not only in its design of cross-hatching lines, but in its function as the new town square where you can instantly find a like-minded community online, broken down in terms of interest, not race. This is the great public global equalizer; we can no longer hold our ideologies precious because people can disagree immediately in tweets, hashtags, or online blogs. It's harder to self-protect by staying with people who are like us. This has created a freedom to invent, morph, and deepen identities.[23]

Our presence online has created what Dalton Conley calls a "network nation." Flexible identities are possible "that treat race as just one of a seemingly infinite number of possible self-identifications." As one millennial put it, "We came along in a generation that didn't have to follow that path of race."[24] We connect to people without seeing them (and can do that in a variety of different identities) and only later (if at all) find out what they "are." DNA testing, increased travel, and the resurgence of finding one's culture is a trend away from the reign of whiteness. It shows a desire to break that down, to remember you are from somewhere, reminding us that the category of whiteness was once a vast range of ethnicities.

Millennials grew up with exposure to the concept of gender as a construct and have seen the rise in the acceptance of trans people. Because trans people are self-identified, it has modeled the idea of one's internal identity not always matching what can be seen. They have a new belief in their right to self-determine or create new categories if the old ones don't match. This is evidenced in the LGBTQIA communities' adding of letters to embrace new kinds of sexuality and gender and in words like cisgender[25] that shift the dominant perspective. Since 1997, census takers are reminded on the form that these answers about race are "self-determined."[26] As satirized in a *Black-ish* episode, sometimes the specificity of this new generation in encompassing all of themselves can feel exhausting: "I'm Stacy, a Tri-racial, gender fluid, panoramic demisexual and my pronoun is they,"[27] says a college tour guide.

The many factors reviewed here set the stage for taking down the binary. In addition, our denial of the inherent paradox of our claim to equality and our racial caste system is harder to maintain. In the past, one could turn on the TV to get programs that promoted an idealized version of America that mostly erased our racial hierarchy by eliminating nonwhites from the landscape. But the information age has changed that. The internet allows for a quick dispensation of information and a spate of alternative voices. Injustices have also been caught on cell phone videos by ordinary citizens, such as in the footage of the shooting of Philando Castile[28] where all Americans could witness a policeman murdering an innocent man while his wife and son sat next to him.[29] Secrets can't be kept for long; there is no longer one media news outlet controlled by the white elite, but a splintering of points of view and voices that can be heard through Twitter, blogs, YouTube videos, podcasts, and Instagram.

Part of being American is holding these two diverging ideas in one's psyche. This has been called "The American Dilemma." In 1944, Gunner Myrdal explained Americans' unique quandary of having their values state one thing and their actions another. He describes this paradox as an:

> ever-raging conflict between, on the one hand, the valuations preserved on the general plane which we call the "American creed," where the American thinks, talks, and acts under the influence of high national and Christian precepts and, on the other hand, the valuations on the specific planes of individual and group living, where personal and local interests; economics, social, and sexual

jealousies; consideration of community prestige and conformity; group prejudice against particular personas or types of people; and all sorts of miscellan-
eous wants, impulses and habits dominate his outlook.[30]

In some ways, this can be seen as the public and private American. The vision
of democracy and fairness is in the rhetoric of American politics and in the
practice of patriotism in its Pledge of Allegiance in its classrooms and the
National Anthem on football fields, but then, privately, there are deeply held
beliefs about racial superiority and inferiority.

The contradiction inherent in American life has created a deep sense of
fracture and guilt for many white Americans who respond with deep denial.
This was particularly clear when I went for a tour of a Southern plantation
outside of New Orleans. After being shown the sitting room in the "big
house" and hearing a lecture on the variety of parlor games people played,
the menu at the debutante parties, and the Southern Belle's typical wardrobe,
I was then given a Mint Julep to sip and the tour seemed to end. "What about
the slaves," I asked our tour guide. "Oh," she answered "that's a separate
tour." This division between genteel Southern life and the brutal sadism of
slavery is represented in the genre of literature called Southern Gothic,[31]
which illuminates the contradictions in the American myth and reality.
This literature, mostly written by white Southerners, explores the psychosis
needed to adapt to America's racial caste system. This is illustrated in a short
story "A Good Man Is Hard to Find," by Flannery O'Connor, where a serial
killer (who has escaped from prison) takes the time to apologize for his state
of undress with his soon to be victims.

" 'I'm sorry I don't have on a shirt before you ladies,' he said, hunching his
shoulders slightly. 'We buried our clothes that we had on when we escaped
and we're just making do until we can get better. We borrowed these from
some folks we met,' he explained. 'That's perfectly alright,' the grandmother
said. 'Maybe Bailey has an extra shirt in his suitcase.' "[32] Both of them know
perfectly well, he will be shooting every member of the family in the head
and leaving them to die. Here the surface manners and gentility are clung to
even when a gruesome crime is about to be committed.

Because of this denial of racism and our racial culture, many Americans
have an unconscious bias. As much as they claim to have no issues with race,
many progressive white Americans carry the vestiges of racial messages
unawares. Dovidio and Gaertner in their work on aversive racism speak
about the orientation that many white people have toward black people,
which they describe as "characterized by inconsistencies and ambivalence"
that they admit "has existed virtually from the beginning." They quote
Joel Kovel, whose work distinguishes between dominative and aversive
racism: "dominative racism is the 'old fashioned' blatant form while aversive

racists sympathize with victims of past injustice, support the principle of racial equality, and read themselves as nonprejudiced, but that the same time, possess negative feelings and beliefs about blacks, which may be unconscious."[33] However, the consequences of aversive racism are "as significant and pernicious as those of the traditional, overt form." Aversive racists are a significant portion of well-educated liberal white Americans. Sometimes called "unconscious bias," these attitudes that persist can explain partly why inequalities between black and white people are changing so slowly. So along with the many reasons the binary is losing its foothold, we also have a history of denial and an unconscious bias[34] that still plays out in all arenas of power, which complicates the story of our progress.

Although no one could have anticipated the long list of ways the binary is being broken down, everyone could imagine the mixing of races. This moment in time when racial minorities would become the majority was imagined by our forebears in two distinct ways: it would create a utopian heaven or a dystopian nightmare. Reviewing this early thinking of the two groups helps us understand the incarnations of these two groups today.

As early as 1782, the writer Crèvecoeur asked in his *Letters from an American Farmer*:

> What then is the American, this new man? He is either a European, or the descendant of a European, hence that strange mixture of blood, which you will find in no other country. I could point out to you a family whose grandfather was an Englishman, whose wife was Dutch, whose son married a French woman, and whose present four sons have now four wives of different nations. . . . Here individuals of all nations are melted into a new race of men, whose labors and posterity will one day cause changes in the world.[35]

Crèvecoeur saw this blending as a kind of transcendence. He was the first to use the metaphor of a melting pot and its product; through mixing, blending, melting of nations and races, there would emerge one new individual called an American, that new and superior citizen made of disparate blends from around the world. Almost a century later in 1869, Frederick Douglass spoke of this amalgamation:

> There is no division of races. God Almighty made but one race. I adopt the theory that in time the varieties of races will be blended into one. Let us look back when the black and the white people were distinct in this country. In two hundred and fifty years there has grown up a million of intermediate. And this will continue. You may say that Frederick Douglass considers himself a member of the one race which exists.[36]

Douglass, an ex-slave and abolitionist, saw this as a way out of the toxicity of race and placed himself in that new "one race." The idea that the American was something special being forged in God's hands through this blending process called Americanization was popularized in 1908 in Israel Zangwill's play *The Melting Pot.* Zangwill wrote: "America is God's Crucible, the great Melting-Pot where all the races of Europe are melting and reforming . . . Germans and Frenchmen, Irishmen and Englishmen, Jews and Russians— into the Crucible with you all! God is making the American."[37]

The protagonist David leaves no secret as to what these new beings will do, nothing short of creating heaven on earth. He paints the picture for his love, Vera, "Here shall they all unite to build the Republic of Man and the Kingdom of God. Ah, Vera, what is the glory of Rome and Jerusalem where all nations and races come to worship and look back, compared with the glory of America, where all races and nations come to labour and look forward!"[38] God's alchemy was creating this different breed of human that would stand for something new. Likewise, Richard von Coudenhove-Kalergi in his 1925 *Practical Idealism* predicted, "The man of the future will be of mixed race. Today's races and classes will gradually disappear owing to the vanishing of space, time and prejudice."[39] He explained that this new race will replace the "diversity of peoples" with a "diversity of individuals," language that is being used today by millennials. For example, when asked what race they are, a popular answer is "the human race."

In 1964 Milton Myron Gordon moved the idea from literature and philosophy to sociology where his study spells out the Seven Stages of assimilation.[40]

1. Acculturation—newcomers adopt language, dress, and daily customs of the host society (including values and norms).
2. Structural assimilation—large-scale entrance of minorities into cliques, clubs, and institutions in the host society.
3. Marital assimilation—widespread intermarriage.
4. Identification assimilation—the minority feels bonded to the dominant culture.
5. Attitude reception assimilation—refers to the absence of prejudice.
6. Behavior reception assimilation—refers to the absence of discrimination.
7. Civic assimilation—occurs when there is an absence of values and power struggles.

This utopian civilization is a place where "power struggles" have disappeared. These power struggles aren't the only thing to disappear; anger about past wrongs or any discussion of reparations has also dissolved. Robert E. Park, founder of the acclaimed Chicago School, followed up this work with his "race relations cycle," which consisted of the stages of Contact, Competition, Accommodation, and finally Assimilation. Race, like all other differences, would for all intents and purposes, disappear. These theorists and sociologists agreed that blending was a positive thing, difference would be discarded, and the new culture would be free of the hegemonic rule of whiteness as well as the deep scars of our racialized past.

The current incarnations of these utopian idealists are seen in those who talk about a "postracial" society, call themselves "colorblind," or use expressions like "I don't see race." White people who believe we are postracial also want redemption and a free pass from racial trauma. It is understandable that, like their predecessors, they want the racial wrongs of the past and present to no longer implicate them. Although the vision of this new mixed generation as a solution was a soothing thought for many, running parallel, there have always been fears and hostilities to the ideas of mixing.

Early theorists connected the idea of blending or miscegenation with reverse Darwinism or deevolution. This was reflected in early antimiscegenation[41] laws and the system of Jim Crow. Instead of ascending toward higher beings, we would devolve toward animals, it was claimed. Madison Grant was a eugenicist who believed in controlling the mating of human populations through sterilization of some and intentional breeding of others to create one superior white race. He fought to restrict immigration, and in his 1916 book *The Passing of the Great Race*, he argued for quarantining of undesirable races to avoid their overtaking the superior "nordic" (Aryan) race. He describes the typical mixed-race person whose different bloods are literally battling inside of him:

> It is scarcely necessary to cite the universal distrust, often contempt, that the half-breed between two sharply contrasted races inspires the world over. Belonging physically and spiritually to the lower race, but aspiring to recognition as one of the higher race, the unfortunate mongrel, in addition to a disharmonic physique, often inherits from one parent an unstable brain which is stimulated and at times over excited by flashes of brilliancy from the other. The result is a total lack of continuity of purpose, an intermittent intellect goaded into spasmodic outbursts of energy.[42]

The mixed blood of the mongrel causes chaos; he is like the equivalent of a dog chasing his tail. In 1920, Lothrop Stoddard, a Klansman warned of the apocalypse of racial mixing in his *The Rising Tide of Color Against White World-Supremacy*. His argument is that the black has no culture of his own so will assimilate easily and take over unlike the stubborn Asiatics:

> Now, what will be the attitude of these augmenting black masses toward white political dominion? . . . To begin with, the black peoples have no historic pasts.

Never having evolved civilizations of their own, they are practically devoid of that accumulated mass of beliefs, thoughts, and experiences which render Asiatics so impenetrable and so hostile to white influences. The negro, on the contrary, has contributed virtually nothing. Left to himself, he remained a savage. . . . This lack of constructive originality, however, renders the negro extremely susceptible to external influences.The negro, having no past, welcomes novelty and tacitly admits that others are his masters.[43]

Quickly dispensing with the great kingdoms of Africa, Stoddard worries that the cultural emptiness of black people will make them readily take on white identity and interlope into this precious realm.

This terror of the masses interbreeding and then dominating is a fear we see rising today. Many people on the right see the previous two terms of President Obama and the changing faces in positions of power as signs of the apocalypse. Emboldened by the election of a white racist president who may not wear a white hood, but feels the same unearned sense of God-given superiority, privilege, and entitlement,[44] this group has become more vocal. President Donald Trump's characterizing black people in derogatory ways and also implying they don't belong here connect him clearly to both Stoddard and Grant. He is reported as having said, "Laziness is a trait in blacks" and "Black guys counting my money! I hate it."[45] But this is combined also with his suspicion of black people as foreign and thus un-American, clearly demonstrated in his birther movement where he challenged President Obama to prove that he was American by showing his birth certificate.

Trump's belief in white supremacy can be heard in his slogan "Make America Great Again" or in ideas like building a wall to keep out Mexicans, or having a Muslim ban at airports. This nostalgic belief in a past America illustrated by popular artist Norman Rockwell was a fantasy enabled by segregation and Jim Crow. This was blasted into living rooms in shows like *Leave It to Beaver* and movies like *Mrs. Miniver* that showed an America devoid of people of color except as devoted domestics. Many white Americans are shocked by Trump's arrogance and freedom to express misogyny, Islamophobia, anti-Semitism, and racist venom, but a good majority of black Americans are not surprised because they have been on the receiving end of these thoughts and words all along. When white supremacists march through Charlottesville chanting, "Jews shall not replace us," and Nazis hold rallies in New York City, this is not a sign of something new, but simply a continuation of a set of beliefs that were always there. But these right extremists aren't the only ones helping secure the binary in place and carrying forth the messages of mixing as dystopia.

Extremists on the left, sometimes calling themselves Social Justice Warriors, are also showing signs of fear. They use their involvement in antiracism or antisexism movements to entrench the binary further. They are part of a new "callout culture" that throws labels of cultural appropriation very freely and police who is allowed to speak for a group, further defining groups and keeping them separate. They promote victim culture and seem to be policing racial boundaries in their own way. When Social Justice Warriors claim no one can write from the perspective of a Native American except a Native American, they are pointing to old views of essentialism at the same time that they are claiming to be liberating these groups. When white artist Dana Schutz depicted the lynched/mutilated body of Emmett Till, there were protests for it to be removed, even destroyed, calling it cultural appropriation. When an artist is being controlled in her subject matter because she is not of the same race as her subject, we are further entrenching notions of essentialism.[46]

There is another group today that doesn't fall into these two strands of thought about racial mixing as utopian and dystopian visions of America. These people see the binary is changing because the nature of how we *think* is changing. There is evidence of this change all around us: Rachel Dolezal's belief she can change races, Obama's ability to "switch" races, black sitcoms laying bare the performance of blackness, new racially ambiguous dolls that are cutting into the market and toppling the reign of the white doll. This change makes some hopeful, but it is greeted by fear in others (both on the right and on the left), which makes them hold fast to the color line. These anxious groups that cling to the binary represent the death rattle of black and white thinking about race. But new directors, producers, academics, actors, manufacturers, students, and citizens are leading us beyond the binary toward real change.

CHAPTER OVERVIEW

Chapter 1. Tracing Race: A Tour of the Racial Binary

To foreground our discussion in how the binary is changing, this section will review the construction of the binary from its inception in the seventeenth century to the present. Blackness and whiteness were defined by science, religion, politics, and culture. It began in pseudoscientific readings of skull shape and measurement to equate blacks with monkeys. Other bodily markers were interpreted in ways that served the notion of inferiority or exoticism (genitalia, hair, fingernails). Narratives in popular culture like Jefferson's *Notes on the State of Virginia*, the film *Birth of a Nation*, and Harriet Beecher Stowe's *Uncle Tom's Cabin* helped bolster these ideas. In addition, carefully orchestrated human zoos presented "simulations" of life in Africa that helped entrench the idea of savagery. This biological essentialism and scientific "proof" later gave way to religious and political justifications for racial segregation. The Civil Rights Movement made enormous changes in de jure racism, but created an experiential essentialism (or the belief that all black people were united in their experience of blackness) that in some ways made black equal victimhood and pathology. These stories changed with groups like Black Power and the Black Panthers, which gave alternate narratives of black as beautiful, exotic, and soulful. However, even those movements that claimed to "uplift" often had ways that kept the binary in place. Today, the emphasis seems to be on acknowledging the variousness of black life in ideas like postblack that explores meaning beyond the restrictive definitions of blackness.

Chapter 2. The Trial of Rachel Dolezal: The First Transracial

Looking at the case study of Rachel Dolezal will lay bare her own racial construction, but also evaluate the media response as entrenched in essentialist notions. In 2015, Dolezal, a "black" NAACP president, was outed as white, which set off a media attack that flourished for a full week on TV and social media. The remorseful apology never came and Dolezal was ousted from her job as lecturer in Africana Studies, her work for the NAACP, and her community. Her choosing her race is proof of a new way of seeing racial identity in our times. Dolezal grew up in a generation who were exposed to the revelations about race that were made possible by genetic testing and also the work of sociologists like Winant and Omi. Having taught in an Africana Studies department, she intellectually understood the flimsy construction of race. But along with these deeper understandings about race and biology, her personal experience added to her concept of fluidity. She had experienced interracial families (she married a black man), multiracial children (she has had two sons with black fathers), and transracial adoption (her white parents adopted four black children). With this background coming together with this moment in time, it is no surprise that Dolezal is in effect testing the limits of our acceptance of race as socially constructed. However, looking closely at the media and public's response to Dolezal and the criteria for determining her whiteness shines a light on our collective anxiety about dissolving racial categories and giving up notions of essentialism.

Chapter 3: Obama as Racial Rorschach: The First *Blank* President

Former president Barack Obama also fomented discussions about race and illuminated how Americans are thinking about racial category. Although it looked transformative on the surface, people's interpretations of Obama revealed just how stubborn their hold was on the black/white binary. Although many accepted Obama as their president, their complex justifications of his "unique" race revealed that the deep roots of racial category are still with us. "Although many see Obama as the first Black president, he is really the first *blank* president" as people filled in the blank of his race according to their own racial identity. In fact, many racial groups found ways to claim Obama as their own. He encouraged this by codeswitching easily between black and white tropes. He also felt free to express all sides of himself without apology; having come from Hawaii where people were all "mixes," he was used to thinking in a nonbinary way. However, after moving to the United States, his time in college made him feel he had to choose his blackness as he explains in his autobiography *Dreams from My Father*. Obama's own story, like Dolezal's, shows the emergent racial fluidity in America as well as the backlash against it.

Chapter 4: Casting Color: Black Barbie and the Black Doll as Racial Barometer

In the doll industry, blackness was transcribed into plastic toys in mostly racist objects like Golliwogs and Aunt Jemima dolls, which let children practice racialized ways of thinking. This soon changed to tokenized or fetishized versions of blackness. By contrast, white dolls expressed the privilege and perceived beauty of whiteness. However, things shifted in the 1980s when multiculturalism became an industry. Now corporations that produce dolls have to add ethnically ambiguous dolls or they can't make a profit. This chapter will review attitudes about essentialism by following the trajectory of the most popular doll in America. Barbie's inception as a privileged blond Christian to the latest Fashionistas that are raceless and nameless parallels the changes in American attitudes about race. Mattel's blundering attempts to integrate and represent blackness show how complex the cultural messages are that children are getting about race from the social world around them. The multiracial and ethnic doll business (Barbie, Bratz, and American Girl Dolls) is a manifestation of corporate America's responsiveness to changing ideas about racial category. These new dolls are a sign of progress, but it is the way these children see and play with the dolls that is the site of real transformation.

Chapter 5: Really Black: *Black-ish* and the Black Sitcom as Racial Barometer

The animated equivalent of the black doll, the black family sitcom, is another crucial cultural site of reorientation. Looking at the path of the black sitcom from comedies inspired by nineteenth-century minstrel shows, followed by radio, and finally television; this chapter traces how blackness was being defined. Television began with early stereotyping of black families in shows from the fifties, sixties, and seventies, but began changing in the 1980s when black directors began running their own shows and exploring their own issues and identities rather than reproducing white racist narratives. An analysis of the current hit *Black-ish*, whose subject is the very performance of blackness, will reveal some aspects of racial thinking today. This novel program has as its subject the slipperiness of racial category and exposes to a white audience what black people have always known—that blackness is partly performance. *Black-ish* addresses the complexity of life for some black people who have made it past financial and daily racial struggles only to find a different set of issues arriving with their success, such as a fear of losing their blackness when integrated into white suburbia. Self-scrutiny, awkwardness, confusion, and obsession all result from the need to determine how black one is. Both black and white people monitor the hair, music, language, proximity to poverty, activism, and familiarity with street culture of black people. This restricted definition is mocked in *Black-ish*. But *Black-ish* also explores the fear white people have of being associated with racism and the contortions they will go through to avoid being labeled as such.

Chapter 6: Talking About Race: Black, White, and Mixed-Race Focus Groups

This chapter reviews trends in focus groups conducted in New York City in which people's views about racial boundaries were elicited using Dolezal as a catalyst for discussion. These groups of black, white, and mixed-race people are seeing these boundaries today often through the lens of their own racial trauma. These discussions provide a nuanced and deeper understanding of the way black and white Americans defend firm boundaries even among people who are "most likely" to be accepting of fluidity. These groups illuminate the extent to which Americans are anxious about where the country is headed in terms of multiracial identity. These groups recognize intellectually that race is performed rather than biological, but they also reveal ideas that point toward more fixed racial categories. The white groups in particular were full of careful language and a fear of being associated with racism, but showed assumptions about black people in line with Dovidio's theory of aversive racism. The black group, partly as a result of their constant awareness of racism and the overall mistrust of white people, saw Dolezal in a long line of white people taking advantage. They revealed attitudes of experiential essentialism in their feeling that the black experience is one that no white person could have. Finally, their territorialism around the black community was a major reason for resisting her "transracialism."

TERMINOLOGY

For the purpose of this book, I am using the word race to refer mainly to the black/white binary. Because of slavery, the one-drop rule, and the country's history of Jim Crow apartheid, black is a term that meshes culture, race, ethnicity, and nationality. Black and (its conjoined twin) white are a particularly fertile place to assess these questions of identity. Although there are many other "races" for whom these changes are also taking place (Jews, Latinos, Asians, Native Americans, Arabs), I am focusing on blacks as these other groups weren't central to American identity, although they played key roles at different times. Whiteness came to include Jews, and some Latinos, Asians, and Native Americans were considered closer to white than to black. However, black people were never read as white. Also unlike Jews, Asians, Latinos, Arabs, and Native Americans, many black people who are descended from slaves did not have access to their ancestral culture, so black culture became something unique and separate in America.[47] While these other groups could go back and forth and reinvigorate their traditions, black Americans were cut off from their ability to strengthen that tie, so their American identity was different. I have chosen the term black instead of African American, Afro-American, or Black (in caps) because I am emphasizing the binary of black and white. They are not capitalized because they are not proper nouns or ethnicities, but shifting signifiers. These race myths created each other and are inextricable.

I have chosen to use the word N*gger instead of the N-word out of respect for the devastating history this word holds.[48] Using the term "the N-word" sanitizes it of its toxicity, which I want to emphasize. However, I am not spelling it out completely out of respect for those who have been on the receiving end of this word and its damaging effects. We can try and change the word (as was infamously done in a version of *Huck Finn* that changed N*gger to Slave), but that choice is a dangerous one as it defangs the word and revises history. The word is a microcosm of the historic relationship between black and white Americans.

NOTES

1. Hegel's Master/Slave dialectic (sometimes called Lordship/Bondman) in his *Phenomenology of Spirit* (1807) is the antecedent of this racialized hierarchy. In it, he talks about the interdependence of each to the other. The notion of the Lord (white) depends on the notion of the Bondman (black) to exist and vice versa. Both are incomplete without the other and neither can become fully recognized or fully conscious in this relationship because one has been made into an object (or thing). Without the dignity of full humanity, the thing doesn't allow the self of his master to be recognized and thus conscious.

2. Lazarus, Emma, "The New Colossus."

3. Wyche, Steve, "Colin Kaepernick Explains Why He Sat During National Anthem."

4. For a discussion of how white privilege creates racialized hierarchies in public policy and private identities, see George Lipsitz's *The Possessive Investment in Whiteness: How White People Profit from Identity Politics.*

5. Cohn, D'Vera, "It's Official: Minority Babies Are the Majority Among the Nation's Infants, but Only Just."

6. For a discussion of mixed "race" nonbinary identity, see Gloria Anzaldúa's *Borderlands/La Frontera: The New Mestiza*, which explores cultural marginalization around both ethnic and gender identity. Here a border is not only a divide, but a psychic, social, and cultural landscape we create.

7. Jones, Robert P., *The End of White Christian America.*

8. Pauker, Kristen, "Intergroup Social Perception Lab."

9. Campbell, Alexia Fernández, "Census Was Wrong: 7 Percent of Americans Are Multiracial, Not 2 Percent."

10. Leslie, Mitchell, "The History of Everyone and Everything."

11. TEDx Talks, *Using Ancestry DNA to Explore Our Humanness: Anita Foeman at TEDxWestChester.*

12. *Using Ancestry DNA to Explore Our Humanness.*

13. American Anthropological Association, "AAA Statement on Race."

14. Winant, Howard and Michael Omi, *Racial Formation in the United Sates*, 13.

15. Yancy, George, and Joe Feagin, "American Racism in the 'White Frame.'"

16. This has become a bestseller.

17. This was nominated for an Oscar in 2017.

18. Hobbs, Jeff, *The Short and Tragic Life of Robert Peace*; Coates, Ta-Nehisi, *Between the World and Me*; Rankine, Claudia, *Citizen*; Blackmon, Douglas, *Slavery by Any Other Name*; Tatum, Beverly Daniel, *Why Are All the Black Kids Sitting Together in the Cafeteria*; Anderson, Carol, *White Rage*; Kendi, Ibram X., *Stamped from the Beginning.*

19. McIntosh, Peggy, "White Privilege: Unpacking the Invisible Knapsack."

20. Focus Group 2B.

21. Forbes, Kenyatta, interview.

22. Painter, Nell Irvin, "What Is Whiteness?"

23. This is not to say that the web has become a racial utopia. See Daniels, Jessie, "Race and Racism in Internet Studies: A Review and Critique"; Newman-Carrasco, Rochelle, interview.

24. Hsu, Hua, "The End of White America?"

25. A person whose sense of personal identity and gender corresponds with their birth sex.

26. Although it is tempting to see the census as a neutral body, Melissa Nobles reminds "categorizing race is as much a political act as it is an enumerative one," Nobles, *Shades of Citizenship*, 1.

27. Griffiths, James, "Liberal Arts."

28. ABC News, *Philando Castile Shooting Livestream Video*.

29. Although the officer was not indicted, movements like Black Lives Matter are calling attention to these injustices with their protests.

30. Myrdal, Gunnar, *An American Dilemma*, x.

31. See Crow, Charles L., *History of the Gothic: American Gothic*; and Lloyd-Smith, Alan, *American Gothic Fiction: An Introduction*.

32. O'Connor, Flannery, *A Good Man Is Hard to Find and Other Stories*.

33. Dovidio, John F., and Samuel L. Gaertner, "Aversive Racism," 3.

34. See Goff, Phillip Atiba, et al., "Not Yet Human: Implicit Knowledge, Historical Dehumanization, and Contemporary Consequences," for a discussion of the deeply entrenched association of blackness to primates.

35. De Crèvecoeur, *Letters from an American Farmer*, 46–47.

36. Douglass, Frederick, "Mr. Douglass Interviewed."

37. Zangwill, Israel, *The Melting Pot Drama in Four Acts*, 33.

38. Zangwill, *The Melting Pot*, 185.

39. von Coudenhove-Kalergi, Richard, *Practical Idealism*, 20.

40. Gordon, Milton M. *Assimilation in American Life: The Role of Race, Religion and National Origins.*

41. Miscegenation is defined as the interbreeding of people who are considered different races.

42. Grant, Madison, *The Passing of the Great Race*, xxix.

43. Stoddard, Lothrop, *The Rising Tide of Color Against White World-Supremacy*.

44. Coates, "Donald Trump Is the First White President."

45. Nittle, Nadra Kareem, "Donald Trump Has Long History of Racist Remarks and Behavior."

46. Kennedy, Randy, "White Artist's Painting of Emmett Till at Whitney Biennial Draws Protests."

47. Although this is changing with the influx of wealthy educated Africans immigrating to America.

48. For a fuller discussion, see Kennedy, *Nigger: The Strange Career of a Troublesome Word*.

Chapter 1

Tracing Race

A Tour of the Racial Binary

Before looking at our cultural case studies, it is useful to give an overhaul of binary thinking in order to understand the changes that are taking place today. Understanding how these myths were built, sustained, policed, and defied is the story of American identity. Today's removal of Confederate statues and Confederate flags is part of our changing of the narrative. A hero is now taken as a villain; a flag becomes understood as a racial slur. I look here at the movements and philosophies that built and reinforced the binary.

The black/white binary in the United States is an edifice built over five hundred years and won't be dismantled easily. The idea that there are biologically different human "races" that we can label by physical type and also connect to superior and inferior traits such as intelligence, morality, physical prowess, and work ethic is an idea that was crucial to the building of American identity. Sometimes called biological essentialism, the conversion of a vast array of people from the continent of Africa with rich and distinct tribal cultures were reduced to one thing: an object called a N*gger. This distortion of a human with a distinct language, identity, and culture to a piece of cargo is made clear in figure 1.1 of a diagram of the *Brookes* slave ship.

Here the cold practicality of storing live humans (who all look identical to each other and are pictured with no distinguishing characteristics) is seen in a similar way to canned goods, stored for maximum profit. In fact, at first glance, you don't realize they are people; they are simply property to be exchanged. Once this creation of the black sprung out of the slave ship, it needed defending through propaganda, stories, songs, biblical proof, and pseudoscience.

In the early days of the founding, the notion of blackness and whiteness was deeply entrenched by the aftermath of Bacon's Rebellion in 1676, in which enslaved Africans, Native Americans, and white indentured servants

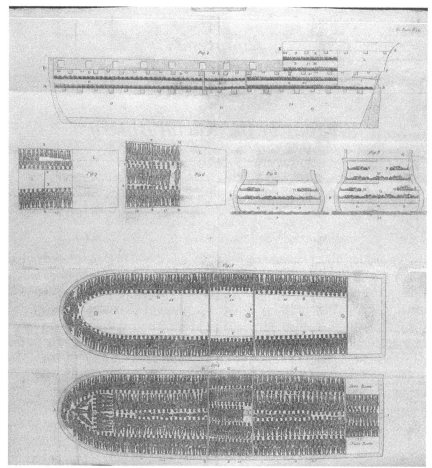

Figure 1.1 "Diagram of the *Brookes* Slave Ship" (1788), which depicts the ship loaded to its full capacity of 454 people. The diagram is a practical guide on how to efficiently store cargo.
Source: The British Library Board (shelfmark: 522.f.23, page 112). Published in 1787 by James Phillips, George Yard, Lombard Street, London (http://www.bl.uk/learning/citizenship/campaign/myh/photographs/gallery2/image2/brookesship.html).

bonded together to protest the current governor of the colony; their uniting successfully into a political force left the English nervous about the potential of this new group. If these dispossessed groups formed an alliance, they would seize control—after all, many of them had reason to be dissatisfied with their status and were hostile toward the elites. A divide and conquer strategy was created and made into law with the Virginia slave codes of 1705.

Before that, people were referred to by their country of origin, their free or slave status, or by their Christian or "heathen" status. Theodore Allen in his *The Invention of the White Race* argues that the "white race" category was invented as a means of social control.[1] From that point on, white indentured servants were encouraged to identify with the elites as fellow white people and not with blacks or Native Americans. Blackness became equated with slavery, contamination, and inferiority; and whiteness with freedom, privilege, and superiority. These codes forbid blacks and slaves from bearing arms, congregating in large numbers, exacted harsh punishments if they assaulted Christians or attempted escape, and black servants were made slaves for life. Later came antimiscegenation laws, forbidding blacks from marrying or having sex with whites. Blackness became a kind of contamination and the one-drop rule assured whites that they would always be separate even from those who were ambiguous phenotypically. Even in states where this was not translated into law, the belief that the mixing of races was unnatural became widespread. Any African ancestry made you black, so free men from Africa were suddenly pulled into the vortex of that chasm of blackness too. The rule of hypodescent ensured that any child born to a white parent and a black parent was automatically black—useful for slave owners to increase their property. The child always followed the condition of the mother, so this legislation was key for keeping the number of enslaved robust.

Although western art had shown the nobility and prestige of African people as evidenced in the five-volume collection *The Image of the Black in Western Art*[2] (which includes sculpture, paintings, drawings of the vast array of black figures since the time of the pharaohs), these images were not seen by most of the inhabitants of the early colonies. Instead, the new drawings of black people were to entrench the belief that they were animal like and identical in character or more precisely in their lack of character.[3] Figure 1.2 shows Nott's "scientific" drawing of skull shape, which attempted to connect blacks to monkeys, a trope about blackness that is still very much alive today.

Although the pseudoscientists of the eighteenth and nineteenth centuries published extensive "evidence" to prove the fixedness of racial categories,[4] these ideas were still being recycled as late as 1994 in *The Bell Curve*, which looked at, among other things, racial differences in intelligence. Long buried are the race scientists such as Linnaeus,[5] Meiners,[6] and Cuvier[7] who created these first taxonomies of humans, along with their charts of flowers and animals, but their ideas still operate powerfully.

Once these categories were created for the purpose of justifying imperialism and slavery from the mid-seventeenth century to the nineteenth century, they needed to be controlled. Borders needed to be drawn and the law needed to have clear criteria for placing someone in or ousting someone from a racial category. Most white and black people were taught to believe race

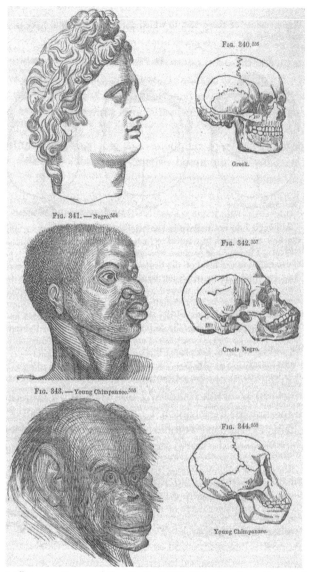

Figure 1.2 *Indigenous Races of the Earth*, 1857. This drawing attempted to connect
black people to chimpanzees by comparing skull shape.
Source: The British Library (shelfmark: General Reference Collection 10007.k.4).
Book: "Types of Mankind," page 458, published in 1854 by Philadelphia: Lippincott,
Grambo & Co.; Authors: Josiah Clark Nott 1804–1873; George R. Gliddon (George
Robins), 1809–1857; Samuel George Morton 1799–1851; Louis Agassiz 1807–1873;
William Usher; Henry Stuart Patterson, 1815–1854.

was something you could see whether it was in the moons of the fingernails or simply darker pigmentation on the skin. Because it was believed that different species were not supposed to interbreed or it would reverse evolution and degrade mankind into a mongrel race, many did. Jim Crow in the United States after the Civil War did its best to separate and reinforce this ban on miscegenation, but because of a high incidence of white men raping black women[8] as well as illicit consensual relationships between races, a racially ambiguous people emerged. This necessitated creative legal ways to keep people in their human categories even if those categories were becoming less clear.

Along with this insistence on race came the struggle against the values placed on this concept. From early slave revolts[9] like the Stono Rebellion in 1739 to more famous ones such as the one led by Nat Turner in 1831 to the sustained organization of the Underground Railroad for over several decades in the mid-nineteenth century, blacks and sometimes whites insisted on the equal humanity of the races. Sojourner Truth asked "Ar'nt I a woman"[10] in 1851, calling attention to the fact that black women had been erased from the women's suffrage movement.[11] Nearly a century later during the Memphis sanitation workers' strike, black men still needed to declare on placards "I am a man" when their rights and masculine identity had been taken away.

In the 1900 Paris Exposition, W. E. B. Du Bois attempted to counteract the toxic and powerful effect of the human zoo exhibits by showing a counter-narrative based on real black people's lives in photographs (see figure 1.3). His exhibit displayed photographs of successful black people with different features, different hair, different bodies—proving there was no common denominator or monolith to blackness—the polar opposite of the image of blacks that was contrived and manipulated to promote colonialism. Although he won an award for his exhibit, the crowds still flocked to the "African" village, which hired black people to play savages while whites standing behind a fence or glass wall observed them.

These performances of blackness soothed the beliefs of white people that all was as they thought it was: black people were simple and wild in contrast to the great culture makers, white Europeans. The world fairs that housed these zoos were held in the great cities of North America and Europe and often stayed open all summer, with an estimate of one and a half billion people flocking to celebrate the spoils of colonialism. In figure 1.4, a woman leans over a fence to feed a small black girl like one would a goat or cow. The white woman's thrill is a different world from the object of her attention, a small child of about three, seemingly unaware of what is being done to her. Figure 1.5 shows "gentlemen" leering at the grown versions of the little girl, who stands topless behind glass. The expression on these women's faces

Figure 1.3 "Four African American women seated on steps of building at Atlanta University, Georgia," an attempt to show the variousness of black life.
Source: Library of Congress (LC-DIG-ppmsca-08778). Photo taken by Thomas E. Askew in 1899 or 1990; Collected by: Du Bois, W. E. B. (1868–1963) for use in African American photographs for the Paris Exposition of 1900 (LOT 11930, no. 362 [P&P]).

shows they understand exactly what is happening even as the gentlemen's dress and stance show they are charading as cultural sophisticates.

Three cultural works that did the most for this early propaganda and helped sustain the idea of the black were Thomas Jefferson's *Notes on the State of Virginia* (1782), Harriet Beecher Stowe's *Uncle Tom's Cabin* (1852), and D. W. Griffith's film *Birth of a Nation* (1915). All were extremely popular and their "types" of blacks still influence racial definitions today. Jefferson gives a full description of the differences: "Comparing them by their faculties of memory, reason, and imagination, it appears to me, that in memory they are equal to the whites; in reason much inferior, as I think one could scarcely be found capable."[12] Along with this verdict, he explains they are lustful, unimaginative in the arts, pick up tunes easily, and have less need of sleep. All of these qualities help justify overworking them (need less sleep), raping them (they are lustful), and not educating them (reason much inferior). His account is quite exhaustive, at times comparing them to the Native Americans as well and finding them lacking.

Stowe's novel with its use of melodrama created pity in its readers, which promoted the cause of white abolitionists[13] particularly by allowing the white child Eva to convert the black child Topsy, but also in her urging her parents to give Tom his freedom. Tom (who now is the source of the pejorative term Uncle Tom) was unthreatening and faithful to his white masters, which

Figure 1.4   Human Zoo, Brussells World Fair, 1958. Patrons attempt to feed black child.
Source: http://politicalblindspot.com/through-the-1950s-africans-and-native-americans-were-kept-in-zoos-as-exhibits/.

Figure 1.5   Human Zoo, Brussels World Fair, 1958. Male patrons looking through glass at African women in an exhibit. Their toplessness was a big part of the attraction for many.
Source: https://popularresistance.org/deep-racism-the-forgotten-history-of-human-zoos/.

assuaged the fear that blacks who were freed would want revenge. Stowe's image of Tom was to incite pity, but not sympathy or equality. Although she was against slavery, she was against miscegenation and hoped that once slaves were freed, they would repatriate to Africa. It also created the idea of the pickaninny or wild devil-like black child in the form of Topsy, an immoral and animalistic child in contrast to the angelic white child Eva. These would later set the stage for the grown-up versions of these two female tropes: the voracious black woman whose sexual appetite could justify white men raping her and the virginal white Southern belle.

The first American full-length feature film, *Birth of a Nation*, taken from the novel *The Clansman* by Thomas Dixon Jr., was so popular that President Woodrow Wilson showed it in the White House. It depicted the imagined nightmare that would ensue if blacks were given rights and privileges after the Civil War—they were either animals turning civilized life into a barnyard with their filth and lawlessness or sexual predators who needed to be kept away from that prized commodity: the white Southern virgin woman. In the film, the white Flora encapsulates these Southern values and shows she would rather kill herself than submit to the touch of Gus, a black man. Gus is eventually lynched by the newly founded Ku Klux Klan. The glorification of the Klan in the film, who are emissaries of Jesus Christ himself, resulted in a 1920s revival of the Klan. These toxic images and racial tropes were built into children's dolls and games as well as adult movies and books. People were being fed this binary on a conveyor belt of popular culture.

The Civil Rights Movement of the 1950s and 1960s grew out of the black Christian church's insistence on everyone equally being God's children. Martin Luther King understood how large the task was ahead, knowing change couldn't happen immediately. As he famously stated, "The arc of the moral universe is long, but it bends toward justice."[14] Because of increased ownership of television, everyone could see the contrast of violent white police and white racists bullying and beating black people who were practicing passive resistance. This shifted the racial trope of black people as unruly children or threatening predators to black people as strong, faithful, and noble.

Along with this activism that fought against biological racism, biological race was being debunked in academia. As early as 1950, UNESCO deemed race a myth. Decades later, Winant and Omi's *Racial Formation in the United States* showed how the fiction of race was constructed and sustained as a powerful creation myth of the United States that enabled the enslavement and exploitation of a designated group now called black. Intellectually, race is now understood by many to be a "lived experience of a people" or "a series of networks and a set of relationships," but "not anything organic to humans biologically."[15] This was further emphasized when the Human Genome Project proved that all humans come originally from Africa and are 99.9 percent the same in their DNA.[16] [17] It made it hard for anyone to claim there is such a thing as biological race.

Many humanists believed the black/white binary wouldn't last, but new Afrocentric movements reinforced them. The Harlem Renaissance had already begun to give vigor to the idea of biological race again, ironically through the celebration of black culture in Harlem. Although blacks had been deemed inferior and had felt this status since slavery, it was now reinvented as superior in some ways; black people were cooler, more creative, more soulful than whites. Black literature, art, textiles, and dance became honored and praised through publishing houses, performance venues, and films. Whites were under the influence of a "Negro Vogue" in the 1920s where the so called primitivism of black arts was "discovered" by whites like writer Carl Van Vechten, who would go to Harlem and exploit his experiences in his novel *N*gger Heaven*. Whites flocked to Harlem to jazz clubs to have blackness rub off on them. In Alain Locke's *The New Negro*, he presented a new version of Negroes, no longer degraded and submissive, but fully embracing their folk roots and boldly creative.

In the 1970s, the Black Power Movement, backed by the Nation of Islam, claimed that the black race was superior. Malcolm X,[18] inspired by Muslim leader Elijah Muhammad, preached a new creation story of whiteness. A black scientist named Yacub selectively bred a separate white species, sometimes called the white devil, that could never be trusted. Similar to the Harlem Renaissance, this period was a celebration of black culture: arts, dance, textiles, food, music, and reconnection to Africa such as choosing African names, wearing dashikis, and celebrating the newly created hybrid holiday Kwanzaa. What came with Black Power was a deeper entrenchment of black community and a belief that separation from whites was the best way forward. This movement was powerful in counteracting the image of black as ugly. Black women were encouraged to grow out their afros, celebrate their curves and facial features, and not try to mimic the look of white women by straightening their hair.

Defining blackness was a subject not just for these writers and theorists, but the legal world. This was particularly important for the race trials of the nineteenth century that helped define who was enslaved and who was free. In Ariel Gross's essay "Litigating Whiteness: Trials of Racial Determination in the Nineteenth-Century South," she lists the five determinants in these trials: physical markers (skin color, hair, nose, lips); documented ancestry (birth certificate, parentage); performance (how one speaks, dresses, gestures, speaks about the past); ascriptive identity (reputation, community and reception in society); and "science" (this involved superstitions such as looking at the angle of a foot).[19] Performance and ascriptive identity were complex categories that were discussed and analyzed in these trials. They included how others saw you because of your lived experience of membership, work, and social life. In other words, the most important criteria were how others recognized you and determined your authenticity. It was believed that someone's race showed up in their behavior, caused by the blood of their birth race. Even if you couldn't see race clearly on the face, the behavior would out your biological nature or black blood. Later in important Supreme Court cases like *Dred Scott v. Sandford* (1857), *Plessy v. Ferguson* (1896), and *Brown v. Board of Education* (1954), the law took on questions such as: Is a black person a citizen or property? How much black ancestry makes you black? Do black children have an equal right to education?[20]

A solidarity was created among people labeled black that began on the slave ship over, and was sustained by resistance movements, the black church, the black ghetto, black culture, and black activism. But it was counteracted by the decision made by some light-skinned blacks to escape systemic racism and choose to live as white. The history of people moving past their ascribed racial boundaries is well-documented and has been going on for centuries. Often called "passing," the numbers of light-skinned blacks who have lived as white can't be definitely determined because we can assume many successfully "passed" and were never caught. Some estimates say black passing to white pre-1950 ranged from hundreds of thousands to several million.[21]

Passing takes its name from trespassing because one who passes is an interloper into another race, but it also has the connotation of dying. When one passed, they had to disconnect from their home, family, friends and former identity. They had to die in one racial identity in order to be born into another. American literature has often focused on the psychological and physical danger inherent in such a choice[22] such as, Nella Larsen's *Passing*, James Weldon Johnson's *Autobiography of an Ex-Colored Man*, Twain's *The Tragedy of Pudd'nhead Wilson*, Danzy Senna's *Caucasia*, Mat Johnson and Warren Pleece's *Incognegro,* Roth's *The Human Stain*. Twain and Larsen mocked the confidence with which racists spoke of how 'they could tell' just as they were being duped by racial passers.[23] Although being caught passing was often fatal, successfully keeping a racial secret also exacted a psychological payment and sometimes resulted in suicide.[24] Some scholars see passing as liberation or radical subversion,[25] while others see it as an act of cultural treason or tragedy.[26] Still others see it as outdated or passé,[27] and finally some see it as utopian as we enter a new multiracial world of race fluidity.[28] No matter how they are interpreted, when passers are caught, they shake up people's assertions about race. As Werner Sollors explains, passers are "ideal questioners of the status quo."[29] Their being outed forces us to reevaluate how we determine categories of identity.

Race trials in the nineteenth century were popular entertainment as people vicariously experienced the frisson of crossing the color line without being caught themselves.[30] However, families and communities often kept hidden their losses to the other side as it only brought shame and trouble. This kind of black to white passing was understandable as it not only helped people escape enslavement or lynching[31] but also made possible privileges like work, education, real estate, and love. Despite the benefits of passing, psychologically a person who crossed the color line found it very hard to recover a sense of identity. Such was the case with *New York Times* journalist Antony Broyard, who kept his Creole past undisclosed till he was on his deathbed. His daughter Bliss Broyard had to uncover the fuller truth in her own book, *One Drop: My Father's Hidden Life*.

Although black to white passing was done for obvious reasons, white to black passing (or reverse passing) was done for a variety of different reasons. One of the most famous cases was explored in John Howard Griffin's memoir *Black Like Me* where a white journalist darkened his skin, buzz cut his hair, and then spent six weeks in the segregated Deep South recording the racism he endured and how it began to degrade his notion of self. This bestseller made whites believe in the suffering of black people because it was coming from a *legitimate* white man who walked in the shoes of a black man rather than a black man whose words couldn't be trusted. Temporary passing in order to "get the story" is also detailed in Laura Z. Hobson's *Gentleman's Agreement* where a Christian journalist passes for a Jew to expose postwar anti-Semitism.

However, Baz Dreisinger in her book *Near Black* shows how this reverse passing also occurred in the entertainment world. She focuses mostly on white men passing for black to gain a certain authenticity. In this kind of passing, Dreisinger argues, "Race changes occur by means of cultural and social transformation, not physical ones."[32] She emphasizes how this is different from "putting on blackface." These musicians, writers, and DJs, including Mezz Mezzrow, Waldo Frank, and Johnny Otis, were fully adopting blackness, not simply idealizing and imitating black culture.[33] Becoming black was possible unlike becoming white because "Central to the enterprise of white passing in American culture from the 1830s to the present day are ideas about proximity. Because "blackness" is imagined as transmittable, proximity to blackness is invested with the power to turn whites black."[34]

White to black passing was less dangerous because the black community has always had "mixed" people. Because of America's one-drop rule, black could look identical to white. But also, this kind of passing is inherently safer because it is a person of privilege masking as one who is oppressed; they still have their privilege intact if they choose it. The belief that black culture was spreading to and affecting whites was delineated by Norman Mailer in his 1957 essay "The White Negro." And in 1970 Ralph Ellison wrote, "The melting pot did indeed melt, creating such deceptive metamorphoses and blending of identities, values and lifestyles that most American whites are culturally part Negro American without even realizing it."[35]

Defining blackness is very different today where blackness has become a hot commodity. Changes in the binary have created a kind of contest for blackness. The intraracial competition between blacks is played out often between blacks with lighter skin and those with darker skin,[36] but it is also determined by language, neighborhood, personal history, and ancestry. E Patrick Johnson[37] sees the roots of this tension as being born in the House N*gger/Field N*igger division created on the plantation. Lighter skinned blacks were given privileges, education, clothing, and language that aligned them more with whites than blacks. Darker skinned blacks often were forced to work the fields, beaten savagely, and forbidden from basic education and literacy. Even today, the expression "talking white" as an insult to educated blacks seems to come partly from that old division made by slave owners.

Post–civil rights and Black Power and after the two terms of President Barack Obama, the definition of blackness is a fraught subject. Although the wealth gap between whites and blacks is even larger than it was in the 1960s. Today 38.4 percent of black families are now considered part of the educated middle class.[38] Educated upper-middle-class blacks often express fear that they are losing their blackness as they live and work among predominantly white people and fall into the belief that it is more authentically black to be poor. This belief that "the folk" are the keepers of authentic blackness has been explored by J. Martin Favor, Houston A. Baker, and even earlier by W. E. B. Du Bois.[39] Today this "folk" being the touchstone of blackness often gets translated by one's closeness to the "hood." Finally, much of the definition of blackness has focused on black hypermasculinity and left out black women. Writers like bell hooks and black legal scholar Kimberlé Crenshaw, who coined the term "intersectionality," have encouraged an awareness of seeing how blackness and gender together create different challenges. Although authenticity was often determined by scholars writing on the subject of blackness, literary writers were also speaking from a personal point of view about what defined blackness.

The black experience was seen as one that robbed black people of the freedom to be truly one's authentic actualized self because they were constantly having an ascribed identity thrust upon them. This brings with it the loss of opportunity or a piece of the dream—and makes them, as Frantz Fanon wrote, truly "the wretched of the earth." In 1952, Fanon in *Black Skin, White Masks*[40] showed how the idea of blackness as always inferior creates the equivalent of a mental illness in those who are treated this way. By stripping away the culture of indigenous groups and making them believe in the new colonizing culture (white European) as superior, it robs them of their authentic selves. Then they are stuck with imitating the colonizers, which is never taken as authentic by the ruling group.[41] Writers like Ann Petry, Toni Morrison, Richard Wright, Alice Walker, and Ralph Ellison wrote about the shared degradation that came from living as black. Although Baldwin acknowledged the myth of race when he referred to white people as "those who think of themselves as white,"[42] he did believe in experiential essentialism or the unifying experience of being black. In *The Fire Next Time*,[43] he writes to his nephew warning him of the psychological damage that comes from being black and his own rage toward whites. Ta-Nehisi Coates echoes this experiential blackness when he asks in his book *Between the World and Me*, "How do I live free in this black body?," a question as old as slavery and lynching.[44]

The writers of the Harlem Renaissance and the period around the Civil Rights Movement encouraged the idea that blacks experienced the world differently from whites—that there was an essential black experience—and this was the subject of black writers during that time. Talk show hosts, teachers, and friends felt free asking a black person to speak for other blacks as it was believed they all shared this common terrain. Many themes unite these works of fiction and autobiography: invisibility, loss of self through the projected hate and suspicion of white people, and the belief that black features and black skin equal ugliness. These classic works reinforced the idea of a black experience that was devastating and violent: black people were always in danger of being enslaved, lynched, shot, and arrested—ultimately they were degraded psychologically and lived with a kind of posttraumatic stress from living as black. However, Albert Murray suggests in his *Omni-Americans*,[45] that this pathologizing of black culture (as evidenced in the Moynihan report, which spoke of broken homes and mentally unstable families) is just another tool of white supremacy.

Along with these negative aspects of being black was the belief that there was richness gained at times by this life of struggle. Writers like Ellison and even Baldwin suggest that the ability to play the blues or have more compassion are results from this deeper lived life. Black life because of its constant challenges produced a richer soul or "interiority" not as available to whites, and with it came a rich culture of food, humor, music, and community. This view of the soulful, wise black figure, sometimes called the Magical Negro, was popularized in films like *Ghost*, *The Help*, *The Secret Life of Bees*, and *The Legend of Bagger Vance*, but also connects back to literary characters like N*gger Jim in *Huck Finn*, Dilsey in *The Sound and the Fury*, and Uncle Remus in African American folktales.

Journalist Eugene Robinson shows the complexity and variety in black life today by dividing black into different populations, which he says have "different profiles, different mind-sets, different hopes, fears, and dreams":

1. a mainstream middle-class majority with a full ownership stake in American society;
2. a small transcendent elite with such enormous wealth, power, and influence that even white folks have to genuflect;
3. two newly emergent groups—individuals of mixed-race heritage and communities of recent black immigrants that make us wonder what "black" is even supposed to mean;
4. a large, abandoned minority with less hope of escaping poverty and dysfunction than at any time since Reconstruction's crushing end.[46]

It is this last group that both blacks and whites stubbornly seem to interpret as the most authentic version of black and the one that is most promoted in the media. Both blacks and whites are saturated with these ideas just by walking down the street and seeing billboards and window displays. Ta-Nehisi Coates speaks of this widening of his version of black when he went to the Yard at Howard University and saw for the first time a vision of blackness that wasn't circumscribed by the ghetto or the media's false world:

> I first witnessed this power out on the Yard, that communal green space in the center of the campus where the students gathered and I saw everything I knew of my black self multiplied out into seemingly endless variations. . . . The black world was expanding before me and I could see now that the world was far more than a photonegative of that of the people who believe they are white.[47]

NOTES

1. Allen, Theodore W., *The Invention of the White Race*, Volume 1.
2. Bindman, David, and Henry Louis Gates, *The Image of the Black in Western Art* (series).
3. See David Bindman's book, *Ape to Apollo: Aesthetics and the Idea of Race in the 18th Century.*
4. Tucker, William H., *The Science and Politics of Racial Research.*
5. Linnaeus, Caroli, *Systema Naturae: Sive Regna Tria Naturæ Systematice Proposita Per Classes, Ordines, Genera, & Species.*
6. Meiners, Christoph, *Grundriß Der Geschichte Der Menschheit.*
7. Cuvier, Georges, *The Animal Kingdom Arranged in Conformity with Its Organization*, translated from French by H. M. Murtrie.

8. See Nell Irvin Painter's *Southern History Across the Color Line* for a deeper look at sexual politics on the plantation.

9. See Herbert Aptheker's *American Negro Slave Revolts*, in which he identifies 250 that took place.

10. The more popularized version of this is "Ain't I a woman?"—this change in linguistic representation was made twelve years after the original transcription to create sympathy for her and make her sound like a Southern slave. In fact, she only spoke Dutch until she was nine and was raised in New York.

11. bell hooks states, "No other group in America has so had their identity socialized out of existence as have black women." hooks, *Ain't I a Woman*, 7.

12. Jefferson, Thomas, *Notes on the State of Virginia*, 146.

13. Black radical abolitionists often intersected with white abolitionists, but also had a set of different priorities.

14. Luther King Jr., Martin, "Sermon at Temple Israel of Hollywood." Despite the impression that King was patient in contrast to Malcolm X, he did not believe in gradualism. See King, *Why We Can't Wait*.

15. Hobbs, Allyson Vanessa, *A Chosen Exile: A History of Racial Passing in American Life*.

16. Highfield, Roger, "DNA Survey Finds All Humans Are 99.9Pc The Same."

17. Sykes, Bryan, *The Seven Daughters of Eve: The Science That Reveals Our Genetic Ancestry*.

18. Malcolm X changed his views in 1964 and broke from the Nation of Islam.

19. Gross, Ariel J., "Litigating Whiteness: Trials of Racial Determination in the Nineteenth-Century South."

20. Later, these legal debates were important for the Affirmative Action agenda. Without racial classifications, how can we redress historical injustice?

21. Fikes, Robert, "The Passing of Passing: A Peculiarly American Racial Tradition Approaches Irrelevance"; Gross, "Litigating Whiteness"; Kennedy, Randall, "Racial Passing."

22. Larsen, Nella, *Passing*; Johnson, James Weldon, *The Autobiography of an Ex-Coloured Man*; Twain, Mark, *The Tragedy of Pudd'nhead Wilson: And, the Comedy, Those Extraordinary Twins*; Senna, Danzy, *Caucasia*; Johnson, Mat, and Warren Pleece, *Incognegro*.

23. Passing makes for good drama as evidenced by the highly successful movies on this topic such as *Pinky*, *Lost Boundaries*, and *Imitation of Life*.

24. Hobbs, *A Chosen Exile*.

25. Dreisinger, Baz, *Near Black: White-to-Black Passing in American Culture*; Wald, Gayle *Crossing The Line: Racial Passing in Twentieth-Century U.S. Literature and Culture*; Sánchez, María Carla, and Linda Schlossberg, *Passing: Identity and Interpretation in Sexuality, Race, and Religion*; Ginsberg, *Passing and the Fictions of Identity*; Kroeger, Brooke, *Passing: When People Can't Be Who They Are*.

26. Hobbs, *A Chosen Exile*.

27. Fikes, "The Passing of Passing."

28. Hsu, Hua, "The End of White America?"; Dawkins, Marcia Alesan, *Clearly Invisible: Racial Passing and the Color of Cultural Identity*; Myrdal, Gunnar, *An American Dilemma, Volume 1: The Negro Problem and Modern Democracy*.

29. Sollors, Werner, *Neither Black Nor White Yet Both: Thematic Explorations of Interracial Literature*, 245.

30. Gross, "Litigating Whiteness"

31. Craft, William, and Ellen Craft, *Running a Thousand Miles for Freedom*.

32. Dreisinger, *Near Black*, 3.

33. Dreisinger, 5.

34. Dreisinger, 3.

35. Ellison, Ralph, "What America Would Be Like without Blacks."

36. Spike Lee's film *School Daze* explores this tension with his dance off between Jiggaboos and Wannabes.

37. Johnson, E. Patrick, *Appropriating Blackness: Performance and the Politics of Authenticity*.

38. Black Demographics, "The African American Middle Class."

39. Favor, Martin J., *Authentic Blackness: The Folk in the New Negro Renaissance*; Baker, *Blues, Ideology, and Afro-American Literature: A Vernacular Theory*; Du Bois, *The Souls of Black Folk*.

40. Fanon, Frantz, *Black Skin, White Masks*.

41. See Scott, Daryl Michael, *Contempt and Pity: Social Policy and the Image of the Damaged Black Psyche*.

42. Baldwin, James, "On Being 'White' . . . and Other Lies," 179.

43. Baldwin, *The Fire Next Time*.

44. Coates, *Between the World and Me*.

45. See also the work of Charles Johnson and E. Franklin Frazier for alternate views of the New Negro.

46. Robinson, Eugene, *Disintegration: The Splintering of Black America*.

47. Coates, *Between the World and Me*, 40–42.

Chapter 2

The Trial of Rachel Dolezal

The First Transracial

Exploring the outing of Rachel Dolezal will help us take the pulse of the black/white binary today. Dolezal's own racial construction through her childhood, involvement in college with a black community, and her activism show why she made the choices she did and how steadfast and personal her commitment was to be her true self. However, when it was made public, it revealed just how tightly we grip the binary. This was seen through the mainstream media's hounding interviews that obsessed on getting her to admit her whiteness and avoided any possibility of a richer discussion. It can also be seen in the public's hostile reaction and resistance to her choice as a viable possibility. Because Dolezal wasn't given room to speak and her story became distorted in media feed, this chapter attempts to look more closely at her choice, the media's framing of her, and how this reflects our racial trauma as Americans.

On June 16, 2015, the tension between the ideas of biological race (or essentialism) and social constructedness became sharply reinforced in the public arena when Dolezal tripped the landmine that is our racial trauma in America. The "black" Spokane NAACP president who was born to white parents was publicly outed as white in a small local Idaho paper. It was revealed that she had bronzed her skin a shade darker, worn an afro hair weave and been understood to be black for eight years. Although there have been racial "passers" before, Dolezal's claim to be of a particular race, even if her ancestry was different and to continue to believe she was that race once her ancestry was revealed to the public, was radical and hugely disorienting to Americans. In addition to a media frenzy that went on internationally for a solid week, people have called her the worst expletives English can afford, suggested she should be raped, lynched, and murdered, and diagnosed her as psychotic for thinking she could be black. This chapter will look at how

Dolezal expressed her blackness in contrast to how the media and public determined her whiteness. These two perspectives enact the historical battle between the social construction of race and our attachment to the belief in biological race. (Figures 2.1 and 2.2 show the two versions of Dolezal when identifying as white and black.)

The media circus that followed was a mixture of shaming, ridicule, and anger. What inflamed people the most was her refusal to even acknowledge the reality of fixed racial category and her "stubborn" belief that she was black. Later the media labeled her sarcastically as transracial. What Dolezal represents to people may be viewed through the lens of their own race, but to all she is a meaningful symbol. The intensity of the reaction to Dolezal was reminiscent of race trials in the nineteenth century in which light-skinned black people who had been passing as white were outed in publicly attended race trials, and the punishment was severe. For some, it meant a return to slavery while others were victims of vigilantes who would physically assault or even kill them. Although Dolezal was verbally threatened, the punishment given to her by her employers and community was ostracization. This response to race has a quality of the hysteria around the concept of witch during the Salem witch trials in colonial Massachusetts.[1]

When Dolezal's racial shift was deemed race fraud, she promptly lost her job as instructor of Africana Studies at Eastern Washington University; her position as president of the NAACP chapter in Spokane, Washington; her position as chair of the police Ombudsman Commission; her job as a writer for the *Inlander*; and most of her community. Although this sentence was less extreme than those given during these race trials, the language people used revealed a similar disdain shown for racial passers more than a century earlier. Stanley Cohen in his study *Folk Devils and Moral Panics* shows how mass media operates to create what he calls a moral panic by the media over-simplifying, distorting, and predicting some kind of downfall of society by blaming a "folk devil." The position of these folk devils or their "deviance" is created by a set of particular laws that themselves are questionable. Howard Becker explains:

> Deviance is created by society. . . . I mean, rather, that social groups create deviance by making the rules whose infraction constitutes deviance and by applying those rules to particular persons and labelling them as outsiders. From this point of view, deviance is not a quality of the act the person commits, but rather a consequence of the application by others of rules and sanctions to an "offender." The deviant is one to whom the label has successfully been applied; deviant behavior is behavior that people so label.[2]

Figure 2.1   Dolezal (2004) when she was married and identifying as white. She saw this version of herself as more of a performance than when she identified as black. Her then husband wanted her to be as white as possible.
Source: "Reduced to Size 0," in book: *In Full Color: Finding My Place in a Black and White World*, by Rachel Dolezal, published in 2017 by BenBella Books, Inc. (p. 10 of photographs section).

Figure 2.2   Dolezal with her son Franklin after identifying as black, 2006.
Source: "Me and Franklin—Christmas," in book: *In Full Color: Finding My Place in a Black and White World*, by Rachel Dolezal, published in 2017 by BenBella Books, Inc. (p. 11 of photographs section).

For a woman of European ancestry to claim to be black is only deviant because of the laws that created and enforced the notion of race to begin with. These laws were based on the fear that mixing these races would devolve the human species toward animals again. And so the demarcation between races was taken as a matter of life and death. Although Jim Crow no longer exists keeping the races apart and the movement between races forbidden, the public outcry attempted to serve the same purpose and restrict Dolezal to the race she was ascribed at birth.

Except for trans people who have publicly claimed to be different from their ascribed gender identity and believed it to be true, Dolezal's insistence that her nature was black seemed unique. Although there have been many "passers" or light-skinned black people that purposely led people to believe they were white, inside they believed they were black and could be found out anytime. Passers were choosing to cross over the color line in order to gain privileges and avoid the suffering and injustice associated with blackness; Dolezal left behind the privileges of whiteness to claim what she felt was her true identity as black, which begged the question, "Can anyone be black?" The media and public responded with a resounding no. This response to Dolezal and the criteria for determining her whiteness shine a light on our collective anxiety about dissolving racial categories.

Dolezal's full story complicates the media's overblown simplification of her motives. Her own reasons behind making this choice refute the public's accusations of her putting on temporary blackness that was labeled blackface, cultural appropriation, and racial passing. From Dolezal's perspective, it is hard to find anything strange about her choice to check the black box on the census when from a young age all that she felt that was meaningful to her identity was related to blackness.

Dolezal's race changing is nothing new. We have been moving between races since the concept of race was first invented. Not only have people changed races by marrying someone of another race, crossing a state line, being in the proximity of a racial community, or even having someone of stature vouch for one's race, but one could also be read as a different race by a shift in clothing, hair, or gestures. In Arthur Miller's novel *Focus*, a man becomes a Jew in others' eyes by getting a pair of glasses, and soon he begins to feel Jewish and identify as such. Although darkly pigmented black people have rarely had a choice on how they are read, choice has been a factor in race for many racially ambiguous people. Children with parents of different races will often choose to identify with one or the other.[3] Although we are born and immediately ascribed labels, we haven't always chosen to follow them. What we call the black community is really a varied group of people who have given different amounts of importance to their blackness. Some are activists and see race in every conversation; others feel it doesn't affect them very much. The media has also successfully suggested someone's race through visual codes. According to white TV watchers, O. J. Simpson entered his trial "as a fellow white man and grew darker as the proceedings went on."[4] Rachel Dolezal became whiter in the media as people clamored for a racial category to be determined.

Writer Trey Ellis alludes to our modern-day pervasive cultural fluidity when he looks at what he call cultural mulattoes[5] who are raised in today's global culture. He sees them as trailblazers whose education makes it possible to navigate easily in the white world. However, they also don't need to deny or suppress any part of themselves or their "complicated and sometimes contradictory cultural baggage to please either white or black people."[6] Here he gets at the idea of permission and acceptance that has always been a part of identity. We can be what we want, but people's recognition of us gives us the nod to go ahead or the warning to stop.

The media attention on Dolezal was abruptly cut off on July 17, 2015, when a white racist named Dylann Roof shot ten black people at a bible study at Emanuel African Methodist Episcopal Church in Charleston, South Carolina, murdering nine of them including the pastor. Black suffering as a result of systemic racism and black people's inability to choose something else are what make many feel the victims of the Emanuel Church shooting were authentically black and Dolezal is not. Roof yelled out his mission as he did it: "I have to do it. You rape our women and you're taking over our country. And you have to go."[7] This reveals the deepest reality about race, not who is black or white, but how our society continues to sustain white supremacist systems and messages that encourage some people to believe and act on them. This fact must be acknowledged before looking at the nuances of how racial identity is constructed and sustained. In the following discussion, we will explore the more subtle aspects of constructing blackness and whiteness even when the media treats them as simplistic obvious categories.

Both pieces of evidence that made others determine Dolezal's racial designation were presented from her parents. Dolezal's visibly fair-skinned white parents showing her birth certificate and their publishing a photo of her at sixteen years old in a local Ohio paper were all people needed as proof. These two things (physical markers in the photo and documented ancestry in the birth certificate) were part of a list of ways to identify black people in the racial trials of the nineteenth century as discussed in chapter 1. Dolezal's parents had been silent on the issue of their daughter's race for ten years, but suddenly went to the media just as their older white son Joshua was undergoing scrutiny for allegedly abusing Rachel's adopted black sister.

Dolezal, admittedly, was not the best spokesperson for a new racial malleability. She let herself be attacked and never got aggressive back.[8] She wasn't a smooth performer on TV and often looked baffled, which added to people's feeling that she was lying. She writes in her memoir about how even in college she had trouble answering questions about her race because it didn't place clearly into the binary: "My responses tended to be awkward, tortuous, strained. Because I didn't fit neatly into a box and didn't know how to articulate who I was or how I felt in a way that made sense to people, I'd end up bouncing from one story to the next until I'd told them nearly everything about my life."[9]

Race trials of the past privileged performance, context, and lived experience over racial markers and ancestry when determining the fate of a racially ambiguous person. However, for Dolezal these other categories were not considered relevant. The media narrative made her into a conniving careerist or a fool. NBC interviewed her, and celebrities like Whoopi Goldberg, Kareem Abdul-Jabbar, Dave Chappelle, and Jon Stewart weighed in with their verdicts. The emphasis of her media interviews was always on getting her to admit she was white, not on understanding her perspective on race and identity. In all of her interviews, the focus was the photograph and birth certificate, not on the other categories that were weighted even more in the race trials of the nineteenth century such as lived experience and community. When she tried to talk about self-identification, authenticity, or community, she was cut off. The tone is a kind of bullying inquest.

First seeking out her confession is the notorious interview from an unidentified reporter from a local TV station, KXLY, in Spokane, Washington. This was mocked by *Saturday Night Live* comedian Maya Rudolph and went viral on the internet:

KXLY: I was wondering if your dad really is an African American man.

RD: I don't know what you are implying.

KXLY: Are you African American?

RD: I don't understand the question.

KXLY: Are your parents white?

She stares blankly and walks away.[10]

In another widely seen interview with Matt Lauer on NBC's *Today Show*, he appears to be only interested in locking in her racial category:

ML: Let me ask you a question in simple terms, are you an African American woman?

RD: I identify as black.

(He shows a picture of her at sixteen.)

ML: Is she a Caucasian or African American?

RD: She would be identified as white.

ML: When did you start deceiving people and telling them you are black?

RD: It's more complex than answering the question of black or white.

ML: Would you make the same choices?

RD: I would.[11]

In another interview on NBC, Savannah Guthrie, co-anchor of the *Today Show*, has the same obsession:

SG: Just as a human being, when someone asks you are you black or African American, you know what they are asking . . . Do you understand . . . why that is a misleading answer given your parental heritage.

RD: I can understand.

SG: You have been acting like you are something you are not.

RD: I definitely am not white. Nothing about being white describes who I am. What's the word for it? The closest thing if I'm black or white, I'm black. On a level of values, lived experience. That's the accurate answer for my truth.[12]

Finally at MSNBC, Melissa Harris-Perry on her weekend news and opinion TV show (with a focus on African American politics) attempts again to get her to cave in:

MH: Are you black?

RD: Yes.

MH: What do you mean?

RD: I have gone there with the experience, being a mother of two black sons, felt instinctual connection with "black is beautiful" and wanting to celebrate that. That was shut down. I was socially conditioned to not own that and be limited to whatever biological identity was thrust upon me, narrated to me. I felt awkward with it. Who is going to be the link for these kids coming into the family? I felt isolated with my identity my entire life.

(MHP ignores all the content and continues.)

MHP: Black women are enraged. Can you understand that?

RD: How dare she claim this? They don't know me. What I've walked through. This has not been a casual come and go.[13]

The trial continued in the blogosphere. Blogger YesImkelly! spends seven minutes ranting about Dolezal being racist, putting on blackface and making a mockery of the NAACP. She accuses her of pretending to be black and laughs out loud at Dolezal. Her diatribe is filled with expletives calling her a "dumb bitch" and wearing a "curly bullshit wig." Although she is particularly harsh, this aggression is consistent with other media coverage such as the interview on the talk show *The Real* where five women attack her simultaneously while the audience applauds.[14]

Dolezal was condemned for a variety of reasons. Some felt she was culturally appropriating when she tanned her skin darker, taught college students Africana Studies, and was a leader in black activism. Some saw her as putting on blackface or caricaturing black people when she wore her hair and styled her clothes in traditionally black ways. Others saw her as passing or knowingly pretending to be black in order to cheat black people out of opportunities and gain advantage herself. Finally, others said she hadn't suffered as black people have because she always had a choice to be white. In other words, the very act of becoming black was an act of white privilege and one she could opt out of if things got difficult.

In her memoir *In Full Color: Finding My Place in a Black and White World*, Dolezal shows the possibility of seeing black as a culture and a choice rather than a race. Dolezal provides the emotional context for her identity shift, something she couldn't do during her media trial and its aftermath because most interviewers were more interested in the sensationalism around her than in hearing from her. The book lays bare how these choices were not made lightly and the deeper meanings of her decision. The story makes the reader probe the key questions that she asks in her prologue, questions that have plagued the country since its importing of slaves, "If scrutinising people's appearance can't provide definitive proof of their racial identity, what does? How do you decide whether certain people are white or black?"[15]

Dolezal's early identification with blackness seems to be partly related to a dis-identification with the whiteness of her abusive parents and older brother. She associated her race with the negatives she saw in her strict white poor community. Her childhood (which is described the same way by her older brother Joshua in his memoir)[16] was a kind of indentured servitude on the isolated planes of Montana where they lived at a subsistence level and were home-schooled according to a strict Christian fundamentalist program. She was hit with a switch for any disobedience and was worked from early day to night. Leaving for college and becoming her "true" self had the exhilarating feeling of escape to freedom.

Dolezal had been exposed to racism close up in her family and her community. From the age of fourteen, her family had the same amount of black and white members and she identified more with the black members, her adopted siblings. Her parents' extremist evangelical sect dictated a pro-life stance and made them choose to adopt four black children (two black Americans, one biracial child, and one black baby from Haiti). Kathryn Joyce has documented that black children adopted into evangelical families are often treated in a highly racialized way, taught to see their own culture as inferior and punished more harshly than their white brothers and sisters.[17] Her parents treated her adopted black siblings in a racialized manner, at times endangering her brother Izaiah. Izaiah (whom she won custody of when she was a teen) listed his safety as one of the reasons he wanted to live with Dolezal. He referred to physical punishments, forced manual labor, and the threat of exile to other state group homes when he didn't cooperate with his adoptive parents' religion and rules.[18] Their parents always made a clear distinction between their black and white children, using harsher methods of physical punishment for the black children, including using a baboon whip on them.

She raised her four adopted black siblings until she left for college and the strong bond she had with them made her feel she wasn't so alone. As she put it "I was truly part of a family, surrounded by people who loved me[19] exactly as I was."[20] From early on, she read about black history in order to be politically aware and help her black siblings manage in the world. As a teenager when she became an artist, her work was on black themes. Her pieces continued with this perspective until she applied and received a scholarship at Howard University for a portfolio that was assumed to be coming from a black artist. Her art continues to be primarily black figures (see figures 2.3, 2.4, and 2.5).

In college in Mississippi, Dolezal immediately went to the one black table in the cafeteria and was accepted by that community. She traded her homemade "Little House on the Prairie" clothes for dashikis and started wearing her hair in box braids. Almost everyone knew she was white, but accepted her as an activist and ally. Later when she joined a black church, some assumed she was black and she noticed the change in tension when black people were not in mixed company. As she puts it, "being seen as Black also made social interactions in the community I lived in much easier. Black people related to me in a more relaxed way. Instead of putting up a wall and thinking of me as an outsider, they treated me as a member of the community, part of the family."[21] This language mirrors her early feelings when her siblings joined their family that she gained the real family she had been longing for.

During college, although still presenting as white, she created a family and community solely of black members. She met and married a black man, had a black son, and later bonded with Albert Wilkerson,[22] a black man whom she took as her adopted father, disassociating once again from her birth parents. She went to a historically black institution, Howard University, for graduate school and immersed herself in black culture and life. She cut off from her family and religion, sought out a new context, and got involved in a black church and activism. She didn't officially change her identification to black

Figure 2.3 *Regret,* by Rachel Dolezal, original oil pastel drawing on fabric.

until Izaiah, the brother she adopted, started a new school and didn't want to be perceived as twice adopted. Together, they decided to allow people to identify her as his biological mother. Tanning her skin facilitated this and for her, this change made her feel complete and whole.

Many cited Dolezal's presenting as black to be a form of cultural appropriation. Dolezal always found darker skin more beautiful and black hairstyles closer to her aesthetic since she started taking care of her adopted sister's hair. In college, she began doing black people's hair and trying out styles on her

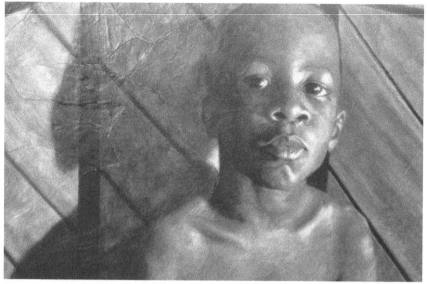

Figure 2.4 *Recognition,* by Rachel Dolezal, original acrylic on elk hide.

own. Her appreciation for black hair also came with an awareness of the history of black hairstyles and the politics of black hair. She had been teaching in Africana Studies a course called The Black Woman's Struggle and Black Women and Hair. Recently, she has published a children's book on black hair, *Ebony Tresses*,[23] which she created as a handmade book in 2001 for her black sister who was six years old at the time.

Susan Scafidi in her book *Who Owns Culture?* defines cultural appropriation as "taking intellectual property, traditional knowledge, cultural expressions, or artifacts from someone else's culture without permission. This can include unauthorized use of another culture's dance, dress, music, language, folklore, cuisine, traditional medicine, religious symbols, etc."[24] This is a general definition that can be easily overpoliced. Does someone need permission to wear their hair in traditional black ways? Does a Chinese woman have a right to wear a Sari to an Indian wedding? Whose permission do we seek to cross over these borders? Recently there have been scandals about authors writing about cultures that are not their own. Elena Ferrante and others have been outed as not "authentic" although their books were happily devoured by the public and "felt true." As a result of globalization, people's ethnic identities feel less secure as they are transmitted, reformulated, and reused throughout the world. This has created a kind of backlash. Although profiting from someone else's culture from a position of power without giving respect to the source

Figure 2.5   *Coming Back*, by Rachel Dolezal, original oil painting on deer hide.

seems ethically questionable, the creative sharing, blending, and creating of new identities has always been crucial to culture evolving.[25]

Being possessive of an experience is again a form of essentialism. Lionel Shriver in her keynote speech at the Brisbane writers festival decries what she sees as a new hoarding and policing of identity. "Those who embrace a vast range of 'identities'—ethnicities, nationalities, races, sexual and gender categories, classes of economic under-privilege and disability—are now encouraged to be possessive of their experience and to regard other people's attempts to participate in their lives and traditions, either actively or imagina-tively, as a form of theft."[26]

White people's sojourn into other cultures could be seen in minstrel shows of the past where they enacted their invented version of blackness. However, this was not done in admiration or deep identification. In fact, it was the opposite, a way to dis-identify. The act of taking off the paint at the end of a show reinforced their feelings that they were safely white.

White people who watched these shows were reassured of the boundaries of blackness and whiteness by seeing someone putting on and taking off blackness. This "closeness" to blackness worked similarly in white people who observed racial trials of the past, which allowed them to feel the vicarious thrill of crossing over the line, but remain safe on one side. Literary critic Leslie Fiedler talks about the racial boundaries for white people as they age: "Born theoretically white, we are permitted to pass our childhood as imaginary Indians, our adolescence as imaginary negroes and only then are expected to settle down to being what we really are: white once more."[27] White people can play[28] at other races as Susan Gubar discusses in her book *Racechanges: White Skin, Black Face in American Culture*, and often this was done in mocking, shallow, and patronizing ways. Norman Mailer wrote about so-called Wiggers (or white people who copied the styles of blacks to gain coolness or cache), which he describes in his essay "The White Negro."[29] These people are playing with the white invented version of blackness, not appreciating the reality of a black experience or black culture.

These definitions of cultural appropriation, putting on blackface, or playing at stereotypes don't quite fit Dolezal, who had a deeper identification with blackness, not just the surface styles of blackness. She describes her earliest memories as having an "awareness and connection with the black experience."[30] Dolezal says in her childhood drawing of herself, she chose the brown crayon not the peach one although her skin was white and freckled[31] (see figure 2.6). Often, she fantasized she was a princess from an African country and she painted over illustrations of white characters in the Bible to make them look black. From her earliest memories, she was drawn to black culture, black aesthetics, and the black struggle in contrast to her parents, who believed that "the people of Ham" were inferior.

In the eight years after she changed her racial markers by bronzing her skin and wearing her hair it an afro weave or in locks, she was read as black. Angela Schwendiman, who was a colleague of Dolezal's at Eastern Washington University, expressed her belief that Dolezal perceived herself as black internally, and that "she was only trying to match how she felt on the inside with her outside."[32] Dolezal wanted to be read as black to fully enter the identity she felt was organically hers. An interview by one of her graduate students who talks to her about being a black woman shows her complaining about going to the grocery store and having people touch her hair or judge her more harshly if she isn't dressed well, common experiences of black women.[33]

Most people saw what Dolezal was doing as passing. However, passers have been defined as those who have been ascribed one identity, but find ways to escape it either briefly or long term. These passers must sever ties with their previous racial context permanently. They see themselves as hiding

Figure 2.6 Self-portrait in crayon made by Dolezal at age 5.
Source: "Self-portrait" in book: *In Full Color: Finding My Place in a Black and White World* by Rachel Dolezal, published in 2017 by BenBella Books, Inc. (p. 4 of photographs section).

their true identity, but are willing to give it up to save their lives (in the case of slavery or Jim Crow), educate themselves, or to be with the person they love. Dolezal never felt she was escaping her real identity, but moving to the one she believes is truly hers. Passers know they are guilty of a transgression, and they wait in fear of getting caught and sent back. Although Dolezal did feel some anxiety about people connecting her to her white parents, it was her inability to explain that worried her. She had no models of people who had done this before. Dolezal did understand that her unusual situation vis a vis her race put her in a no man's land: "If you dared to cross this boundary, as I have done, and were exposed, you were put in a no-win situation: white folk would see you as a traitor and a liar and never trust you again, and Black folk might see you as an infiltrator and an imposter and never trust you again."[34]

In Nella Larsen's *Passing*, the character Clare Kendry passes as white, but craves to return to her black community. She goes on a sojourn into the white world, marries a white man, but in the end wants to come home. Dolezal didn't miss the white community or feel she was faking her black identity. This may explain her lack of remorse when questioned in the media.

Baz Dreisinger in her book *Near Black* shows how even the term passing is passé. She writes, "If we are all mixed heritage, then no one is passing as white or black; he or she is legitimately *claiming* whiteness or blackness. A true anti-essentialist framework must embrace the technical truth that passing makes no sense."[35] Dolezal asserts that she was claiming blackness over whiteness, not claiming an African American ancestry.

Many accused Dolezal of changing her look to get ahead in her career and that she took the job from a deserving black person. However, her position at the NAACP was volunteer and she had been asked to take it because of her excellent work in the community. The organization's website cites her "courageous and empowering leadership" and claims that she "rejuvenated" the organization.[36] In fact, the decision to have her step down was a result of the media calling negative attention to the branch, not Dolezal's competence. When Dolezal was outed, Lonnie Randolph Jr., former head of the NAACP, said to the *International Business Times*: "I don't understand what it is that is so significant to talk about. I could care less what she looks like as long as she does her job and does it well to protect the rights of all people."[37] Her genuine commitment to the cause is clear in her resignation letter on the NAACP website. She does not call attention to herself or what others see as her "lie." Instead, she focuses on the work she has done out of a passion for the cause. This letter has no defense of her choice and again no apology, but a plea to continue the struggle against racism and inequality.[38] Her life's work as an activist and educator on black issues would make her black according to theologian James Cone: "Being black in America has little to do with skin color. Being black means that your heart, your soul, your mind, and your body are where the dispossessed are."[39]

The other claim that she was passing to gain privilege was in her scholarship to Howard University, a traditional black college. However, her interest in studying at Howard was because her art was on black subjects. She presented as white when she applied and gained a scholarship based on the quality of her art. Nevertheless, when they saw she was white, her scholarship was retracted. Her thesis at Howard was a series of paintings presented from the perspective of a black man and the college dean, Tritobia Benjamin, questioned whether Dolezal had a legitimate claim to this view.[40] They also made an assumption about her family—because she was white, she must have parents who can afford to pay her tuition. In fact, when she sued Howard for retracting the scholarship based on race, she was pregnant and supporting her husband with no family financial support. Many of her critics claim she was white when it suited her and black when it suited her. In fact, it would have suited her to be black at that time, but she had not changed her racial markers yet.

Dolezal's transraciality was often compared with Caitlyn Jenner's transsexuality because the July cover of *Vogue* sported Jenner, a former Olympic athlete, in an elegant gown a month after Dolezal's face was plastered over newspapers. This comparison was highly charged because many felt her claiming to be similar was sugarcoating the historical trauma and current transphobia that transgender people have had and continue to endure. Despite the law changing and trans people getting more mainstream attention[41, 42] in hit shows like *Transparent* and Caitlyn Jenner's own reality TV show *I Am Cait*, life is still a struggle for many trans people. Dolezal's experience and Jenner's do have some commonalities, although trying to find the links between the two set off another attention storm, this time in academia.

Rebecca Tuvel in March 2017 wrote an article for the feminist journal *Hypatia*, titled "In Defense of Transracialism," where she compared the response to Dolezal in the media with similar responses to trans people. Immediately there were calls to retract the article, and the editor who had published it was fired. Tuvel issued a statement on May 1, 2017:

> I wrote this piece from a place of support for those with nonnormative identities, and frustration about the ways individuals who inhabit them are so often excoriated, body-shamed, and silenced. When the case of Rachel Dolezal surfaced, I perceived a transphobic logic that lay at the heart of the constant attacks against her. My article is an effort to extend our thinking alongside transgender theories to other nonnormative possibilities.

The similarities between trans people and Dolezal had been explored earlier in 2016 in Roger Brubaker's book *Trans: Gender and Race in an Age of Unsettled Identities*. Both Tuvel and Brubaker go through the parallels between trans people and Dolezal using logic rather than emotion. As Brubaker explains:

> The distinction between sex and gender—and the irrelevance of ancestry to definitions of sex and gender—has made it possible to construe gender identity as a subjective individual property that is uncoupled from the body. Racial identity, however, is understood to be tightly coupled to the body and to be grounded in social relations, specifically in family and ancestry. This holds even more strongly in North America, where racial classification has historically depended not only on phenotype, but also crucially, on ancestry.[43]

Despite, the thoughtful correlations from both a historian and philosopher between these two forms of trans, the main objection to these comparisons was similar to the objections about cultural appropriation: people's own trauma made them have emotional reactions rather than logical ones.

This brings us to the other main objection to Dolezal and it is about people's feelings rather than her rights. Many claim Dolezal is not black because she hasn't been living the experiential blackness that writers like Baldwin and Morrison spoke of. Dolezal has certainly suffered, but she has not been ascribed an identity and the negative construct that goes with it from birth. Many black people speak of the immutability of blackness, the burden, the inescapability from that image others project onto them from the moment they are deemed black. The criticism of Dolezal often centers around her freedom to be white again. However, a decade has passed and she is not identifying as white. She feels psychologically that she doesn't have a choice.

Several years have passed since Dolezal's fifteen minutes of media fame. In this time, she has written two books, given a TED Talk, given birth to another black son, and continues to identify as black and be involved in causes that fight oppression. She has changed her name to Nkechi Amare Diallo to separate her from her birth parents and the media storm around her.

Dolezal can never experience the historical trauma that people who have black ancestors have felt. The history of colonization, slavery, Jim Crow, and lynchings[44] is passed down to successive generations. In a study done on Holocaust survivors, traumas affect the DNA of the survivors and that in turn is passed on to the children of these people and even the grandchildren. They say it takes several generations to unmake the toxic effects of cultural historical traumas like these. However, she is similar to other black people who emigrated from the Caribbean and never experienced these historical traumas. But can Dolezal have some understanding of the daily burden of what one feels in living as a black person? The black body has consequences with police, and mass incarceration, but also the smaller micro-aggressions[45] that take place in schools, grocery stores, and hospitals. But also it is the framing of blackness in the film industry, television, and social media that makes someone black feel their twoness. The consciousness that they are negatively portrayed and must always be battling against these stereotypes is an exhausting but necessary part of being black. Dolezal did not grow up watching her parents live in black bodies that kept them from opportunities, but she did watch it in her four black siblings and her sons Izaiah, Franklin, and Langston.

Spokane NAACP leader Quarles-Burnley told *The Spokesman-Review*: "But you can't portray that you have lived the experience of a particular race that you aren't part of."[46] What is the "experience of a particular race"? Today, there are racially ambiguous black people that may identify in a variety of ways, dark-skinned black people who live in primarily white communities, black people like Oprah Winfrey who because of their fame aren't always viewed as black. Their wealth admits them into a world where money is the main identifying feature. Not every black person living today has experienced racism regularly. This begs the other essentialist question: Is black suffering different from the suffering of people who have been "othered" or had constructs about them that are as old as their histories. Jewish disabled suffering? Arab geriatric suffering? Black trans suffering? Asian "little people" suffering? Native American blind suffering. We would need to create an infinite amount of categories to cover them all, just as the census keeps expanding, but can never capture the truth in people's particular identities. The white journalist Griffin, who darkened his skin and was taken for black, immediately suffered from this new identity and began to experience the psychological damage from the continuous "hate stare" from white people as well as the physical brutality. But after he was outed as white, he was burned in effigy by white racists and had to move to Mexico for his safety. Was his suffering and terror any different because he was "really" white? Dolezal has suffered much in her life from her abusive childhood and marriage to surviving cancer to being humiliated and eviscerated in the media. She has suffered watching people she loved discriminated against in her own home and raised sons who face discrimination every day as black boys and men. She herself has been read as a light-skinned black woman for thirteen years. Who is allowed to determine if she has suffered enough to be legitimately black?

Today in the United States, we have the most multicultural, multiracial society ever, not to mention a recent president with one white and one black parent. Because of this, people have felt the ground shifting under the binary racial system. In 2013, the US Census,[47] the determinant of human categorization, acknowledged on its website that race is a choice, not a reality. It reads: "The Census Bureau collects race data . . . based on self-identification. The racial categories included in the census questionnaire generally reflect a social definition of race recognized in this country, and not an attempt to define race biologically, anthropologically or genetically."[48] In the last decade, it has also begun to accept several boxes ticked in racial category instead of one or the other as part of its understanding of the new "mixed" population.

The boundaries of racial definition today are slipping and allowing for a more fluid identity where people can feel a more authentic one than the one ascribed at birth. Although race trials of the past didn't acknowledge self-identification, today self-identification is an important part of identity. Joe Kincheloe in *White Reign* distinguishes the ways white people can choose to be black:

> To choose blackness or brownness early on as a way to escape the stigma of whiteness and to avoid responsibility for owning whiteness is still very much an act of whiteness, but to choose blackness or brownness as a way of politically misidentifying with white privilege is, on the other hand, an act of transgression, a traitorous act that reveals a fidelity to the struggle for justice.[49]

This struggle is one that has great meaning for Dolezal in her work. The result of this media trial is that Dolezal lost her standing in the community and her work. She has been excluded from the Baltimore Book Festival where she was invited to speak and promote her book (and nearly every other book signing) and blocked from participating in the Martin Luther King Jr. Dreamfest in North Carolina. On her trip to South Africa to visit her son Izaiah, who was doing a study abroad there, she was invited to be made an honorary tribe member by the Khoisan tribe because of her work as an activist. However, right after the ceremony, a white South African woman grabbed the microphone and began screaming at Dolezal, insisting she is white and must claim whiteness. She now earns her living as a hairstylist of African hair. It's clear what has been lost, but what has been gained?

The response to Dolezal speaks of the cultural anxiety that is coming from a shifting landscape. As Jenkins states in his introduction to the book of essays on *Authentic Blackness*, "Questions about authenticity tend to arise when culture is under assault—as it is everywhere as a consequence of economic globalization and the commercialization of every area of life that is one of globalizations' major consequences."[50] Although white supremacy is deeply entrenched, Americans are beginning to question the black/white binary in its social construction. Hobbs writes in her book *A Chosen Exile* about this new way of viewing race:

> The essence of identity is not found in an individual's qualities, but rather in the ways that one recognizes oneself and is recognized as kindred. These forms of recognition may begin with superficial markers such as skin color, speech, and dress, but these are only indicators of associative relations, ways of being in the world, and an imagined sharing of a common original and iconic experience.[51]

Dolezal may not seem like it, but she is on the frontier of what has become the new incarnation of race: one that allows for authenticity and self-empowerment—a move away from ascribed identity. The inherent trauma that the nation has gone through because of the construct of race is still an open wound. Dolezal is the ghost that haunts our assumptions about race and tells us we aren't standing on firm ground anymore.

NOTES

1. Fields, Karen Elise, and Barbara Jeanne Fields, *Racecraft: The Soul of Inequality in American Life.*
2. Becker, Howard S., *Outsiders: Studies in the Sociology of Deviance*, 8–9.
3. This choice is explored eloquently in Danzy Senna's *Caucasia* where two sisters coming from one black and one white parent move fluidly through identities: white, Jewish, black.
4. Rosenblatt, Roger, "A Nation of Pained Hearts," 43.
5. The word mulatto is a derogatory term for a person who is mixed race with a black and white parent. It comes from the Spanish for mule, which is the result of a donkey mating with a horse resulting in a sterile animal. Here Ellis repurposes the word in a positive light.
6. Ellis, Trey, "The New Black Aesthetic," 235.

7. Sanchez, Raf and Peter Foster, "You Rape Our Women and Are Taking over Our Country" Charleston Church Gunman Told Black Victims."

8. In an interview, Dolezal explained to me this was because she was trying to deescalate their attempts to create drama as is done in shows like *Jerry Springer*.

9. Dolezal, Rachel, and Storms Reback, *In Full Color: Finding My Place in a Black and White World*, 84.

10. KXLY, "Raw Interview with Rachel Dolezal."

11. Mathis-Lilley, Ben, "Dolezal Says She's Felt Black from Early Age, Evades Tougher Credibility Questions on *Today*."

12. NBC, "Rachel Dolezal: 'Nothing About Being White Describes Who I Am.'"

13. MSNBC, "Rachel Dolezal on Her Connection with the Black Experience."

14. NPR, "WATCH: In Interview, Rachel Dolezal Admits She Was Born White."

15. Dolezal and Reback, *In Full Color*, 4.

16. Dolezal, Joshua, *Down from the Mountaintop: From Belief to Belonging*.

17. Joyce, Kathryn, "The Homeschool Apostates."

18. Brumfield, Ben, "Race of Rachel Dolezal, Head of Spokane NAACP, Comes Under Question."

19. Passers often chose to join a race so they could be with their loved one. This didn't always turn out well. See Rhinelander versus Rhinelander where mixed race Alice Jones married the white Leonard Rhinelander. After pressure from his family, he sued her for divorce for misleading him on her race. In court, she was made to disrobe and show her body to the court in an attempt to prove her husband must have known she was black.

20. Dolezal and Reback, *In Full Color*, 8.

21. Dolezal and Reback, 9.

22. Wilkerson who was a civil rights activist writes the preface to Dolezal's book, emphasizing the important role Dolezal is playing in race history.

23. Dolezal, Rachel, *Ebony Tresses*, n.d.

24. Baker, "A Much-Needed Primer on Cultural Appropriation."

25. See the work of Stuart Hall and Paul Gilroy on hybridization.

26. Shriver, Lionel, "Lionel Shriver's Full Speech: 'I Hope the Concept of Cultural Appropriation Is a Passing Fad.'"

27. Fiedler, Leslie, *Waiting for the End: The American Literary Scene from Hemingway to Baldwin*, 134.

28. See Gubar, Susan, *Racechanges*, for an excellent exploration of whites' enjoyment of playing black.

29. Mailer, Norman, *The White Negro*.

30. Samuels, Allison, "Rachel Dolezal's True Lies."

31. Koerner, Claudia, "Student Who Posted Rachel Dolezal Interview Wanted Public to See Her 'Be Herself.'"

32. Fieldstadt, Elisha, and Lamarre Giselle, "NAACP Chapter President Rachel Dolezal Plans to Address Race Controversy Monday."

33. Koerner, "Student Who Posted Rachel Dolezal Interview Wanted Public to See Her 'Be Herself.'"

34. Dolezal and Reback, *In Full Color*, 2.

35. Dreisinger, Baz, *Near Black: White-to-Black Passing in American Culture*, 124.

36. "Response Re: Rachel Dolezal."

37. Winsor, Morgan, "Is Rachel Dolezal White or Black? Africana Studies Colleague, NAACP Respond to Controversy."

38. "Response Re: Rachel Dolezal."

39. Cone, James H., *Black Theology and Black Power*, 151.

40. Crowley Coker, Hillary, "When Rachel Dolezal Attended Howard University, She Was Still White."

41. Barnard College, a woman's college, hired their first trans professor Jennifer Boylan in 2014.

42. The "Bathroom Bill" or North Carolina's Public Facilities Privacy & Security Act (which allowed trans people to use bathrooms that match their gender identification) was made law in 2016, although portions were repealed in 2017.

43. Brubaker, Rogers, *Trans: Gender and Race in an Age of Unsettled Identities*, 6.

44. Thomson, Helen, "Study of Holocaust Survivors Finds Trauma Passed on to Children's Genes."

45. Indirect, subtle, or unintentional discrimination against members of a marginalized group. See Rankine, Claudia, *Citizen*.

46. Esrada, Sheryl, "Rachel Dolezal's Replacement Naima Quarles-Burnley Speaks Out."

47. The census is still a problematic form. Although many other categories are expanding and showing overlapping identities, "white" still stands as a one-check category and is the only one that isn't divided further into ethnic identities except for "white hispanic." The amount of $400 billion will be allocated by this constitutionally mandated service, but it becomes harder and harder to use it to go to the populations that need it. It is one of the reasons people feel they need to choose a race.

48. US Census Bureau, "Race." Melissa Nobles in her book *Shades of Citizenship* reminds that "census bureaus are not simply producers of racial statistical data; they are also political actors" and that census bureaus are "often overlooked as participants in the creation and perpetuation of race." Nobles, *Shades of Citizenship*, 1–2.

49. Kincheloe, Joe L., *White Reign*, 72.

50. Japtok, Martin, and Jerry Rafiki Jenkins, *Authentic Blackness—"Real" Blackness*, 1.

51. Hobbs, Allyson Vanessa, *A Chosen Exile: A History of Racial Passing in American Life*, 14.

Chapter 3

Obama as Racial Rorschach
The First **Blank** *President*

President Barack Obama, like Dolezal, modeled a new form of racial identity that hasn't been attempted so publicly and pervasively before. He was transparent in his racial fluidity and spoke about it in his autobiography, but also in speeches leading to his election and during his two terms as president. Analyzing the way Obama consciously formed his racial identity and the way this identity was received by American voters tells us something about the firmness of the binary at the same time that it models a way it is becoming permeable to change.

Obama is a racial Rorschach. He was the first black president to some, but the first fill-in-the-*blank* president to others. Everyone sees something in him that reflects his or her own racial identity or ideas about race. Because of America's historical one-drop rule[1] and black/white binary, this uncategorizable president has been unique and illuminating about Americans' racial thinking. The question of Obama's race hasn't reached any consensus, but has been a fervent topic of discussion throughout his election and two terms as president; this discourse has brought with it the age-old American debate about what makes someone black and what makes someone white. Many groups claim him with pride: black, multiracials, Irish, Hawaiian.[2] Many others place him disdainfully in a set of other groups: alien immigrant, Arab, Indonesian, and Kenyan. Obama's ability to shift between racial categories is distinct from racial "passing" for he feels he is genuinely many things, whereas passers believe they belong in one group but move secretly into another. In other words, passers claim an identity they believe they don't possess. His authentic ability to manifest multiple identities[3] is a new possibility for a generation who identify themselves as "fusion," "mixed," or refuse the notion of racial category altogether. As Shelby Steele puts it, Obama "speaks in some way to the fissures of race that have characterized the

American experience, as well as the fluid state of identity—the leaps through time, the collision of cultures—that mark our modern life."[4] [5] And David Remnick reiterates this in his biography of Obama, *The Bridge*, calling him "someone who represented the variousness of American life."[6]

Obama himself in his speeches and public appearances consciously linked his vision of America with his racially integrated vision of himself. He modeled racial fluidity by code switching easily between singing gospel in a black church and using his Princeton law school voice, which is associated with "sounding white," and referred to himself jokingly as "mutts like me." He is aware of both the constructedness of racial identity and the potential for a multiplicity of identities, which he emphasizes in his autobiography *Dreams from My Father*. However, looking at voter surveys and interviews over two terms reveals the complex interpretive strategies citizens have developed for managing Obama's racial ambiguity and thus their own struggle with racial boundaries. Although it looked transformative on the surface, people's interpretations of Obama revealed just how stubborn their hold was on the black/white binary. Although many accepted Obama as their president, their complex justifications of his "unique" race revealed that the deep roots of racial category are still with us.

Scholars have disagreed about what the election of Obama means for America and race. Some see it as a much wished for breakthrough,[7] while others see it as a deluded postracial fantasy[8] or as a polarizing force.[9] Others use Obama as simply a way to further explore how race operates in America.[10] At the 2013 White House Correspondents' dinner, Obama introduced a short comedy film. It features a "promo" for an imagined biopic called *Obama* where the white actor Daniel Day Lewis plays the president. Steven Spielberg in the "promo" for the film asks when introducing the film, "Who is Obama really, we don't know."[11] This joke, and the joke of the Irish actor Lewis playing Obama, allude to Obama's mixed-race enigma. Obama knows he is a racial conundrum and makes it the subject of much of his humor in his two terms in the White House.

Obama's racial elusiveness has also been fundamental to his success as president. His election campaign and his speeches play around the edges of racial boundaries both by alluding directly to it as he does in the "promo" video, but also by moving fluidly between tropes of blackness and whiteness. Christopher Metzler emphasizes how this one president could mean something so different for differently racially identified people: "While many whites voted for Obama as a way to move beyond race, many Blacks voted for him as a way to vindicate the entire black race."[12] Many white people also saw him as without a race. This chapter evaluates the discourse, visual representations, and attitudes around the racial identity of Obama. It will look at how his mixed race played out as suspicious, he symbolizes his mixed race as the ideal America of inclusiveness and fluidity, and how being born to a white mother in Hawaii and black father who was absent forced him to choose his blackness and perform it along with whiteness. Obama may have revealed how strong the binary is for most Americans, but he also modeled a new way of being in terms of race. In this new approach, our idiosyncratic personal stories dictate how much and how deeply we are identified with race; it shows how it is possible to be fluid in our use of black and white.

DETERMINING OBAMA'S RACE

In a 2009 study by David C. Wilson and Matthew O. Hunt,[13] we can see how opinions about Obama divide by race.

Whites see him as:

Black 24%
Mixed 53%
Both/neither 18%
Refused/don't know 5%

Blacks see him as:

Black 55%
Mixed 34%
Both/neither 8%
Don't know/refused 3%[14]

Here we can see that no one agrees on his race and a full 18 percent of white people don't know what to call him, although 8 percent of black people also couldn't assess his race.

In a national survey of 2,230 Americans in March 2010 done by the Harris Poll, the mystery of Obama was revealed as mostly negative. The percentage of the group that perceived him as various suspicious incarnations are reflected in the following breakdown:

40% he's a socialist
32% Muslim
25% and not born in the states, ineligible to be president
20% doing many of the things Hitler did
14% may be the antichrist[15]

This view of Obama as a nonwhite alien who is un-American was spearheaded by Donald Trump's birther movement. This early perspective of Obama shows that his race and loyalties created some confusion for people. The answers "socialist," "Muslim, and "not born in the United States" are how people read his itinerant childhood and middle name (Hussein). Ishmael Reed attributes these misreadings to simple racism. He cites former senator Bob Kerrey, who tried to associate Obama with Islamo fascists: "His name is Barack Hussein Obama and his father was a Muslim and his paternal grandmother is a Muslim" and "he spent a little bit of time in a secular madrassa."[16] Later he points to Wesley Pruden in the *Washington Times*, saying, "It's not the fault of the president that he has no natural instinct or blood impulse for what America of the 57 states is about. He was sired by a Kenyan father, born to a mother attracted to men of the third worlds and reared by grandparents in Hawaii, a paradise far from the American Mainstream."[17] Even earlier than this was the *Time* magazine October 20, 2008, cover.[18]

In this manipulated photo, we can see not only the representation of Obama as mixed race, but also the idea that his whiteness is a cover up. The photograph of Obama's face has been painted white on the left side to suggest minstrel shows of the past where white men caricatured black men. This idea of Obama as putting on blackface is echoed in the words of state senator Donne Trotter, who called him "the white man in blackface in our community."[19] No one agrees which color he is painting on, only that he is hiding something and faking some race. The fact that his head is also floating without being rooted in a neck and body makes him slightly sinister as does his almost imperceptible smile. The headlines add to the suspicion with phrases and words like "foreignness," "worried white voters," and "Obama loses."

In 2009, a digitally manipulated photo of Obama (taken from a *Time* 2006 cover) similarly covered in white paint like a minstrel show performer went viral. The image is a reference to the film *Batman*, which featured a villain called "The Joker," who is a sadistic sociopath who has a yen for blowing things up. Like the supervillain, Obama's eyes are circled with an eerie blacking and his mouth surrounded by a sloppy red painted grin.[20] This view of Obama sees him as possibly "blowing up" the country as it stands by bringing in a "socialist agenda" such as national healthcare. Obama again is in disguise and we don't know what he may do.

However, this representation of Obama as shifty and unknown ran parallel to another view of him as some people got to know his story and hear his vision of America, symbolized by his mixed race. He began to represent moving beyond the compartmentalized thinking about race and emphasized shared humanness. Michael Eric Dyson argues that "the goal should not be to transcend race, but to transcend the biased meanings associated with race."[21] It is these biased meanings that are driving Obama's racial image. He is aware of others labeling him, but continues to evade these labels. In the documentary *Chasing Daybreak*, Obama explains, "What I am always cautious about is persons of mixed race focusing so narrowly on their own unique experiences that they are detached from larger struggles, and I think it's important to try to avoid that sense of exclusivity, and feeling that you're special in some way."[22] In a 2007 interview with CBS's *60 Minutes*, he claimed, "I am rooted in the African American community. But I'm not defined by it. I am comfortable in my racial identity. But that's not all I am."[23] He reiterates this in *Dreams* when he says, "I learned to slip back and forth between my black and white worlds, understanding that each possessed its own language and customs and structures of meaning, convinced that with a bit of translation on my part, the two worlds would eventually cohere."[24] The familiar Obama image (figure 3.1), which was designed by street artist Shepard Fairey and came to be the iconic election poster, is in stark contrast to the 2008 *Time* cover, illustrating this everyman notion.

Here there is no black and white, but red, white, and blue. Obama does not have his face split down the middle, but a kind of melding of colors in both the background and on his face. The word hope in all capital letters emphasizes the symbol of the new president. His expression is looking upward into the future with a solemn reflective gaze. Obama crystallized this view of America in his speech delivered at the 2004 Democratic National Convention (DNC). "There's not a black America and a white America and a Latino America and an Asian America; there's the United States of America."[25] This worldview is reiterated in his book *The Audacity of Hope* the title of which came from a sermon he attended during which he describes having an epiphany. He imagined "the stories of ordinary black people merging with the stories of David and Goliath, Moses and Pharaoh, the Christians in the lion's den, Ezekiel's field of dry bones."[26] In other words, he was able to see black people as part of a continuum of all people, not just those ascribed as black. In his 2004 DNC speech he also talks about "recognizing ourselves in one another" and having "common hopes."[27] Through a concept of American identity that is bound up with diversity and change, he has become the embodiment of those ideals.[28]

In his second inaugural speech, Obama emphasized the value of equality expressed in the Declaration of Independence: "We hold these truths to be self-evident, that all men are created equal." Despite America's shameful history of slavery, lynchings, and Jim Crow, Obama emphasizes the founding values.[29] In Obama's America, "America in an ethnically inclusive, unifying manner helps neutralize the equation of America with whiteness, by claiming that idea for citizens of any hue."[30] Reifowitz explains that this view of America is modeled by Obama's upbringing, describing him as "the man with a white mother and black father, growing up in diverse Hawaii and Indonesia

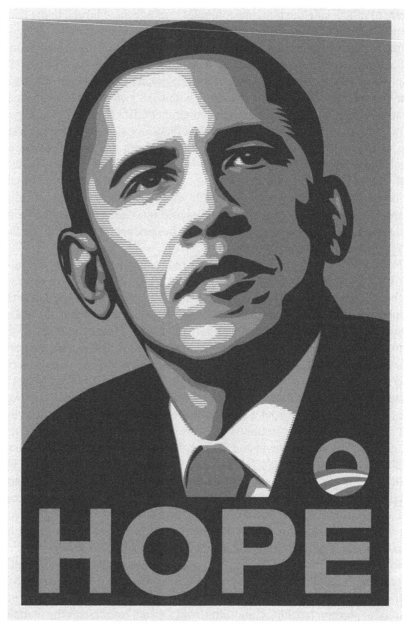

Figure 3.1 "Hope" poster of Barack Obama, designed by street artist Shepard Fairey, which became an iconic symbol.

and conscious of ethnic and national identity." He concludes it's a "national belonging that all Americans can embrace."[31]

Obama not only urges people to think in this racially transcendent way, but also forces it by playing with people's attempts to categorize him. He often jokes about being "too black" or "not black enough." He code switches easily when he uses slang when in a predominantly black neighborhood ("nah, we straight," he says to a cashier who tries to give him his change after buying a chili dog),[32] but then also gets welcomed in Dublin and shouts to the crowd, "My name is Barack Obama, of the Moneygall Obamas, and I've come home to find the apostrophe we lost somewhere along the way."[33] Zadie Smith talks about what a virtuoso Obama is for vocal range: "The new president displays an enviable facility for dialogue . . . Obama can do young Jewish male, black old lady from the south side, white woman from Kansas, Kenyan elders, white Harvard nerds. This new president doesn't just speak for his people. He can speak them. It is a disorienting talent in a president; we're so unused to it."[34]

Obama's fluidity around his own racial identity is a model for how one can be both authentic and transcendent about self. He started using the notion of being an American as meaning someone who is fluid and inclusive. His positive slogan "Yes We Can" for his first election emphasizes the "we" in America or "we the people," a phrase he repeats in his "A More Perfect Union" speech in 2008. Obama can emphasize both blackness and whiteness, and at times evades the binary to emphasize a "transcendent cosmopolitanism."[35]

Obama had an awareness of the constructedness of identity from an early age, which he then shaped and altered as explored in *Dreams*. "I was trying to raise myself as a black man in America and beyond the given of my appearance, no one around me seemed to know exactly what that meant," he says in the preface to the first edition.[36] He admits to being an admirer of Malcolm X because "his repeated acts of self-creation spoke to me." Obama strives for authenticity, and his autobiography is really a quest for his true self within and beyond race. But what is race? As King asks in his essay "Becoming Black": "is 'black' made of colour, culture or allegiance?"[37] In his book on mixed race, Peter Aspinall outlines the different reasons people see their own race the way they do.

1. It is my own sense of personal identity
2. It is the way society sees me
3. It is the group I feel I belong to
4. My parents are from different racial/ethnic groups
5. My ancestors before my parents were from different racial/ethnic groups
6. My friends/peers identify me in this way[38]

Interestingly, Obama could claim all of these and has emphasized these reasons at different times in his life. His goal as he put it in the preface to the first edition of his autobiography was to find "a workable meaning for myself as a black man." It took him until his early community organizing work to feel he knew what his personal identity was (number one). In *Dreams*, he talks about the moment he understood the burden of blackness (number two). He describes seeing a magazine spread on a black man who tried to peel off his skin to change it to white. This self-mutilation shocked him, and it was then he wondered staring at his own skin in the mirror if "something was wrong with me." Here was where he became aware that society read black as something bad. His internalized understanding of the shame of blackness made him try to avoid being associated with the only other black child in school whom the other children decided should automatically be coupled up with him. In college in the US, he chose to be part of a black group and black peers (number three and number six). His awareness of his parents difference took him some time to acknowledge (number four). He admits that before the age of six, he didn't know he needed a race. And he says it "barely registered in his mind" that his father was "black as pitch and my mother white as milk."[39] It was only in adulthood that he tried to understand the influence his absent Kenyan father had on him and went to visit his country and kin (number five).

Culture was key to his black identity. He not only makes many references to pop culture in his public appearances, but talks about its early influences on him in high school. Obama in *Dreams* emphasizes how important this was to feeling black and being read as black:

> TV movies, the radio; those were the places to start. Pop culture was color coded, after all, an arcade of images from which you could cop a walk, a talk, a step, a style. I couldn't croon like Marvin Gaye, but I could learn to dance all the *Soul Train* steps. I couldn't pack a gun like Shaft or Superfly, but I could sure enough curse like Richard Pryor. And I could play basketball, with a consuming passion.[40]

He learned to perform the "cool black brother" during Punahou High School when he made his first real black friends who comprised most of the black population in the school. He learned from them how to identify as black partly by understanding the damage and mistrust of whites. He looks back on this with an awareness of it being a role he was practicing: "I was living out a caricature of black male adolescence, itself a caricature of swaggering American manhood."[41] He continued to explore this politicized black identity by consciously choosing friends in college who were more politically active black students. In *Dreams*, he shows one of his strategies of emphasizing his membership was to put down other black students who he felt reminded him of his formerly "unwoke"[42] self. At one point he makes fun of a black student named Tim, quipping that "he should be called Tom." But he was aware of the insincerity of it and then was shamed by another black friend, named Marcus, for turning on a fellow black person, and he began to understand the concept of racial loyalty.

Later during his time in the White House, he points to his blackness by having the symbols and objects of blackness prominently displayed in the Oval office: books on civil rights, recordings of Mahalia Jackson, a bust of Martin Luther King, a framed quote and a book by Martin Luther King, and a book from Muhammad Ali. After joining Trinity United Church of Christ, Obama learned how to resonate like a black Christian church preacher and took on the black Christian identity. We see this in his remarks and rendition of "Amazing Grace" when he eulogized at a memorial service for the Emmanuel Church murder victims.

He talks about learning to be comfortable with a new language or how he learned to speak "black": "White folks. The term itself was uncomfortable in my mouth at first; I felt like a non-native speaker tripping over a difficult phrase."[43] Later at the White House Correspondents' dinner, he shakes his head as he says in a common black vernacular "Mmm mmm mmm." His acquiring of the cool black crooner is clear when he breaks into Al Green at the Harlem's Apollo Theater and sings a line of "I am so in love with you" or repeats "I'm just tellin' the truth," or "Y'all know what I'm talking about."[44] But it's also his references to rap culture (his playlist, his preferring Jay Z to Kanye, and mentions of Young Jeezy). The most recent is his last White House Correspondents' dinner where he ends with the two words "Obama out" and then drops his mic (a gesture made by rappers after a really crushing performance).

Outside of his performance of black are the facts of his features. Obama is seen as black in his skin color combined with his kinky hair and what people read as black features. CBS correspondent Steve Kroft asked him at what point he decided he was black. Obama's answer was simple. "Well, I'm not sure I decided it. I think, you know, if you look African-American in this society, you're treated as African-American."[45] He emphasizes the way you can't escape your blackness when you are marked racially as black when he famously said, "If I had a son, he would look like Trayvon."[46] This statement emphasized that to be a black boy or man, you are endangered just by that fact of pigmentation.

His conscious choice to often call attention to his dark-skinned wife Michelle during speeches adds to his black credibility. He alluded to her growing up in the South Side of Chicago and her hardworking father who despite his disability never missed a day of work. Not only is the South Side of Chicago seen as a particularly authentic black credential, but Michelle, who then transcended her poor childhood to go to Princeton and Harvard Law and become a successful lawyer, is also living the American dream. In his farewell speech to the nation, he says "Michelle . . . (*points to her, audience goes wild with applause*) Michelle LaVaughn Robinson, girl of the South Side," before he continues to list her accomplishments during his term as president.[47]

Michelle and their two daughters emphasized his color also, something that wasn't the case when he was a child in Hawaii being raised by white grandparents and a white mother. He takes many photos with them and calls attention to Michelle by his constant romantic gestures and physical affection to her as well as mentioning her more than any other president mentioned his wife.[48] Most important, he modeled a black man completely in love with a dark-skinned black woman, which combats the historic narrative of black women being undesirable. Michelle's beauty and body were celebrated on covers of *Vogue* (three times), *In-Style*, *Ebony*, and the *New York Times Magazine*, among others. Articles were written about how to get her arms[49] and she was proclaimed a fashion icon.[50] Because she took on the role of spokesperson for child obesity, she was often seen exercising, dancing, and showcasing her body (and skin) in videos and photographs. Her bringing in many black superstars from the music industry (Beyoncè, Jay-Z) further emphasized this pride of culture. All this was part of Obama's identity as black and proud.[51]

Obama understands the importance of allegiance to being black, calling it community, "whatever my father might say, I knew it was too late to ever truly claim Africa as my home. I had come to understand myself as a black American and . . . what I needed was a community . . . a place where I could put down stakes and test my commitments."[52] He knew he needed to find a black community post-college after hearing his college friend Regina's stories of her intact black community in Chicago. Obama admits that he envied her "vision of black life in all its possibility, a vision that filled me with longing—a longing for place, and a fixed and definite history."[53] It's no surprise that he chose a wife that was from that same neighborhood. He then decided after Harvard Law School to do community service for voting in Chicago.

Finally in his black credentials is that he has experienced racism as a black man. As mentioned earlier, he only became aware of this deeply entrenched hatred of the black man at the age of nine when he saw a magazine photo of a man who had destroyed his face by attempting to change his skin. Obama describes the experience as "violent for me, an ambush attack."[54] At school when word got out that his father was from Kenya, students made monkey sounds and asked if his father ate people: "My sense that I didn't belong continued to grow."[55]

It was later as a teen that he began to observe this antiblack message in the culture he was absorbing around him. He noticed on TV programs how the role of black men was never a strong, empowered one. "Cosby never got the girl" and "Santa was white."[56] His black identity never connected to Kenya even though his father was from there, but he realizes that white antagonism to black skin is something that unites him to all Africans as well. He asks what if "the only tie that bound me to him [his father] or to Africa, was a name, a blood type, or white people's scorn."[57] In adolescence he became aware that even his white family members had been affected by the messages of white supremacy as well. He found out from his grandfather that his grandmother Toot was afraid of someone at a bus stop because he was black. "I knew for the first time that I was utterly alone."[58]

Later, in college, he reframed how he saw his mother's attitudes toward blacks (which he thought were innocent) when she suggested they go see the Brazilian film *Black Orpheus*. In this, he saw a work that exoticized blacks as happy dancing children, close to nature, and close to animals. He began to see that even her love for his father was touched by this exoticism. He became aware of his mother's constant promotion of his absent father as extraordinary and those qualities somehow connected to his father's blackness. He writes that for his mother, "to be black was to be the beneficiary of a great inheritance, a special destiny, glorious burdens that only we were strong enough to bear."[59] To have his own mother's view of blackness be so distorted was when he realized he really needed a black community that he could trust.

Perhaps because of his conscious strategy to find his blackness, blacks began to see him as black. It is noticeable that in his second term, he began showing his "black self" more, although he seemed to avoid "race" before that. Obama's first term had a series of black distancing moves that the black community responded to. He did not attend the black union symposium and his Father's Day speech in 2008[60] was perceived as shaming black fathers and playing into the racist stereotype of the absent irresponsible black man. This had begun earlier when he ran against incumbent Bobby Rush for senator. Black voters didn't perceive him as very black. A media consultant called it "the Black Panther against the professor."[61]

This detachment was particularly evident in reference to public race scandals, including the response to Hurricane Katrina and the arresting of Harvard professor Henry Louis Gates Jr. outside his own home, which was seen as weak and not in solidarity with the black community. About the arrest, he claimed, "I don't know, not having been there and not seeing all the facts, what role race played in that," and later he seemed to play down the seriousness of it: "The Cambridge police acted stupidly in arresting somebody when there was already proof that they were in their own home."[62] His lack of out-rage wasn't helped when he attempted to make amends by having Gates to the White House for a beer. He was perceived as not taking the "black side" on political issues such as the firing of Shirley Sherrod or denying that race was a factor in the slow government response to Katrina. He even called Kanye West "a jackass" when the rapper aggressively tried to get attention moved from the white singer Taylor Swift to Beyoncé during the MTV Music Video Awards.

Because Obama wasn't a candidate like Shirley Chisolm or Jesse Jackson who were running on a black platform, blacks didn't overwhelmingly support him in his early candidacy for senator against the much more race conscious former Black Panther candidate Bobby Rush, who claimed, "I'm a race politician, he's not."[63] He admits that people can't take him at face value when they discover his white mother, claiming they "no longer know who I am."[64] Blacks were busy rejecting him as authentically black, such as Debra Dickerson, claiming he was not descended from slaves, so not black; but others referred to his birth, upbringing, and elite education as dissociating him from blackness.[65]

By late 2011, black people saw Obama as unequivocally black. In Mark P. Orbe's focus groups, this perception of black people is clear. Although Obama plays his part in controlling perceptions of his whiteness or blackness, people have their own ways of translating Obama depending on their racial background as well. In his study, *Communication Realities in a "Post-Racial" Society: What the U.S. Public Really Thinks About Barack Obama*, Orbe shows a clear division in how whites see Obama and how blacks see him. Although many polls have been done, this study gets an in-depth insight in the thoughts and strategies that help people envision Obama as raced.

One recurring theme in these conversations is black pride. As one black participant put it, "My brother and some of his friends thought it was a big deal. They have to wear IDs in school, and you're not supposed to write on them at all. But, he and his friends . . . all of the black guys wrote on them saying 'My president is black.'"[66] Obama's blackness here is a source of cele-bration even to the point of subversive rebelling. Their connection to Obama, needs to be declared. Another participant felt strongly the effect of Obama embracing his blackness publicly:

> I remember someone actually asking him about how he identified. And it created a challenge for him, because when he tells his story, his narrative is clearly on where he is biracial. He acknowledges, and accepts, and embraces all of the aspects of his culture. But when he answered that question, he actually said, "I'm a black man. I'm treated like a black man." I think that at that moment it was very interesting, because there seems to be a little bit of a disconnect

between how he embraces all of the different aspects of his identity and who he is and then versus how other people see him. "People see me as a black man," is what he said. "So, I see myself as a black man." What was most impressive about this is that he said it with a sense of pride, not shame.[67]

Again, this speaker gains great pride from seeing a black man declaring himself black, proudly and in an office of great importance. This is echoed in another participant's words:

> I find myself getting offended when I hear people of white descent talking about Obama like they don't see him as black. Maybe, it's just me, but I do feel like every time I see Obama I feel proud because I'm black and he's black. I always see a black president. I feel like we always say that we don't—but we see color. WHY? WHY? Even like his swag, or the way that he communicates. I feel like that is the ultimate swag of a positive black man. I see a BLACK president, not that he just happens to be black, he is a black man.[68]

Here the participant expresses not only a frustration with the colorblindness of whites, but also the extreme pride the participant has with identifying with Obama, whom he deeply admires. His anger and resentment at having this association taken away is clear in the all caps WHY? WHY? But also his insistence on not having the blackness washed away because Obama is president. Not only does he shout in the all capitalized BLACK, but says the word eight times in one paragraph. Obama's blackness is a fact in the most positive sense, and the participant doesn't want this black label taken off of someone so admirable and (to him) obviously black.

Although Obama doesn't talk about his white identity, he knows how to code switch easily to language that is often associated with sounding white. When campaigning he saw his mother's face in the many people who invited him to talk and was able to feel at home. Although his black mentor Frank told him to "keep your eyes open"[69] and not trust white people, he couldn't hate them as a group because he would "remember [his] mother's smile."[70] He also knew that he didn't have the characteristics people associated with black: "I was more like those black students who had grown up in the suburbs, kids whose parents had already paid the price of escape. You could spot them by the way they talked, the people they sat with, they refused to be categorized. They weren't defined by the color of their skin, they would tell you. They were individuals."[71] This clearly was an assumption that "individuals" was the default position of white. He didn't identify with multiracials like his friend Joyce who told him, "I'm not black I'm multiracial . . . *they're* making me choose."[72]

Because he was raised by white grandparents and a white mother, he felt they had the biggest impact on his behavior. He only met his father twice briefly and felt he was a stranger.

Although much of the focus of the autobiography and its title are about his father, by the time the second edition came out, he reframed his life story in the preface and shifted the emphasis to his white mother "What is best in me, I owe to her."[73]

But mostly what makes middle-class white people see him as white is his squeaky clean, conservatively dressed family in the White House: wife and daughters with straightened hair, homework, vacations, dinners together. The negative tropes about black politicians are avoided. Shelby Steele writes, "He is interesting for not fitting into old racial conventions. Not only does he stand in stark contrast to a black leadership with which Americans of all races have grown exhausted—the likes of Al Sharpton, Jesse Jackson, and Julian Bond—he embodies something that no other presidential candidate possibly can: the idealism that race is but a negligible human difference. Here is the radicalism, innate to his pedigree, that automatically casts him as the perfect antidote to America's corrosive racial politics."[74] The image the Obamas present is like a black Norman Rockwell world of innocence, family, and American traditions. In an early interview on ABC with the family,[75] Michelle mentions their family activities as picnics, fairs, and ice cream parlors. She shares that he often brings her flowers and they go on romantic dates. The only vice his young daughters out him for is preferring minty gum to other sweets, like ice cream, and leaving his bag in the hallway for them to trip on.

David Brooks highlights how Obama steers clear of any black stereotypes that would set off white people: "In all that time there hasn't been a moment in which he has publicly lost his self-control. This has been a period of tumult, combat, exhaustion and crisis. And yet there hasn't been a moment when he has displayed rage, resentment, fear, anxiety, bitterness, tears,[76] ecstasy, self-pity or impulsiveness."[77] In other words, he did not fit the corrosive stereotype of what a black man was supposed to be. Obama plays into this by wearing always a conservative gray or blue suit, stands with perfect posture, barely uses his hands when he speaks, and keeps his face relatively impassive.

His Harvard and Columbia pedigree separate him from working-class blacks and the elitism of these institutions puts off middle-class blacks. Whites still under the influence of racist tropes about black men find him an acceptable black or honorary white because his cool unemotional demeanor and Harvard Law speech patterns make him nonthreatening. Obama's studied impassiveness is partly to avoid being associated with the angry black stereotype, which is spoofed in the comedy duo of Keegan-Michael Key and Jordan Peele. Peele plays the unperturbed Obama and Key plays the expected stereotype of black rage as Luther, Obama's Anger Translator. In one skit, Peele as Obama—cool as ever—delivers his speech in a suit, tie, and placid tone. Meanwhile his "anger translator" Luther unleashes a stream of epithets and uses a high-pitched screaming voice, his eyes bugging out, calling on old stereotypes of both the coon and the black buck.[78] He jumps up and down and warns, "Hold on to your lily white asses! She gonna get that, aw yeah!"[79]

Obama himself admits in *Dreams* that he knew how to not threaten white people. He calls it his trick and he explains, "People were satisfied as long as you were courteous and smiled and made no sudden moves. They were more than satisfied; they were relieved—such a pleasant surprise to find a well-mannered young black man who didn't seem angry all the time."[80]

Obama's constant vigilance to not fall into behavior that could be suggestive of these negative images of blackness was something he was aware of and in fact invited Keegan-Michael Key (as Luther, the Anger Translator) to come to his last White House Correspondents' dinner to perform next to him stoically reading a speech. People's expectations of a black president were the opposite of Obama. In fact, Toni Morrison in her 1998 essay for the *New Yorker*, ironically suggests it is Bill Clinton that was really the first black president. Clinton *did* fall into almost all of those tropes of blackness she outlines as including "single-parent household, born poor, working-class, saxophone playing. McDonald's-and-junk-food-loving boy from Arkansas."[81] Obama, although he came from a single-parent household with his mother, emphasizes instead his two-parent household with his white grandparents. He even manages to distance himself from Clinton's image of overeating junk food with Michelle's campaign on childhood obesity and her planting an organic vegetable garden at the White House.

Finally, Obama's white roots were from Ireland and pictures surfaced of an ancestor of his that looks uncannily like him (see figure 3.2), leading people to call him "O'Bama."

Whites, in contrast to blacks, do many contortions to convince themselves Obama isn't simply black, so they can better identify and claim him. MSNBC commentator Chris Matthews infamously declared after Obama's 2010 State of the Union Address: "He is post-racial, by all appearances . . . I forgot he was black tonight for an hour. You know, he's gone a long way to become a leader of this country, and past so much history, in just a year or two. I mean, it's something we don't even think about."[82] Ironically as he consciously deracinates Obama, Matthews declares that he isn't thinking about it. This is echoed in the words of a young white woman from Massachusetts from Orbe's focus groups when she says: "Barack Obama represents a transitional bridge. The United States wasn't entirely ready for a black president. But they could be ready for Obama."[83]

Figure 3.2 Fulmoth Kearney, Obama's Irish ancestor from Moneygall, which was revealed in 2014 by Obama's third cousin once removed.
Source: Irish; Article by Megan Smolenyak: http://www.huffingtonpost.com/megan-smolenyak-smolenyak/photo-of-barack-obamas-ir_b_6358220.html.

Another participant goes on a slippery reasoning slope to work out how to think about Obama's race.

> I think that he goes beyond race. Yes, he is black but actually he is mixed. But so often people generalize your race based on the color of your skin, not actually science. Because he is president, though, he goes above and beyond race. Not only that though, but his "black characteristics" (if you will) are not there. The way that African Americans speak, the way that they behave—a lot of things about him radiate "white" not "black." And maybe that's why I don't even think about his race.[84]

This is complex logic. She begins by claiming Obama is "beyond race," then reluctantly accepts that he is black, and revises it to say he is mixed. Then she dismisses the idea of race altogether, "not actually science," then declares the president is an exception category. Then she goes back to bioracism by claiming his black characteristics aren't there. Then she returns to him being an honorary white. Then she says, "I don't even think about his race." Her lack of awareness of the complex work of justification she is managing is especially interesting. Some people refer to this as the "magic negro." In company with Sidney Poitier and Morgan Freeman, these benign figures assuage white guilt over slavery and segregation by replacing stereotypes of dangerous, highly sexualized men with sexually neutral and nonthreatening figures.[85]

Another white participant uses the president category as a "get out of black free" card when she says: "I was going to say that when I hear him, I hear him as The President. And I have to remind myself that he black. He speaks to me as a person, and it didn't bother me. Same thing for my daughter; she says 'Obama, he is the president.' She doesn't see a black president."[86] This participant has to "remind" herself about blackness. She reveals her biases when she says Obama speaks to her as a person, so the blackness "didn't bother me." Is this a reference to Obama being in a superior role of president, so he is a person, not a black person? Her daughter has mimicked her mother's logic that separates the notions of blackness and presidential.

In another participant, we get the same logic as the previous that equates president with white.

I think what was even more obvious was his communication style was what he sounded like. Unfortunately, this is based on a stereotype but white people listened to him and heard a white person talking. Obviously, they saw what they saw, but they heard a white person talking. And black people identified with what he looked like, but white people heard . . . maybe they didn't "hear white," but what they heard was "presidential." He sounded like every other presidential candidate that we ever had. He was an excellent public speaker. He wasn't too different.[87]

This speaker echoes the previous ones that Obama sounded like every other presidential candidate (white). They have left out Jesse Jackson and Shirley Chisolm—both campaigning on race and politics who presented in ways people associated more with black. One interpretation of this statement is that she is not associating him with stereotypes of black people. As Joe Biden infamously said, "the first mainstream African American who is articulate and bright and clean and a nice-looking guy."[88] In other words, he is not an angry or militant black or one that makes whites feel guilt.

This careful hedging by white voters about not caring about Obama's blackness is in keeping with the way many whites in the twenty-first century think about race. They speak in careful terms, distancing themselves from racism, but reveal their racism unknowingly. These white citizens are in turmoil about how they think about Obama and reveal their self-consciousness and ambivalence about his race. Obama's presidency revealed much of the quicksand of our racial history and how early divisions of black and white are still intact. People have just become very self-conscious about how to present what they think and feel. But Obama himself, like Dolezal, is modeling a new frontier of more of a personal choice in terms of race.

Obama had to prove his blackness to black people, so he was rendered authentic. He had to distance himself from black stereotypes for white people to prove he wasn't "that kind of black guy." The obsession with Obama's race in both the black and white community reveals the contortions people make to keep these racial boundaries intact. Zadie Smith looks at the idea of authentic blackness as a kind of incarceration:

> To me, the instruction "keep it real" is a sort of prison cell, two feet by five. The fact is, it's too narrow. I just can't live comfortably in there. "Keep it real" replaced the blessed and solid genetic fact of Blackness with a flimsy imperative. It made Blackness a quality each individual Black person was constantly in danger of losing. And almost anything could trigger the loss of one's Blackness: attending certain universities, an impressive variety of jobs, a fondness for opera, a white girlfriend, an interest in golf. And of course, any change in the voice. There was a popular school of thought that maintained the voice was at the very heart of the thing: fail to keep it real there and you'd never see your Blackness again.[89]

Here Smith reveals the rigidity of racial category for blacks, which is often policed by other blacks. It was easy early on in Obama's campaigning for blacks to disqualify him from blackness. However Obama, always aware of these tropes of blackness, changed his voice and gestures as he entered his second term, less afraid of alienating voters. The complex set of moves necessary to keep blacks and whites unthreatened by his race was unparalleled in any other president or candidate. Although he will go down in the history books as the first black president, this major breakthrough didn't shift the firmness of these racial boundaries for many Americans. They just found a way to identify him with their own race rather than allow him to be the fullness of his identity. Obama modeled racial freedom and fluidity, but we have to wait for Generation Z to be able to see him in a way that Rogers Brubaker calls the "trans of beyond." This kind of thinking involves "positioning oneself in a space that is not defined with reference to established categories. It is characterized by the claim to transcend existing categories or to transcend categorization altogether."[90]

NOTES

1. Although not all states had official laws, in 1662 Virginia was the first to try and make official the treatment of mixed-race people. Although laws had different

names in different states, the belief in the contaminative quality of black blood or ancestry was prevalent in the United States and continues today.

2. Yang, Jeff, "ASIAN POP/Could Obama Be the First Asian American President?"

3. Although many may see this as a manipulative, political ploy to relate to his various constituencies, Obama has expressed an interest in identity and particularly how his own was formed being raised by a white mother and later white grandparents while meeting his Kenyan father only twice.

4. Steele, Shelby, *A Bound Man: Why We Are Excited About Obama and Why He Can't Win*, 48.

5. Gregory Stephens refers to this kind of person as an integrative ancestor—a person whose mixed-race identity and ability to relate to all people gets claimed from different racial groups.

6. Remnick, David, *The Bridge: The Life and Rise of Barack Obama*, 90.

7. Ifill, Gwen, *The Breakthrough: Politics and Race in the Age of Obama*; Reifowitz, Ian, *Obama's America: A Transformative Vision of Our National Identity*; Wilson, John K., *Barack Obama: This Improbable Quest*; Henry, Charles P., Robert L. Allen, and Robert Chrisman, *The Obama Phenomenon: Toward a Multiracial Democracy*; Steele, *A Bound Man*.

8. Metzler, Christopher J., "Why Obama Has Not Yet Given Us a 'Post-Racial' America"; Wingfield, Adia Harvey, and Joe R. Feagin, *Yes We Can? White Racial Framing and the 2008 Presidential Campaign*.

9. Tesler, Michael, and David O. Sears, *Obama's Race: The 2008 Election and the Dream of a Post-Racial America*; Reed, *Barack Obama and the Jim Crow Media: The Return of the Nigger Breakers*.

10. Jeffries, Michael P., *Paint the White House Black: Barack Obama and the Meaning of Race in America*; Daniel, Reginald G., and Hettie V. Williams, *Race and the Obama Phenomenon: The Vision of a More Perfect Multiracial Union*; Barreto, Amílcar Antonio, and Richard L. O'Bryant, *American Identity in the Age of Obama*; Jolivette, Andrew J., *Obama and the Biracial Factor: The Battle for a New American Majority*.

11. C-SPAN, *President Obama at 2013 White House Correspondents' Dinner (C-SPAN)*.

12. Metzler, Christopher J., "Barack Obama's Faustian Bargain and the Fight for America's Racial Soul," 160.

13. Wilson, David C., and Matthew O. Hunt, "The First Black President?: Cross-Racial Perceptions of Barack Obama's Race," 229.

14. Barreto and O'Bryant, *American Identity in the Age of Obama*, table 9.1, 230.

15. Avlon, John, "Scary New GOP Poll."

16. Reed, Ishmael, *Barack Obama and the Jim Crow Media*, 51.

17. Reed, 81.

18. See http://content.time.com/time/covers/0,16641,20081020,00.html.

19. Ifill, *The Breakthrough*, 160.

20. The image was originally created by college student Firas Alkhateeb on Flickr in January 2009. It was then further amended by another online hacker to include the tag word socialist—this became a viral phenomenon and proliferated into posters,

bumper stickers, T-shirts, and mugs. See https://www.google.co.uk/search?q=obam
a+as+joker+image&tbm=isch&source=iu&pf=m&ictx=1&fir=H84XqpplHLePtM%
253A%252CSYG9YzIRaIuveM%252C_&usg=__n8C70tizsP99R60DWkof83fZA1I
%3D&sa=X&ved=0ahUKEwjjwZC--qnXAhXhD8AKHeAXC94Q9QEIKjAA#imgr
c=H84XqpplHLePtM.

21. Dyson, Michael Eric, *I May Not Get There With You*, 15.

22. LeRoy, Justin, *Chasing Daybreak: A Film About Mixed Race in America*.

23. CBSN, *2007: Barack Obama*.

24. Obama, Barack, *Dreams from My Father: A Story of Race and Inheritance*, 103.

25. C-SPAN, *Barack Obama Speech at 2004 DNC Convention*.

26. Obama, *The Audacity of Hope: Thoughts on Reclaiming the American Dream*, 294.

27. C-SPAN, *Barack Obama Speech at 2004 DNC Convention*.

28. Lewis, George, "Barack Hussein Obama: The Use of History in the Creation of an 'American' President."

29. *New York Times, Obama Inauguration 2013/Barack Obama's Complete 2013 Inauguration Speech*.

30. Reifowitz, *Obama's America*, 42.

31. Reifowitz, 43.

32. *Barack Obama Real Cool*.

33. Horsley, Scott, "Obama Gets in Touch with His Irish Roots."

34. Smith, Zadie, "Speaking in Tongues," 105.

35. See Anderson, Elijah, *The Cosmopolitan Canopy* for his analysis of the spaces and places where we are free of racial negotiations.

36. Obama, *Dreams from My Father*, 48.

37. King, Richard H., "Becoming Black, Becoming President."

38. Aspinall, P. J., and Miri Song, *Mixed Race Identities*, table 2.3, 30.

39. Obama, *Dreams from My Father*, 10.

40. Obama, 78.

41. Obama, 79.

42. Woke is black slang meaning you are aware of the apparatus of white supremacy. "Unwoke" means being oblivious or in denial of white supremacy.

43. Obama, *Dreams from My Father*, 80–81.

44. Alonso, Mauricio Trujillo, *President Obama Campaign Event at the Apollo Theatre*, video.

45. Schorn, Daniel, "Transcript Excerpt: Sen. Barack Obama. Read a Transcript Excerpt of Steve Kroft's Interview with Sen. Obama."

46. TPM, "Obama: 'If I Had a Son, He Would Look Like Trayvon.'"

47. Guardian, *Teary Barack Obama Thanks Michelle in Farewell Speech*.

48. Chastain, Mary Ann, *Barack, Michelle and Oprah Winfrey, 2008*.

49. Raskin, Donna, "The Michelle Obama Arm Workout."

50. Givhan, Robin, "First Lady Michelle Obama Serves as Fashion Icon."

51. This isn't to say all Michelle Obama's coverage was body positive. There were harsh, racialized criticisms of her body and attitude. See https://www.

washingtonpost.com/lifestyle/style/michelle-obamas-posterior-again-the-subject-of-a-public-rant/2013/02/04/c119c9a8-6efb-11e2-aa58-243de81040ba_story.html?utm_term=.8ce201b423c1.

52. Obama, *Dreams from My Father*, 115.

53. Obama, 104.

54. Obama, 51.

55. Obama, 60.

56. Obama, 52.

57. Obama, 302.

58. Obama, 91.

59. Obama, 51.

60. *New York Times*, "Obama's Father's Day Remarks (Transcript)."

61. Scott, Janny, "In 2000, a Streetwise Veteran Schooled a Bold Young Obama."[This should be note 61]

62. CNN, "Obama: Police Who Arrested Professor 'Acted Stupidly.'"

63. Williams, Juan, "Black Voters Aren't Fully Sold On Obama."

64. Obama, *Dreams from My Father*, xv.

65. Dickerson, Debra J., "Colorblind"; Hendon, Rickey, *Black Enough/White Enough: The Obama Dilemma*; Beinart, Peter, "Why White People Like Barack Obama"; Preston, Mark, "Reid Apologizes for Racial Remarks About Obama During Campaign."

66. Orbe, Mark P., *Communication Realities in a "Post-Racial" Society*, 111.

67. Orbe, 114.

68. Orbe, 118.

69. Obama, *Dreams from My Father*, 98.

70. Obama, 81.

71. Obama, 99.

72. Obama, 99.

73. Obama, xii.

74. Steele, *A Bound Man*, 7–8.

75. Boone, Jamal, *Barack Obama Michelle Malia Sasha Family Full Interview*, YouTube.

76. Obama did famously tear up when he spoke about the massacre of children in Sandy Hook, Connecticut, as well as in his farewell speech when talking about Michelle. Both tasteful displays in which he quickly regained control.

77. Brooks, David, "Thinking About Obama."

78. Bogle, Donald, *Toms, Coons, Mulattoes, Mammies and Bucks: An Interpretive History of Blacks in American Films*.

79. *President Obama and Anger Translator Luther*, YouTube.

80. Obama, *Dreams from My Father*, 94–95.

81. Morrison, Toni, "On the First Black President."

82. Calderone, Michael, "Matthews: 'I Forgot He Was Black Tonight for an Hour.'"

83. Orbe, *Communication Realities in a "Post-Racial" Society*, 91.

84. Orbe, 92.

85. Ehrenstein, David, "Obama the 'Magic Negro.'"
86. Orbe, *Communication Realities in a "Post-Racial" Society*, 93.
87. Orbe, 102.
88. Thai, Xuan, and Ted Barrett, "Biden's Description of Obama Draws Scrutiny."
89. Smith, "Speaking in Tongues," 188.
90. Brubaker, Rogers, *Trans: Gender and Race in an Age of Unsettled Identities*, 10.

Chapter 4

Casting Color

Black Barbie and the Black Doll as Racial Barometer

Dolezal and Obama showed the flexibility and fluidity of race in their personal choices while many resisted their identities by tenaciously holding on to the binary. I now turn to two major cultural industries to show how the binary is shifting in mass-produced dolls and mass-produced television. These two wide-reaching mediums have had a huge impact on the way we determine blackness and whiteness. Dolls have mimicked the cultural changes in American life. The movement away from rigidly raced dolls to ambiguous multiethnic dolls (or dolls whose race isn't stigmatized or exoticized) is a significant sign of progress.

Casting color refers not only to the process of molding and sculpting plastic black dolls in a white mold, which raises interesting questions about likeness or authenticity, but also for its other meaning. The decision-making process for casting someone (or something) as a representative of race is a complex negotiation between real people and reigning myths. Casting is fitting a part to a person, but most importantly, there should be a feeling of recognition for there to be success (or high sales). For children, these play items help them reflect on their own racial identity and learn how to encode it in ways people recognize as authentic. Just as in casting people for films and plays, when casting dolls, toy manufacturers are looking for the stereotypes that children will recognize. Brian Herrera explains that casting directors look for "features [that] match pre-existing impressions of what cultural groups or types are."[1] So it's not always about what something is, but what people in power have agreed it is.

The "racial relics"[2] of blackness in black dolls had lasting effects on both white and black children. What does the trajectory of the black doll tell us about shifting views about racial boundaries? How has blackness been encoded in the past and how is it encoded today?

The markers of blackness that are weaved into the construction of dolls such as skin color, facial features, hair, clothing, material, and language (through talking dolls, partnered books, and merchandising) are key to suggesting identities to young girls and sometimes boys. But children also bring their own creative responses and find ways to use these dolls to have some agency in their play of race. The change in their play and attitudes toward racially encoded dolls reflects not only the objects themselves, but the new cultural messages about race they are getting from the social world around them.[3] This relationship that children have with their dolls is seminal in helping them identify race in themselves and others, practice racial roles, and absorb or resist racial messages through their play.

"Colored dolls need no clothing because they are so black nobody can see," said one of the children surveyed in the first scholarly study on dolls and children's play from 1897. Another quote from the report mentioned children who "never allowed their dolls to drink coffee, for it made their skin dark." These remarks of difference and a fear of black contamination in a survey of eight hundred teachers and parents were the only attention paid to race except to say that dolls were "nearly universal among both savage and civilized peoples."[4] A scholarly eye was again turned to dolls in Donald Ball's 1967 essay, "Towards a Sociology of Toys," in which he claimed that a doll's influence on children from birth is seminal in their development because children are more often in the presence of dolls than humans. With the increase in single-parent households, working mothers, and less extended family residing in the home, he argued, toys were the true companions of children. Children play with the imagined identity of dolls and their time in this "symbolic world of miniature people" helps them define, experience, and relate to their social environment.[5] Today, half a century later, this influence is even more powerful as technology steals parents' attention increasingly from their children, who turn to "the surrogate of a favorite doll to help them practice affective expression."[6]

After Ball's seminal study, the several decades of silence that followed on the subject of dolls and girls' play revealed just how little value was placed on girls as well as youth culture,[7] but in the 1980s, dolls once again came to be seen as a formative way to understand changing culture. At this time, the focus was on "dismantling the patriarchal imperative of dolls," which coerced girls into being mothers and homemakers but ignored their roles as players with their own creative imaginative agendas.[8] Since the 1990s, the Girl Power Movement gave girls agency and voice through magazines, rock bands, and TV shows like *Buffy the Vampire Slayer*, which showed girls with "badass" attitudes and ambition. At this time scholars began to use intersectional approaches to looking at Barbie, the most popular doll in America, such as Ann DuCille's "Black Barbie and the Deep Play of Difference," Elizabeth

Chin's "Ethnically Correct Dolls: Toying with the Race Industry," Mary F. Rogers's *Barbie Culture*, and Erica Rand's *Barbie's Queer Accessories*. These all look at the problematic way dolls influence and question notions of identity about race, sexuality, gender, and normative culture. According to Brunell, they set off a critical examination of dolls as players in the "socialization, sexualization, commodification, exotixation, commercialization, racialization and essentialization of girlhood in the 21st century."[9] In figure 4.1,[10] artist Sheila Pree Bright morphs the plastic and the real in her *Plastic Bodies* exhibit, which questions where the line is drawn in forming identity between commercially produced products and reality.[11] Children see themselves in dolls and dolls suggest identities to children.

Today, scholars[12] are looking at the way children seem to be moving toward the idea of dolls as more fluid compared to the rigid racial structure implied in the manufacturing of black and white dolls. Given the looser boundaries about defining race in the twenty-first century, children are resisting easy definitions or fetishized versions of race and preferring dolls that give them freedom to interpret identity, like the line of vaguely ethnic Bratz dolls or Mattel's racially ambiguous Fashionistas.

Dolls are made up of their physical embodiment (the doll-as-physical-object) and the personality ascribed and imagined with it (doll-as-invented-personality).[13] The doll-as-physical-object involves the choice of materials. Early dolls were simply wooden paddles with eyes; today they are highly sophisticated with moveable parts, more like lifelike "sculptures." The doll-as-invented-personality is a combination of what the company tells the child about the doll, how it dresses the doll and what stories it tells about the doll in its merchandising. But then there is the story children tell themselves about the doll, the voices they use in their imaginations or in play with others. Much of this comes from what they've been told or signaled about a particular race or kind of doll. Most early black dolls that weren't homemade were not based on reality but tropes about blackness invented in the white imagination and sustained through white media.

The casting of black dolls from the nineteenth to the twenty-first century has been mired in the agendas of white supremacy, which sent out clear messages to black and white children. In chapter 1, I emphasized the crucial role played by Stowe's bestselling novel *Uncle Tom's Cabin* and its incarnations for American culture.[14] Stowe's book was more popular than the Bible and it morphed from page to songs, dances, plays, films, and toys for over a century. In particular two child characters, white Eva and black Topsy, had an immeasurable influence on the doll industry and how people conceived of black and white children. The incarnation of these characters is alive today in TV, film, and fashion. These two fictional children, black and white, reinforced the binary between black/savage versus white/Christian.

Figure 4.1 From artist Sheila Pree Bright's *Plastic Bodies* exhibit, a set of digitally manipulated photographs of multi-ethnic women and dolls, morphing human skin with plastic. This shows "the fine line that is often drawn between reality and fabrication in American culture."
Source: http://www.sheilapreebright.com/?lightbox=dataItem-ihkku2dy4.

The novel's two descriptions of a black and white child provided the template for the dolls that followed. Chapter 20 of *Uncle Tom's Cabin* describes Topsy as follows:

> She was one of the blackest of her race; and her round, shining eyes, glittering as glass beads, moved with quick and restless glances over everything in the room. Her mouth, half open with astonishment at the wonders of the new Mas'r's parlor, displayed a white and brilliant set of teeth. Her woolly hair was braided in sundry little tails, which stuck out in every direction. The expression of her face was an odd mixture of shrewdness and cunning, over which was oddly drawn, like a kind of veil, an expression of the most doleful gravity and solemnity.[15]

Topsy's physical description meshes perfectly with the description of a minstrel coon. Her skin is ultra dark in contrast to her white teeth, her eyes pop out, her hair is unruly and comical, and she is shrewd and untrustworthy.

In contrast to Topsy is the description of Eva (as seen through Tom's eyes): "to him she seemed something almost divine; and whenever her golden head and deep blue eyes peered out upon him from behind some dusky cotton-bale, or looked down upon him over some ridge of packages, he half believed that he saw one of the angels stepped out of his New Testament."[16] Eva's description is focused less on the body than on what she represents, which is perfect innocence and goodness with words like almost divine, golden head, and angel. Her peering down on Tom makes her an omniscient godlike creature watching over him in his toil.

If this binary weren't obvious enough, toys reinforced the duality. The Bruckner Topsy Turvy doll emphasized the difference by having them share a body. What follows is a 1907 Babyland Rag Doll catalog advertisement:

> TOPSY-TURVY—What is this?
> Looks like just a pretty miss.
> But turn her over and you'll find,
> She is quite another kind.
> First she's White and then she's Black,
> Turn her over and turn her back.
> Topsy that side—Betty this—
> Yet complete, each little Miss.[17]

The black doll's ugliness is embedded in the lines "she is quite another kind"; this also alludes to the idea that black people were often seen as another species. In an illustration of the book, we can see Eva's ladylike clothes and shoes and even a hat to protect her complexion (figure 4.2).

Figure 4.2   Little Eva and Topsy illustrated by John R. Neill originally published in 1908 in a single volume as *The Story of Topsy from Uncle Tom's Cabin.*
Source: Public Domain, book: "Story of Little Black Sambo," page 51, published in 1908 by Chicago, Ill.: The Reilly and Britton Co.; Authors: Helen Bannerman (1862–1946); John R. Neill.

The predominantly white colors emphasize her innocence and purity compared to Topsy's suggestive rag of a red dress and bare feet. The upright Eva contrasts with the hunching figure of Topsy whose face is pictured as masculine with her muscular neck and arms (this brings to mind how white men played black women in minstrel shows). Finally Topsy's features are exaggerated to make her ugly in contrast to the fine and delicate Eva. Her lips are exaggerated with a sloppy stain of red, and her hair is made to look wild and haphazard compared to Eva's flowing groomed blond locks. Finally, her expression is almost lustful, having none of the restraint of Eva's expression. As if to emphasize this, Eva is using her arm to keep Topsy (who seems to be moving forward) at a distance. These two characterizations of black and white children dominated the play of nineteenth and twentieth-century boys and girls.[18]

In catalogs selling both black and white dolls, this difference was additionally emphasized in their names. The Butler Brothers' toy listing in 1895 advertised the white dolls with names that suggested royalty, kindness, poise, and innocence: Empress, Sweet Alice, American Countess, Society Belle. Black dolls were simply reduced to their race or color: Nigger Baby, Nigger Doll, and Darky Head.[19] While black children were forced to play with white dolls (given the lack of nonracist alternatives), white children were given plenty of opportunity to play with both white and black dolls.

In Robin Bernstein's *Racial Innocence: Performing American Childhood from Slavery to Civil Rights*, she explores how white children acted out the power dynamic between slaves and masters with their black and white dolls. Their language mimicked the way masters spoke to slaves, but also the behavior. It was so common for them to beat and sometimes lynch the black dolls that doll manufacturers made black dolls out of materials that could withstand brutal play. The minstrel doll was later incarnated in Golliwogs and Raggedy Anns, which were often relegated to the role of victim, target, or sacrifice. Author Florence Upton who created the *Golliwog* books treated her own minstrel doll brutally. "Seated upon a flowerpot in the garden, his kindly face was a target for rubber balls . . . the game being to knock him over backwards. It pains me now to think of those little rag legs flying ignominiously over his head, yet that was a long time ago, and before he had become a personality. . . . We knew he was ugly!"[20] Upton describes the Golliwog as "a horrid sight" in her book *Two Dutch Dolls and a Golliwog*. This first *Golliwog* book plays into the inherent contrast of black and white with the exaggerated black color of the Golliwog in contrast to the blond, blue-eyed Dutch dolls, and she went on to create a very popular series of books with the Golliwog at its center. As seen in figure 4.3, the Golliwog (just as the description of Topsy) was clearly drawn from minstrel shows with its exaggerated lips, clownish hair, popping eyes, and vested suit. In the first half of the twentieth century, it was the most popular American toy, second only to the teddy bear. Its furry skin and absence of nose, hands, or feet make it more animal than human.

This minstrel coon made its way into children's books such as Frank Baum's *Oz* books as seen in the scarecrow character, who doesn't have a brain. Raggedy Ann and Andy dolls who are floppy harmless scarecrows also perpetuate the stereotype of the perpetually smiling dancing slave. Another black doll that competed in sales with the Golliwogs and Pickaninnies was Amosandra, the supposed child of Amos and Ruby Jones of the infamous radio show that featured two white men performing Black Voice.[21] Seventy-five percent of Amosandra dolls were sold to white people.[22] These books

Figure 4.3   Vintage Golliwog Soft Toy. The Golliwogg was a Black fictional character that appears in children's books in century during the nineteenth century.
Source: Public domain: http://www.publicdomainpictures.net/view-image.php?image= 44002&picture=vintage-peluche-golliwog&large=1

and toys helped incarnate these categories for white children, ideas they rehearsed every day. And for black children, they whittled away at feelings of self-esteem and worth.[23]

The innocent, angelic character of Stowe's Little Eva was replicated in baby dolls created by German and French companies in expensive porcelain that put forth the precious white baby with its long eyelashes and perfect petticoats. Grown-up Evas came from manufacturers like Horsman, Vogue, and Madame Alexander who were modeled after famous white people—singers, stars from TV and film—and characters in books were produced as expensive collectible status symbols. Dolls, mostly white, were often made (and continue to be made) in the image of Hollywood characters such as Scarlett O'Hara and the many Shirley Temple movies, but also royalty. This mix of Hollywood and monarchy can be seen in bestselling Disney princesses, such as the top-selling Elsa doll from Disney's *Frozen*.[24]

While the descendants of Eva are thriving today, the equivalent black doll that positively reflected a black child's innocence barely existed. There was always an understanding among black leaders, black parents, and progressive white people that these black incarnations were damaging to black and white children. In 1910 Booker T. Washington suggested that black dolls could give black girls and the women they grow into "a feeling of respect for their race." Early twentieth-century black nationalist Marcus Garvey, who created the Back to Africa Movement, urged black parents to:

> Take down the pictures of white women from your walls. Elevate your own women to that place of honour. They are for the most part the burden-bearers of the Race. Mothers! give your children dolls that look like them to play with and cuddle. They will learn as they grow older to love and care for their own children, and not neglect them. Men and women . . . God made us as his perfect creation. He made no mistake when he made us black with kinky hair.[25]

With a history of black women serving as mammies to white children while having little time with their own, this resolution understood the importance of forming a bond within black families. Black girls played with grotesque incarnations of black babies or tended beautiful white babies that gave a clear message of their future roles—mammies to white children. However, it did not allow them to practice bonding with their own. Attempts were often made to create black dolls that, like white dolls, would enhance a child's self-esteem by reflecting back a beautiful black child.[26] Garvey's United Negro Improvement Association included a doll factory. And other social movements like Negritude in the 1930s, Black Power in the 1960s, and Black Arts in the 1980s all understood the need to create black dolls that allowed black children to imagine themselves as beautiful, loved, and successful. However, getting black dolls into successful white businesses was difficult.

The mission to create a realistic black baby doll that truly reflected black children was taken up by white activist Sara Lee Creech who was inspired by the testimony of psychologists Kenneth and Mamie Clark. The Clarks had influenced the 1950 Supreme Court decision on *Brown v. Board of Education* by sharing the results of their "doll test" experiment. Here, dolls revealed children's inner feelings about race that ultimately helped change the law on segregated schools. The Clarks used six to nine-year-old children's associations with black or white dolls to show how segregated schools had damaged black children's self-esteem.[27] These dolls were identical except in color (in fact the black dolls were simply made in white doll molds and dyed brown). The test began by showing a brown doll and a white doll on a table and asking the child to identify which he or she liked best, which one was nice, and which one was bad. They then were asked to identify the race of the doll and finally to identity their own race though the question "Which doll looks like you?"—this often elicited tears in the black children. Black and white children overwhelmingly preferred the white doll, revealing the biases they had internalized about race. Later another pair of psychologists, Darlene and Derek Hopson, replicated the test and found little had changed by 1985. Kiri Davis repeated it in 2006, and CNN and ABC in 2010. The results were very similar—children, both black and white, overwhelmingly associated blackness with negative attributes.

Creech proposed to make "the ultimate negro doll" based on a thousand photographs of black children from babies to age ten photographed from the front, side, and back.[28] With the support of Zora Neale Hurston and Eleanor Roosevelt to help with fundraising, she created an Inter-Racial Council in her community in Florida that was half white and half black. She found that many black mothers in her community would buy white dolls for their children because the choice of black dolls were usually the racist Topsy and Mammy options. A white sculptor who had made "praying black boy," which was based on her adopted black son, was selected to create the Sara Lee doll that would positively embody black children. The different dolls in the Sara Lee line were named Little Miss, Little Brother, and Little Sister unlike earlier lines that reduced them to color or racial slurs; this was simply a black family.

Sara Lee, in 1951, was born into a business that already had two black doll competitors, but they were based on white dolls. Patti-Jo, was made from the white mold of Terri-Lee, but had a shade that was dark enough to establish her as black. Her expensive clothes made her appeal to the black middle class. Another group that were key consumers of Patti-Jo, according to *Ebony* magazine, were tourists wanting to bring home an example of what a negro in America looked like. Although black parents bought the Patti-Jo doll and white dolls for their children, the Topsy-type black dolls were still very popular among white patrons. The December 17, 1951, Christmas issue of *Life Magazine* debuted the Sara Lee doll as seen in figure 4.4.

The introduction of the doll mimicked the problems inherent in the society it was being introduced to. Not only was there only one page of text given to it over the three dedicated to carving a lamb, but all the ads in the magazine seem to reinforce the need for this doll. They feature white adults (including white Santa) drinking, smoking, and living the elegant life and white children who looked similar to the Eva image—charming Shirley Temple look-alikes playing with their white dolls. The emphasis in the article is not as much on the importance of the creation of the doll, but on its anthropological realism: "profile shows a large upper lip, eyes wide apart, a characteristic negroid feature."[29] The intense focus on the verisimilitude of the black

Figure 4.4   The realistic, but short lived Sara Lee Doll created by Sara Lee Creech based on photographs of black children and sculpted by Sheila Burlingame, a white woman with a black adopted son.
Source: photo taken by Debbie Behan Garrett, owner of the doll.

features is reminiscent of skull measurements and diagrams that compared black and white features in nineteenth-century anthropology. Black and white photos of black children's faces that resembled mugshots with front, side, and back views sat next to and competed with pictures of the new doll.

One of the biggest challenges in making the black doll was selecting a color when the black community were already very sensitive to shade and the implications drawn from it from both white and black people. The variety of hues found in black people was rarely found in black dolls. In fact early dolls and objects of racist memorabilia often chose the darkest black to accentuate the caricatured features of white surprised eyes and white teeth in contrast. The shade of one's skin was historically politicized for enslaved black people where color determined whether you would work in the house or the field.[30] So the doll's skin shade had to be carefully thought through if it was to pass the inspection of black parents. For Creech, determining the color was a challenging endeavor when colorism (or the preference given to lighter-skinned black people) had loaded this issue for centuries. She consulted with a professor of early childhood development, who said it couldn't be too dark or come in only one skin tone as if all black people were the same color.[31]

The choice of color was a difficult one not only to make (getting the dye to absorb in the plastic), but also getting parents to recognize it as feeling authentic. The first prototype had a color that reminded one black mother of a dead baby.[32] As a result, they created a "color jury" made up of scholars and leaders in racial matters. They ended up with a soft medium brown with a plan to create other shades as they brought the doll to market. However, parents and jury members were divided—they all thought the shade was too light or too dark, each seeing the doll through the lens of their own racialized experience. It is hard not to applaud Creech's attempts at shifting the black doll stigma. However, the disagreements in the community and the obsession in the way the white community focused on "accuracy" of getting blackness down in one doll revealed much of the damage already done. A doll is read according to the racial atmosphere of the time. When Sara Lee showed up, it hadn't shifted much—after all it was early on in the Civil Rights Movement. This focus on getting the doll just right seemed to shift the responsibility to the doll itself rather than black and white people's toxic belief systems. As Chin suggests, "with ethnically correct toys, the logic of the Clark study is reversed; it is the toys that are responsible for children's perceptions, not the society that produces them. Ethnically correct dolls refashion racist discourses and market them to minority buyers."[33]

If you don't want a white doll to represent a black doll and you don't want to reduce blackness to one set of features, how do you approach the doll conundrum? Although some stores carried the Sara Lee doll, Macy's and Saks refused as they worried it would bring an influx of black customers. Black women who were lucky enough to get a Sara Lee doll when they were girls recall her with real affection. Ironically it was her skin color that led to her demise. The dye from her skin ran and ruined the clothing and she was discontinued.[34]

One of the most powerful signs of the dominance of whiteness over blackness was Mattel's Barbie doll, which has controlled the toy industry since the 1960s and is still at the top of the doll food chain. At the *Barbie* exhibit in Paris at the Musée des Arts Décoratifs in the summer of 2016, a display case symbolized her reign. Blond Barbie was pinned to the wall; fanning out in a circle around her was her universe of stuff. Not only does she have an enviable wardrobe, but the people and things that surrounded her are bounteous, a symbol of American industry and success. This included not just her extravagant and varied outfits, but also her pets, cars, family (no parents—too limiting, but an aunt and uncle), boyfriend Ken (quite dull so as not to upstage her), but also friends (including one black friend named Christie). She was at the center of an entourage that orbited around her. However, just as access to wealth and opportunity in America were practically off limits to black people, so were the spoils of Barbie. Her ancestry (a German Aryan sex toy named Lilli) is clearly evident today. Despite her insensitivity to other ethnic and racial groups, she is still what M. G. Lord describes as the "most potent icon of American popular culture."[35] Not only do her sales show this, but Mattel proudly claims that girls ages three to ten have 100 percent brand recognition.

Ruth Handler, a Jewish woman, had the idea of an adult doll that would allow her daughter to play out possible future careers instead of just being a mother, which traditional baby dolls encouraged. She found inspiration in the German Lilli doll, a plastic toy based on a cartoon prostitute who was long legged and big busted; men could hang her up in their cars or give her as gag gifts. Her personality was something that was to be changed and crafted over time.

In the focus groups that discussed the prototype of Barbie, the psychologist and marketing expert Ernest Dichter declared her to be "a feminine poised little lady." Lilli was disengaged from Barbie except through the exotic dancer body. Dichter realized that if mothers could associate her with good grooming in their daughters, they wouldn't be as put off by the sexy body and suggestive clothing.[36] This identity for Barbie was derived from exhaustive interviews with mothers and daughters. In his focus groups with parents, Dichter asked if Barbie is "nice, friendly and loved by everyone, or is she vain and selfish, maybe even cheap? Does she have good taste or is she a little too flashy?"[37] Ultimately, Barbie was an accommodation between mothers' fears that their daughters would become too sexually promiscuous and girls wanting to have a doll that represented their fantasy future selves.

Barbie's dream world very much mimics the white dream life shown on television sitcoms in the 1950s and early 1960s—clean, free of danger, and very homogeneous, a world that her inventor Ruth Handler didn't have full access to. Like the Jewish man who created Superman, Handler created the ultimate insider by an outsider. In doing so, Barbie "colonized the American imagination."[38] Barbie's enviable life allows for flat-chested prepubescent girls to imagine a life where they aren't children anymore, but aren't saddled with children—that window of freedom where they can explore what might happen when they are Barbie's age, which is old enough to drive and own a dream house, but not be responsible for the insurance and mortgage.

Although Barbie's outfits and body changed with the times, her squeaky clean facial expression, clean shimmering blond hair, and slightly preppy life remained at the core of her identity. Even her name Barbara Millicent Rogers shows privilege and noble ancestry (no hint of ethnicity in her name). Barbie's wardrobe is from fashion designers and never veers too far into depravity, but can be trendy. Her ascribed life kept her safely in the parameters of good girl, and her sexiness seemed to mimic the unconscious allure of a *Playboy* centerfold: girl next door who doesn't know the peeping Tom is leering at her.

The white world of Barbie along with shows like *Father Knows Best* or *Ozzie and Harriet* couldn't sustain their popularity when the reality of American life was rattling outside their doors. The Watts riots in 1965 were a response by the black community in Los Angeles protesting another instance of police brutality. Four thousand members of the California Army National Guard were sent in and after forty-three deaths and $40,000 in property damage, the looting, arson, and physical assaults were quelled. This incited Mattel's multiple and awkward attempts to create a black authentic doll. Mattel, nervous about their own safety, sat down with leaders of the black community and asked them what they wanted. They asked to run their own company, so Mattel created Operation Bootstrap, which financially supported black owned and run businesses, including one called Shindana toys. Although Shindana was out of business by the mid-1980s, they were the first to tap into the multicultural market by making ethnically correct dolls.[39]

One of their dolls, Tamu, called attention to her blackness in a positive way, a radical change from the Golliwogs of the past. Tamu had a pull strip and in it she reveals her black credentials, using black slang like "Cool it, baby" and "Can you dig it?" She also calls attention to her cultural connection to Africa with her Swahili name when she explains, "Tamu means 'sweet'"—(one of the words formerly associated with white dolls and Little Eva). Finally, she sends the Black Power message of "I'm proud, like you," which also implies, "I'm black like you." Although these kinds of dolls offer important cultural connections, they don't allow a child as much room for much imaginative play—the doll has a script for the child rather than being a canvas to play out a child's psychic dramas and work out daily stresses.

Shindana was a noble effort, but it didn't cut into the Barbie matrix. How could any doll acquire the mountain of luxury that she had amassed over the years? So black children whose parents didn't want to buy them white Barbies still noticed them in school and at friends' houses and couldn't ignore the messages. One black girl describes the frustration and creative solution she came up with of mixing paints until she found one that matched her own skin and proceeded to race change her doll.[40] Another black girl describes her hostility to Barbie and her inaccessible world; her hostile treatment of the doll shows her anger at the exclusive world of Barbie: she cut off her hair and "popped off her head and tore off each limb, and sat on the stairs for a long time twirling the torso like a baton."[41]

Barbie began integration with the aptly named Colored Francie in 1967, who seemed to declare her need to stay segregated. She was born perhaps as a response to the Civil Rights Movement and changing images on television that were creating more sympathy for black people, shifting the narrative from lazy or comical to righteous and strong. Although she was cast in the exact same mold as Francie Fairchild, Barbie's British and slightly shorter cousin, she had light brown skin. Nothing else marked her as black: her hair was straight, her features were just like Barbie's white cousin. Colored Francie never sold well, even though Mattel made it clear that Colored Francie was not a relative like the other Francie. That would have meant miscegenation somewhere in Barbie's checkered past.

The second attempt at a black doll was 1968 Christie who was introduced as Barbie's black friend (people could now rest assured that Barbie's not racist—after all, she's got a black friend). This again was taken from the same mold as a white doll (Midge) and she had the same body as Barbie, but tinted brown and with an afro. She didn't have outfits made for her, except what she came in, but she could borrow from the extravagant collection in Barbie's closet. Barbie's black friend Christie had a pull string where she could express herself, "Let's go shopping with Barbie" or "Let's visit Barbie and Stacey." All in all, she declared nothing more than her proximity to Barbie, definitely sidekick territory. Although Mattel created a black baby as part of the entourage, it was quickly withdrawn as some might interpret it as Barbie having had a black sexual partner.[42]

In 1981, Black Barbie (her color mentioned in her name unlike white Barbie who was simply Barbie) was introduced, but this time designed by a black doll designer named Kitty Black Perkins who began working for Mattel in 1975. Black Barbie had the Stephie face mold (a white doll), but her color was brown. Parents complained that Black Barbie was cast in the same mold as Barbie, which made it clear she wasn't an original and separate person. Children could see right through this and one disappointed black parent reported that her child asked for a "real Barbie" meaning the white one.[43] Making black dolls in the mold of white dolls was nothing new. Throughout doll history, white dolls would be tinted darker and declared a black doll. Companies rationalized it as too expensive to make a variety of molds. But many children were thrilled with a doll that looked like them. Perkins designed her clothes to try and reflect her race, so she didn't wear pastels as Barbie did, but spicy colors and African style jewelry.

The biggest issue with casting Black Barbie was what people interpreted as her lack of "black hair." Kumea Shorter-Gooden, coauthor of *Shifting: The Double Lives of Black Women in America*, commended Mattel for diversifying the size and look of Barbie, but was disappointed that European-American hair was still the standard.[44] Because black girls are already struggling with messages about the ugliness of black skin and hair, these choices cannot be taken lightly.[45] Mattel defended its choice by explaining that the tiny head of Barbie doesn't make it easy to do black hair styling on an afro as easily. Stacey McBride-Irby, who later designed a line of black dolls for Mattel and then her own brand, reminds that these are designed for play: "I remember as a child, I wanted to comb/play with the doll's hair. Because it is still a doll, an afro didn't lend itself to allowing the girls to braid, cut and style the 11.5" fashion doll hair." She did include an afro in a few of the dolls but she believes doll collectors can appreciate the ethnic hairstyle more than children.[46]

Although Ann DuCille criticizes the Barbie "dipped in chocolate," she acknowledges that making Black Barbie bodies different can veer into the territory of bioracism because it determines difference. Although adults and toy companies have spent much time debating the features, shade, and accompaniments to a black doll, black children have a variety of reactions. Sharon Raynor in her essay "My First Black Barbie"[47] wasn't particular; she noticed the similar skin color to her own and that was enough to suggest likeness and identification. But others like Jasmine Guy knew Barbie was "like a white girl" and couldn't bond in the same way because she didn't look like her. Because there is no representative black girl, the different responses to Black Barbie can be related to a child's own features and shade, but also the way they choose to play with her.

Barbie's next attempt at a successful black doll was the Shani line in 1991, which stepped away from the Barbie entourage and created a group of three black friends with the same long crimped hair (which came with a hair pic) and a variety of skin tones. (Shani was brown, Asha was honey, and Nichelle was deep mahogany.) Unlike the names Francie and Christie, which don't read as African American, Shani, Nichelle, and Asha do. Drs. Hopson, the psychologists who had reimplemented the doll test, were consulted. These dolls had plumper lips, wider hips, and a flatter nose. Chin points out that Shani dolls' features get more stereotypically black, the darker the dolls' skin color.[48] Kitty Black Perkins dressed them in culturally suggestive clothes with ethnic fabrics, using autumn tones rather than colors like pink or lavender. Shani sported dangly gold earrings and had hair that was textured differently from Barbie's although still waist long (which for many black women is impossible without a weave). The doll looks like it has a higher/bigger behind, which was achieved by angling the back slightly.

Almost two decades later, Mattel tried again to make an "authentic" black doll in 2009 with the So In Style dolls; the name alone gives away the trendiness of ethnic dolls as if race can come into style (and go out again). Their fuller lips, kinkier hair, and different shades seemed like a redo of the Shani dolls of 1991. The new black trio of friends Grace, Kara, and Trichelle were not accessories to Barbie and didn't reference her world. But when they were blinged up with fancy trainers and even a ghetto blaster, some cried racial stereotype. The hair, like with Black Barbie and Shani, also ran into trouble with critics calling the dolls too white with their straight long hair over short and kinky. Most controversial was the So In Style hair styling set that allows girls to straighten their dolls' hair completely. "Black mothers who want their girls to love their natural hair have an uphill battle and these dolls could make it harder," claimed Sheri Parks, an associate professor of American studies at the University of Maryland.[49]

Although the other black Mattel dolls came already with straight hair, this brought to mind a process of going from kinky to straight that is highly politicized. Malcolm X in his autobiography discussed the self-abuse involved in hair straightening with lye (which often left scars on the scalp) as an attempt to become white, and a call to grow out afros was a key part of the Black Is Beautiful Movement. Today, black women, often falling prey to racialized notions of beauty, spend untold amounts of money on hair weaves from India or process their natural hair to straight.[50] Previous first lady Michelle Obama, who was a role model for many black women, chose to straighten her hair as did her daughters while they were in the White House but was seen wearing her hair out in an afro when she left.

Black parents wanted more afros and larger noses for the So In Style dolls as they were not perceived as "black enough." The debate about black authenticity within the black community was being played out again, bringing to mind the color jury in Creech's Sara Lee doll. McBride-Irby describes the conversations as "sometimes brutal," feeling that people were forgetting these were dolls designed for play, not real people. In other words, the focus was on the agenda of the adults over the children. In contrast to the results of the doll test, which revealed how a doll's race reflected a child's self-esteem, McBride-Irby claims there are other important factors as well: "Girls do want dolls that they can relate to, even if it's just stating that the doll is a cheerleader and likes to read, just like the girl. However parents want dolls that represent their child [racially], or dolls that they weren't offered in their childhood."[51] The Shani line and the So In Style line of dolls are now collector items. According to Debbie Garrett, a black doll collector and authority on black dolls, Mattel's "lack of commitment in producing a diverse line of dolls probably contributed to the demise of both Shani and So In Style Barbie."[52]

Once dolls are cast as black, they seem to play limited roles in the stories manufacturers tell about them. Brian Herrera comments on the limitations that black bodies must endure in the film industry, which can equally apply to dolls:

> Certain bodies are seen as neutral and universal and certain bodies are anchored in the type they look like such as woman over forty or actors of color. However, the white actor Eddie Redmayne can play both disabled and trans—he's able to tell a universal story. But not so with minority actors, they must be specific in ways that align with their bodies. Certain bodies are authorised to reach beyond

the limits of their own bodies. But there is a rigid separation between who is universal and who is specific.[53]

This rigid casting is seen in the American Girl Doll historical line also from Mattel. These high-end dolls each come with a story book and each plays a key role in history. Although the white dolls contribute to history in myriad ways, there were only two black dolls to choose from—Civil War era Addy who escapes from slavery and civil rights era Melody. These dolls were reduced to their race as if all black stories derive from slavery or the fight for justice. A third, Cecile, who lives in nineteenth-century New Orleans and had a life beyond being black, was discontinued in 2014. Barbie can be anything, but Black Barbie has her parameters; white American Girl dolls are limitless in their reach and role in America's past, but it is only recently that a black doll has a story that goes beyond her race.

Although things have progressed from Golliwogs and Aunt Jemima dolls, the fetishization of race that resulted from Barbie's attempts to be multicultural still didn't free us from rigid racial associations. As DuCille puts it:

> In today's toy world, race and ethnicity have fallen into the category of precious ready-to-ware difference. To be profitable, racial and cultural diversity—global heterogeneity—must be reducible to such common, reproducible denominators as color and costume.[54] Race and racial differences—whatever that might mean in the grander social order—must be reducible to skin color or, more correctly, to the tint of the plastic poured into each Barbie mold.[55]

Mattel's attempts to integrate Barbie's world have been fraught with politics and confusing business choices. However, it could be that they were focused on deciding on a monolithic look for blackness when there is none. Children born into a more multicultural atmosphere seem to understand this and look less to race as a way to ascribe personalities and qualities to their dolls. They don't see race as much as culture and ethnicity.

In Elizabeth Chin's ethnographic study of poor black girls in New Haven, Connecticut, who played with Barbie, they didn't care about her facial features or white plastic body. They complained more that the lifestyle of Barbie did not reflect theirs. This echoes McBride-Irby's point about girls wanting to recognize themselves in the dolls and find a point of contact. One child named Asia states bluntly that Barbie does not represent her life. She complains not about Barbie's whiteness, but about her privilege. Asia says, "You never see a fat Barbie. You never see a pregnant Barbie. What about those things? They should make a Barbie that can have a baby."[56] Later this same child suggests there is an absence of an abused Barbie. This isn't the Freudian notion of imaginative play as wish fulfillment. This is girls practicing the roles they see around them in their community. So Barbie's looks and skin color didn't seem to be a factor that shut out identification. Interestingly, these girls related to their white Barbies by doing their hair in ways they styled their own hair—with beads, braids and foil.[57] One child held the platinum blond Barbie on her hip and called it her "brat"; she didn't seem to care about her facial features matching her own.[58] So children, unlike the adults who see the dolls as static, created meaningful connection to their white dolls through naming them, styling them, and reflecting in their play the world they live in.

This is a noted difference in the play of children a century before who knew the boundaries of crossing races as Jim Crow had taught them. It is also different from the self-conscious tokenism of the Civil Rights Movement–inspired black dolls. The fluid environment of cultural exchange they see around them gives them permission to be flexible about racial embodiment, while children in the past would never consider casually treating a white doll like a black one. Chin claims that this choice of theirs to create race through hair using a limited doll has "a profound and potentially radical meaning that confounds the commercial rhetoric of ethnically correct dolls like the Shani doll."[59] The girls in Chin's study simply groom their dolls in racialized ways.

Now the doll industry has moved past the idea of a doll with one particular race and embraced the multicultural demographic children see around them. When asked why Mattel has created the new racially ambiguous nameless dolls called Fashionistas, Robert Best, Senior Design Director of Barbie/Mattel says that they wanted to "embrace and be open to remove narrow definitions of race following what culture has done." He doesn't pretend this is a moral imperative, but understands it is a business one. Eliana Dockterman agrees that Mattel "did not make those changes, necessarily, because it wanted to be a moral leader . . . but rather as a cynical business calculation any good company is expected to make on behalf of itself and its shareholders." She calls this "cultural change by way of capitalism."[60] In discussing the new multiculturalism of Mattel, Best said that Barbie reflects what is happening in the world. He refers back to the Dolls of the World line that began in 1991, which had dolls in historical costumes of different cultures including many black dolls. They were frozen in time and in their one costume.[61] Best now sees these ethnic line of African dolls as reductive: "It's one thing, native dress: we wanted a more nuanced approach."[62] As DuCille points out, the Jamaican doll did little more than entrench a stereotype.

Like the Disneyland ride and accompanying song "It's a Small World" that highlights difference to create a utopian vision of the world, these dolls can fall into the traps of colorblindness. We are all different in shallow ways like dress and language, but ultimately the same, it declares cheerfully. This kind of message was proclaimed in the famous Coca Cola "Hilltop" ad from 1971. This extremely popular television song and video featured people who look like the Mattel Dolls of the World. The camera first shows a blond white woman singing (who could just as well be Barbie) followed by two more white people, and then the camera reveals an especially dark black man and especially dark Asian man. An Indian woman wearing a bindi is scanned over. The camera zooms out to include a rainbow coalition of coke drinkers. They stand on a hill together, but not too close; no one looks at each other or interacts, but just sings facing forward. There is no racial mixing; each singer is firmly in a racial category emphasized by their native costumes. It would be hard to have an ad like this succeed today because the current generation expects mixed-race faces and fluid cultures. Mattel, who created the white privileged world of Barbie, has changed in the same way that fast food chain McDonald's now serves salads. But McDonald's will always be known for its earlier incarnation where health was not on the menu.

Before Fashionista dolls, Mattel didn't acknowledge racial mixing, choosing instead a token representative of every race: black, Asian, Hispanic, Native American. Best explains how part of the change from white Barbie to racially mixed Barbies reflects the people who work at Mattel. They started with a staff of mostly white middle-aged women who were sewing as a hobby in their free time. Today, their staff are younger and much more diversely trained designers, many of whom are second-generation Japanese American and come from mixed parentage. Best himself is "a mix"—his mother is from El Salvador and his dad is from Tennessee.[63] To determine the bodies and features of these dolls, they get their inspiration by combing through trends from fashion and culture worlds, often using social media like Pinterest and Instagram. Fashionistas don't have names, which often were racial signifiers and they are varied with their seven new skin tones, four body types, and twenty-two eye colors.

Although parents may choose Fashionistas or find dolls that mirror their children's multiracial looks, the kids themselves respond to what dolls are wearing, not body type. They may notice a cute purse or dress rather than comment on hair or skin tone. According to Kelly Power, Associate PR manager at Mattel, as of May 15, 2017, the Fashionista line has been up 83 percent globally since the launch.[64] This popularity of multiracial dolls is echoed in Hollywood. In a study done by SAG, diverse casting makes for better box office.

Multiracial dolls are simply reflecting the trend of what children see around them in the United States. Likewise, Mattel's American Girl Doll line has also updated with an understanding that they need to represent blackness beyond slavery and political struggle. Gabriela, a Doll of the Year, just came out in 2017 and is multiracial and described as having grown up:

surrounded by the arts—dance, painting, music, and theater. But poetry is becoming her art form of choice, for good reason: she struggles with stuttering and poetry helps her words flow more freely. Although Gabriela is a bit quiet, when she does speak, she is sharp, honest, and funny. But can she learn to harness the power of her words and her creativity to help save her beloved community arts center from being torn down?[65]

The description of Gabriela does not fall into stereotypes of blackness (a bit quiet and a stutterer)—the opposite of the trope of the angry black woman. In fact, the description is free of racialization. Gabriela's tawny skin, long wavy hair, and facial features that are from the white doll mold doesn't make it clear she is black. However, the accompanying book has a photograph of a black girl on the cover.

The phenomenon of MGA Entertainment Bratz dolls that were introduced in 2001 is an indicator of consumers' need to see diversity in their dolls. But most important, Bratz have a clear imagined personality with "flava";[66] in other words, not generically white. The Bratz are the first to dethrone Barbie—sales in the UK outsell Barbie two to one and they also took a bite out of sales in the United States across race and socioeconomic status. They represent 40 percent of the toy market versus Barbie's 60 percent. Four ten-inch dolls—Yasmin, Cloe, Jade, and Sasha[67]—each vaguely represent a different racial group. However, their facial features are similar enough to be racially indeterminate as well, which makes it possible for all girls to assume it could be them—their names also don't give away any specific race. No one doll is the queen bee as in Barbie's empire, but the dolls can be bought in a set. They are equals unlike Barbie's world where she remained at the center with the other dolls to do her bidding. Their oversized huge almond-shaped eyes are heavily eye shadowed and dominate their faces. Full lips, permanently shiny from lip gloss, distinguish them from Barbie's own small mouth. They are trendy and entrenched in hip-hop culture and style, their merchandising helps explain. Unlike Barbie, they have no profession and unlike the high-priced American Girl Dolls, they are more affordable at eight dollars each.

Although many parents and educators are horrified by the sexualization of these dolls[68] with their generous breasts and round behinds fitted into skin-tight revealing clothing, children themselves don't seem to be focusing on that at all. Adults see them as having a child porn quality, but they also disdain the values put forth with the Bratz line. Like the Kardashians, their defining characteristic is being a consumer or having "a passion for fashion." Although adults would prefer they are more like Barbie with her impressive incarnations as astronaut and presidential candidate, ironically, girls who play with Barbie most commonly make her go on dates or to parties, very similar to what the Bratz dolls state outright (boyz, parties, and shopping).

Lisa Guerrero argues that the brand exploits racial difference as something "hip," making "otherness" the equivalent to a fashion accessory.[69] She also critiques them for connecting "the sexualization of these dolls with their color, playing on an old racial stereotype.[70] Despite, these objections, she does admit that they are "opening up a space in the popular imagination for the normalization of multiracial identities."[71]

In her ethnographic study, Rebecca Hains' moves past the adult view of Bratz to let the girls playing with them speak for themselves. One girl Madison made clear how playing with Bratz was different from playing with Barbie: "I buy Bratz dolls because all of them—all the Bratz dolls are treated right."[72] She seems to be referring to the lack of hierarchy unlike in Barbie's world. Hains notes that Madison could see that Bratz of various skin tones were treated as individuals, with distinct personalities and equally fashionable styles. She contends that unlike Barbie, "the darker-hued Bratz dolls were not offered as costumed, 'dye-dipped' versions of their iconic blonde sister. The Bratz were a peer group."[73] Margaret Talbot in the *New Yorker* also alludes to the freedom from Barbie's racialized world; kids who buy Bratz "are content with creating their own narratives, however problematic they may be. They are paying for the thrill of owning a doll that has kicked the old Barbie model to the curb with the heel of a leopard print stiletto." She also excuses the Bratz doll's sexiness as "not enough of a deterrent, as sex has become desensitized in its hyper-prevalence in our society."[74]

In the Bratz movie, each "doll" played by actresses of less ambiguous ethnicity than their doll counterpart move through a world that is multicultural (their teachers, fellow students, and families). They represent the culturally fluid Gen Zers. Although no one would call them role models, there is no hierarchy according to race; they each refer minimally in the film to a watered down ethnic identity (Latina, Jewish, black, Asian). On their first day of school, they express the goal of their generation that doesn't feel they have to choose a race: " 'What are we guys going to do?' One asks. 'Blend!' " they answer in unison as they slink into the cafeteria with belly dance music floating behind them. They are free to access any culture as part of their multicultural bill of rights.

Our obsession with using dolls in the past to sustain racial narratives has moved from racist memorabilia to tokenism to fetishishizing of black dolls. Today with the new trend of multicultural dolls like Fashionistas and Bratz, there is less racial "precision" but it frees children to interpret the dolls more personally. Race today can't be commodified, so let's just make it unreadable, these companies seems to say. But in Hains's ethnographic study of (mostly black) girls playing with Bratz, she was surprised to see them working out racial conflicts and reenacting racial history.[75] The girls used their imagination to see these glammed-up party girls as runaway slaves and slave masters. They were aware of the history of race, but could use these dolls in other ways too.

In 2001, curator Thelma Golden and artist Glenn Ligon in their exhibit *Freestyle* in the Studio Museum of Harlem created a space for black artists "adamant about not being labeled 'black' artists, though their work was steeped, in fact deeply interested, in redefining complex notions of blackness."[76] Golden used the term postblack to refer to this freeing of a narrow form of black identity. Touré generalizes this concept and expands it to include not just artists, but successful black people in all areas and fields of American life. In his book *Who's Afraid of Post-Blackness?*, he interviews black people who are public figures on their views about black identity. In the foreword to the book, Michael Eric Dyson writes that postblack "clearly doesn't signify the end of Blackness; it points, instead, to the end of the reign of a narrow, single notion of Blackness. Postblackness has little patience for racial patriotism, racial fundamentalism, and racial policing."[77]

Postblackness, perhaps, is what we can look to with the next batch of dolls. Labeling a doll black already creates a kind of straightjacket for manufacturers and the children that play with those dolls. No one can agree what black looks like. There are larger differences within races than between them, so it is an impossible task. As Hains's group of young black girls showed, the flexibility given to them through Bratz dolls' ambiguous race doesn't erase race, it just puts the power in their hands to create stories that may or may not involve race. As Hains puts it, "Children are not just passive receivers of toys, but creative agents." These children are seeing a very different reality around them where race is no longer a strict category with uncrossable boundaries. It makes sense that the dolls they play with allow them to work out the conflicts in their life and reflect their world rather than create an artificial one.

The Golliwogs of the past created a monstrous version of black skin that damaged self-esteem, the brown-dipped Barbies gave a clear message that white was still first and best; the "anthropologically correct" black doll lines fetishized blackness; finally, the racially ambiguous new dolls are pointing a way forward and also allowing race not to be the first thing children are directed to.[78] As Wahneema Lubiano says, "Post-Black means that . . . everything is up for grabs as a possibility."[79]

NOTES

1. Lueger, Michael, "'You Don't Read Latino': Discussing the History of Latinx Casting with Brian Eugenio Herrera."

2. "Black Doll Collecting."

3. Pree Bright, Sheila, "Plastic Bodies."

4. Hall, Granville Stanley, and Alexander Caswell Ellis, *A Study of Dolls*, 11.

5. Ball, Donald W., "Toward a Sociology of Toys: Inanimate Objects, Socialization, and the Demography of the Doll World," 449.

6. Ball, 450.

7. Forman-Brunell, Miriam, "Interrogating the Meanings of Dolls: New Directions in Doll Studies," 3.

8. Forman-Brunell, 4.

9. Forman-Brunell, 4.

10. Created by using a set of digitally manipulated photographs of multiethnic women and dolls.

11. Forman-Brunell, "Interrogating the Meanings of Dolls."

12. For example, Forman-Brunell.

13. Lord, M. G., *Forever Barbie*, 4.

14. Reynolds, David S., *Mightier than the Sword: Uncle Tom's Cabin and the Battle for America*; Sundquist, Eric J., *New Essays on Uncle Tom's Cabin*; Ammons, Elizabeth, *Harriet Beecher Stowe's "Uncle Tom's Cabin": A Casebook*; Gossett, Thomas F., *Uncle Tom's Cabin and American Culture*; Williams, Linda, *Playing the Race Card: Melodramas of Black and White from Uncle Tom to O. J. Simpson*.

15. Stowe, Harriet Beecher, *Uncle Tom's Cabin*, 206–207.

16. Stowe, 127.

17. "Topsy-Turvy A.K.A. Topsy-Turvey, Double Doll, Two-Sided Doll."

18. Hix, Lisa, "Black Is Beautiful: Why Black Dolls Matter." The Topsy-Turvies first existed because slave masters didn't want slave children to have dolls that reflected them as it would give them a sense of empowerment. They could play with the black side and then flip it if they master came by.

19. Wilkinson, Doris Y., "The Doll Exhibit: A Psycho-Cultural Analysis of Black Female Role Stereotypes," 23.

20. Davis, Norma S., *A Lark Ascends*, 10.

21. This is a term used to describe a language white people used to indicate black people: it emphasized mispronunciations, malapropisms, and put in a "d" for a "th." Along with white actors, many black actors were then told to use this voice themselves when playing stereotyped characters.

22. Thomas, Sabrina Lynette, "Sara Lee: The Rise and Fall of the Ultimate Negro Doll," 45.

23. Thomas, 38. Also popular was the Aunt Jemima rag doll or mammy caricature. From the late 1800s to the mid-1900s, these servant dolls were ubiquitous in the homes of white children.

24. If there is any question about dolls' connection to popular culture, securities analysts consider toys part of the entertainment industry.

25. Garvey, Amy Jacques, *Garvey and Garveyism*, 29.

26. "Moments in Black Doll History—Garvey's UNIA Doll Factory."

27. Clark, Kenneth B., and Mamie P. Clark, "Emotional Factors in Racial Identification and Preference in Negro Children."

28. "Doll for Negro Children: New Toy Which Is Anthropologically Correct Fills an Old Need."

29. "Doll for Negro Children," 41.

30. Alice Walker first coined the term Colorism in *In Search of Our Mothers' Gardens*. Here she discussed the preferential treatment lighter-skinned black people receive within their communities.

31. Thomas, "Sara Lee," 41.

32. Thomas, 42.

33. Chin, Elizabeth, "Ethnically Correct Dolls," 310.

34. "Black Doll Collecting."

35. Lord, *Forever Barbie*, 6.

36. Dichter, Ernest, *Ernest Dichter Papers*.

37. Lord, *Forever Barbie*, 39.

38. Lord, 160.

39. DuCille, Ann, *Skin Trade*, 15.

40. DuCille, 10.

41. Jones, Lisa, *Bulletproof Diva: Tales of Race, Sex, and Hair*, 150.

42. Lord, *Forever Barbie.*

43. Lord, 47.

44. Jones, Charisse, and Kumea Shorter-Gooden, *Shifting: The Double Lives of Black Women in America.*

45. Jones and Shorter-Gooden.

46. McBride-Irby, Stacey, interview.

47. Raynor, Sharon, "My First Black Barbie: Transforming the Image."

48. Chin, "Ethnically Correct Dolls," 313.

49. CBS News, Associated Press, "Mattel Introduces Black Barbies."

50. See Chris Rock's 2009 documentary *Good Hair*.

51. McBride-Irby, interview.

52. Garrett, Debbie, "Lecture and Sara Lee Doll."

53. Lueger, "You Don't Read Latino."

54. Lesavage, Halie, "The First-Ever Hijab-Wearing Barbie Is Here, and Ibtihaj Muhammad Is Beyond Excited."

55. DuCille, *Skin Trade*, 43.

56. Chin, "Ethnically Correct Dolls," 305.

57. Chin, 306.

58. Chin, 308.

59. Chin, 306.

60. Garber, Megan, "Barbie's Hips Don't Lie."

61. They introduced a Nigerian in 1990, a Jamaican in 1992, a Kenyan in 1994, a Ghanaian in 1996, a princess of South Africa in 2004, and a Kwanzaa celebrator in 2006.

62. Best, Robert and Marissa Beck, interview.

63. Best and Beck, interview.

64. Powers, Kelly, "Data for Barbie Chapter."

65. "Gabriela/Girl of the Year/American Girl."

66. Flava is slang for individual style.

67. In 2015, a fifth girl, Raya, was added to the clique with tan skin and unidentifiable race.

68. Talbot, Margaret, "Little Hotties."

69. Guerrero, Lisa " 'Can the Subaltern Shop?': The Commodification of Difference in the Bratz Dolls," 189–190.

70. Hains, Rebecca C., "An Afternoon of Productive Play with Problematic Dolls."

71. Guerrero, "Can the Subaltern Shop?," 194.

72. Hains, "An Afternoon of Productive Play with Problematic Dolls," 129.

73. Hains, 129.

74. Talbot, "Little Hotties."

75. Hains, "An Afternoon of Productive Play with Problematic Dolls."

76. Golden, Thelma, and Hamza Walker, *Freestyle*, 14.

77. Touré, *Who's Afraid of Post-Blackness?: What It Means to Be Black Now*, xv.

78. Hains, "An Afternoon of Productive Play with Problematic Dolls," 138.

79. Touré, *Who's Afraid of Post-Blackness?: What It Means to Be Black Now*, 21–22.

Chapter 5

Really Black

Black-ish *and the Black Sitcom as Racial Barometer*

In this chapter, I turn to the black family sitcom that, like the doll industry, found destructive ways to disseminate mostly harmful incarnations of the black family in shows like *Amos 'n' Andy*, *Sanford and Son*, and *That's My Mama*. Like its cultural older sibling film, black characters in black sitcoms and their antecedents were key propaganda to sustain the stereotypes of black inferiority that justified inequality. Like the title of Donald Bogle's *Toms, Coons, Mulattoes, Mammies and Bucks*, black sitcoms have chosen from the groups on this racist menu. Many of these stereotypes were invented after emancipation. When reconstruction promised freed slaves land and possibilities, white people were threatened and the campaign to create the notion of the N*gger was strengthened. Through cartoons, posters, radio, and finally TV, these negative tropes about blackness were pervasive.

However, since the 1980s that has been changing; black directors began to have agency through opportunities as writers and directors to alter the detrimental narratives about blackness, which allowed for later shows like *The Fresh Prince of Bel-Air* and *The Cosby Show*. I turn here to a close reading of four seasons of the show *Black-ish* to reveal the unmasking of racial performance and the command of these stereotypes though humor. The show looks at the role of stereotypes today when both black and white people have become aware of their constructedness. How do white people tiptoe around them for fear of being called a racist while at the same time have their thinking influenced by them?

In particular, I explore how *Black-ish* attempts to unveil any last vestiges of the binary by exposing how black and white characters address it directly with their conversations, arguments, debates and self-reflection (in the form of narration). In addition, the show expands the definition of blackness to include a world beyond survival and racism. Because it takes poverty out of the equation, it can address the complexity of life for black people who have achieved financial success. A new challenge comes of how to hold on to their blackness, which begs the question, "What defines this blackness I am trying to hold on to?"

In the 1812 Brothers Grimm fairy tale "Snow White," the evil stepmother harangues her magic mirror daily by asking, "Who is the fairest of them all?" This color contest reflects the fear white people have of losing their whiteness. Such a prized commodity was this whiter skin that parents would warn their girls to stay out of the sun or they would get dark. Some desperate nineteenth-century white mothers gave their daughters arsenic, as a beauty treatment, to create a deathlike pallor. For black people, there have been some who tried to chemically or surgically remove their black skin, but many others have merely spent a small fortune on lightening creams and pills to achieve lighter if not white skin. Ironically today, the contest for many is no longer who is the fairest, but "who is the blackest of them all." The anxiety both black and white people feel about determining blackness is different from the historic determination of blackness by white people in power. Now the debate over black identity is about holding on to, rather than getting rid of, blackness. This pervasive topic is present in blogs, TV, radio, online chat rooms, and even card games.

Black comedians like Dave Chappelle make fun of the random power some feel they have to dictate who is in and who is out of "real" blackness. In their skit "The Racial Draft,"[1] Chappelle and his white cowriter Neal Brennan set the sketch up like a presidential delegation where representatives of each race announce their choice of new recruit to their team. The selectors for their party are caricatures of their race: a Jew with religious beard, glasses, and heavy accent; a black man with Jheri Curl, sunglasses, and a red suit; a white man in a pastel suit and tie who uses expressions like "will you cut the malarkey!" They in turn choose a well-known figure who is either racially mixed or culturally fluid while a trio of sports like commentators make racist comments; meanwhile the massive crowd cheers or despairs of the new recruits. While black people choose Tiger Woods (with the caption "Tiger Woods: Now 100 Percent Black"[2]), the white group choose Colin Powell. They negotiate a trade where white people keep Eminem (the white rapper), but give O. J. Simpson back to the black community in a trade. What Chappelle satires here is the fluidity and arbitrariness of being categorized as a race when you are ambiguous and how one's behavior is read as more important than facial features or ancestry. He also highlights how ridiculous it is for another person to bestow race upon another. In the skit, Tiger Woods says gratefully to the black group how happy he is to finally have a racial home.

This racial identity is investigated with poignancy in Issa Rae's sitcom *Insecure* where the main character works in an organization whose name tries to mimic black language (We Got Y'all), but whose staff are mostly white. She and her coworkers work with black kids from the ghetto although these adults in charge have no experience living there. Because she is black, they expect Issa to be the interpreter of blackness. She is insecure about her blackness and constantly negotiating her identity with black and white people in her life. In the film and TV show *Dear White People*, a politicized and militant black student runs a radio program explaining to white people the rules about how not to offend black people, which inevitably leads to explaining black people. Secretly she dates a white guy and tries to hide that her hair isn't adequately kinky. Podcasts like "Codeswitch," "Closer than They Appear," "Still Processing," and "Yo, Is This Racist?" are also places where the game of determining blackness is explored. In her card game TradingRaces, Kenyatta Forbes has made a space to safely discuss our notions about blackness by having cards with characters like Malcolm X, Colin Powell, and Bill Clinton. As the instructions ask, "Can you out-black your opponent?," all players throw down a card and they have to convince the other players why this card's character is blacker than another. The group then must come to a consensus on which card wins. The purpose is to lay bare assumptions about race.

Black-ish is the first hit show on television created and acted primarily by black people whose subject is blackness itself, not the politics of race, but the internal struggles characters face to hold on to and understand their blackness. Although a few episodes address racism, most are interested in the more subtle identity configurations of blackness and authenticity. The characters, both black and white, struggle, fumble, offend, and retreat. The show has a mixed audience, but is popular with black viewers who comprise 24 percent of the show's audience, despite their 13 percent share of the total US population.[3] It has won many awards since it began in 2014 (Emmys, Golden Globes, NAACP, African American Film Critics Association) and garnered special attention when Michelle Obama called it her favorite show;[4] there is even a spinoff, *Grown-ish*, that began in January of 2018. It is one of the few shows that has characters ask each other, "Are you even black?" The irony in this statement is clear. In America, it seems, if your features are read as black, you are black. But *Black-ish* shows the complexity and nuances of performing blackness. Self-scrutiny, awkwardness, confusion, and obsession all result from the need to determine how black one is and how that translates into behavior and appearance.

Black-ish could never succeed with this difficult subject matter if it didn't use humor, particularly satire to do it. The act of playing an exaggerated role to critique and change societal norms has played a key role in political change. When performing for white audiences, black performers played on racist stereotypes; yet they often reserved another kind of satirical humor for the black community "thus, it seems that artistic expressions, historically, have been used among black performers to critique constructions and expressions of race in America."[5] Using stereotype to wield power, rather than be a victim of it, is something black comedians have been doing for a long time.

Wearing the mask of the perpetrator of injustice to highlight hypocrisy and injustice is often more effective than earnest indignation or outrage. In his novel *Invisible Man* (1952), Ralph Ellison shows the inherent power involved in masking one's identity as a way of moving through enemy territory (or dealing with white people) when one of his characters gives this advice to his son that is repeated to his grandson: "Live with your head in the lion's mouth. I want you to overcome 'em with yeses, undermine 'em with grins, agree 'em to death and destruction, let 'em swoller you till they vomit or bust wide open."[6] When you play a role, but you know you are playing with it, you have the power. Those who believe your role are the ones being duped. In his essay "Change the Joke, Slip the Yoke" (1958), Ellison further explains how at times using the "darky entertainer" stereotype could be an act of empowerment and assertion of identity, not one of passive acceptance:

> Very often, however, the Negro's masking is motivated not so much by fear as by a profound rejection of the image created to usurp his identity. Sometimes it is for the sheer joy of the joke; sometimes to challenge those who presume across the psychological distance created by race manners, to know his identity. . . . We wear the mask for purposes of aggression as well as for defense: In short, the motives hidden behind the mask are as numerous as the ambiguities the mask conceals.[7]

Black-ish investigates the complexities of what is beneath this mask while using the mask to play with expectations. It turns suffering—"the yoke"—into pleasure—"the joke."

From the early minstrel shows to shows like *Martin* in the 1990s and contemporary films like *The Blind Side* and *The Help*, stereotypes of black people are still hugely popular.[8] What's radical about *Black-ish* is that it is for both black and white audiences, so it can play with the stereotypes to defang them, but it has to tell something that feels like truth to black and white people. *Black-ish* tries to expand white people's notion of blackness, and Dre, the narrator and father of the Johnson clan, serves as a kind of indigenous interpreter.[9]

Many scholars have analyzed the pattern of black characterizations on film and TV and the toxicity of its effects.[10] Although there is no shortage of these analyses and collected essays on shows of the past,[11] *Black-ish* because it is fairly new has just begun to get attention. Its phenomenal success for both black and white audiences shows that there is a resonance to the identity issues they are exploring. *Black-ish* has acknowledged earlier sitcoms (including an homage to *Good Times*), but created a new medium that calls blackness itself into question and problematizes the idea of authenticity. No one is the arbiter on authentic blackness anymore, and as the show's protagonist Dre Johnson reveals, attempts to play that role make you foolish.

The other radical aspect of the show is that it looks at issues of race that aren't the obvious ones from black shows in the past, such as living in the ghetto or dealing with racial injustice. Lisa Sharon Harper states, "It is a much needed peek at African-American humanity. These are the conversations we have around the dinner table at night. When poverty is removed from the equation, these are the human and cultural concerns that rise to the surface in our families."[12] The Johnsons are a successful family with a two-profession household in a large house in the suburbs with four kids who are happily attending a posh private school with mostly white classmates. Because success has already been achieved, the focus shifts away from what earlier sitcoms of the seventies addressed, the struggle to make it in a racist world. But *Black-ish* asks, What is blackness once those hurdles have been cleared? Instead it takes us inside some of the challenges posed daily to affluent black people: how to maintain a connection to your roots, what you show in front of white people, what your relationship is to black stereotypes, what black cultural traditions you observe and keep. Therefore the show encourages white viewers both to challenge their racial stereotypes and acknowledge black success as a reality that is not mutually exclusive with racial oppression.[13]

Although the show's name created some controversy and Trump infamously called it "racist,"[14] it fits; it's about "losing" degrees of blackness and the loss of a monolithic meaning for black. Interestingly the term *Black-ish* is so slippery that three of the lead actors had different answers when interviewed by Stephen Colbert[15] about the term *black-ish* versus *black*. Although humorous in tone, the actors' responses showed the same tensions that are reflected in the characters of the show. We see an array of black possibilities and no one can agree on the "real" version. Even using "ish" on the end is something that laughs in the face of the one-drop rule, which didn't allow for the nuances of "ish" but believed in racial purity.

Although Dre Johnson is the self-designated explainer of blackness, he is the most confused of all the characters. He begins each episode with a kind of one-minute black tutorial on a subject that is a theme in that show: swimming pools and segregation, Martin Luther King, the black vote, the black church, role models, playing the dozens (otherwise known as trash talking), slavery, representation. It is told with humor (sometimes animation) about some of the harsh truths of black history and how their legacy is manifested today. His pride in this history is also what drives his need to have his children understand it. However, these primers seem directed at white viewers as if he is letting them know the key features that explain black behavior. The other important and worrisome subject Dre takes on is how pervasive and fluid black culture has become; this has diluted its meaning for black people and set no clear boundaries for who is allowed to participate. As he says in the pilot episode:

> Sometimes I worry that, in an effort to make it, black folks have dropped a little bit of their culture and the rest of the world has picked it up. They even renamed it 'Urban'. And in the 'Urban' world, Justin Timberlake and Robin Thicke are R&B Gods, Kim Kardashian's the symbol for big butts, and Asian guys are just unholdable on the dance floor. Come on! Big butts? R&B and dancing? Those were the black man's go-tos![16]

Dre's anxiety about losing his culture and then seeing it reflected back at him from nonblack people is one that tugs at his sense of self.

For Dre, living in the white suburbs is erasing his black insider card, and he admits to sometimes feeling like an oddity. In one of the opening shots, the family is shown as an attraction in a kind of safari where white people come by in a tour bus and the white guide points out the Johnsons standing and waving next to the well-groomed suburban lawn of their beautiful home.

> Tour Guide: And if you look to your left, you'll see the mythical and majestic Black Family out of their natural habitat and yet still thriving. Go ahead and wave. They'll wave right back.
>
> Woman: They're smiling. Hi. Hello.
>
> Man: The little ones are cute.
>
> Tour Guide: They're just just amazing.[17]

Here the show treats the Johnsons as updated exhibits in a human zoo, complete with white gawkers. The oddity of a black family in a place other than the ghetto or projects speaks to the common association of blackness with the disenfranchised and poor.

Blackness has a history of being equated with slavery and the poverty that ensued after emancipation. In Robin R. Means Coleman's 1998 study *African American Viewers and the Black Situation Comedy*, his subjects mostly believe that "all economically ascended Black people have their immediate roots in the underclass and /or ghetto" and that "real blacks never forget or sever themselves from this underclass."[18]

In *The Souls of Black Folk* (1903), W. E. B. Du Bois, a black Northerner, went to the South to find out about the essence of blackness. Du Bois's belief that poverty is equated with realness ("How hard a thing is life to the lowly, and yet how human and real") is felt today in the slang expression "keepin' it real," which loosely translates into "being your authentic self." Alain Locke in *The New Negro* (1925) privileges the South ("those nascent centers of folk-expression") and the poor ("the migrating peasant") as the touchstones of black culture. In *Authentic Blackness* (1999), J. Martin Favor suggests that stereotypes of blackness are partially rooted in slavery and most African Americans' socioeconomic status as lower and working class. This early identification of blackness with poverty made this the credential for many black people in claiming true blackness. As one black young man said to a focus group participant when identifying himself, "I'm black, slave black." These poor Southerners migrating north became the inhabitants of the ghetto. Poverty and authenticity are always linked, so in this logic, the opposite is true: you become more out of touch with your authentic black self as you get wealthier. Dre is vulnerable to this fading of identity partly because he no longer lives in the ghetto. When Dre complains to his coworker Charlie that his son isn't black enough, the solution is familiarization with the ghetto: "Look, all your son needs to do is understand the struggle. You get me? Mm. Take him back to the hood."[19]

This identity quandary is familiar to the experiences of the show's creator Kenya Barris and lead actor Anthony Anderson. These two successful black men have children that were born into privileged Hollywood lives and reside in primarily white neighborhoods. Anderson's son at age twelve told his father he doesn't "feel black" and because his friends are primarily Jewish, he asked for a bar mitzvah.[20]

Barris is equally interested in the way black communities create hierarchies of blackness, not just white people making these determinations. In a *New Yorker* interview, he talks about being jolted when seeing Spike Lee's movie *School Daze*. The dance off between "jigaboos" (dark-skinned black people with "black" hair) and "wannabes" (light-skinned black people with straighter hair) explicitly showed intra-black tension. He explains what ignited his idea for the show:

> I looked at my kids and they were not the idea of what I thought "black" was growing up. They're a little bit filtered—they're "black-ish." They skateboard and surf! They didn't exactly follow my journey of what being "black" was. All their friends are Asian, Jewish and Latino and they're a little bit more black, so they're also a version of "black-ish." It's an additive and a subtractive. That's what our country is right now. We're "Asian-ish" and "Latino-ish." We're all in a melting pot.[21]

This reality of today's America is seen as positive for some, a movement toward less of a black/white binary. However, as Barris admits, it is also a subtraction. The Johnson family are not just struggling against white supremacy, but rather struggling within themselves about finding authenticity in their black identities. In order to see how radical *Black-ish* is, it's useful to look back at the roots of the black sitcom and how it has progressed along with changes in binary thinking.

The distorted incarnations of blackness in theater go back to the 1600s when the antecedents of the minstrel stereotypes were incarnated in leaflets, drawings, books, songs, and poems, but they were particularly solidified and popularized in the post–Civil War minstrel shows beginning in the 1830s. White men blacked up their faces, painted their lips white, and played the lazy stupid black stereotype for mostly white audiences—often a white straight man asked these "coons" or "sambos" questions revealing their idiocy and incompetence. These were popular and if you were growing up black or white in the nineteenth century, this was part of your education. With the rise of vaudeville, white performers left the minstrel shows and which started dying off by the 1920s. In the 1930s, these spectacles moved to radio. *The Jack Benny Program* featured Rochester, a coon stereotype played by black actor Eddie Anderson. One of the longest running minstrel inspired shows was *The Amos 'n' Andy Show*, which ran from 1928 to 1960 and set the tone for many sitcoms to follow.

The mass media spreading of the coon stereotype started on the radio where Amos 'n' Andy were played by white actors using "Black Voice."[22] All black people sounded the same in a created language of mispronunciation with lots of "Dis," "Dat," and "De Oder." The physical movements were also commodified on TV shows: the wide-eyed surprise and double take, the slow walk, the exaggerated gestures with the head. The coon stereotype was often accompanied by the female equivalents, Sapphire (or the angry black shrew who emasculated her husband) or the Mammy character as seen in *Beulah*, a 1940 radio show where the character was played by a white actor Marlin Hurt. [23] Black characters were not shown in the context of their own families, but as accessories to white people. Coleman Means sees black TV as having designated periods with specific agendas.[24] This minstrelsy era (1950–1953) had a fondness and nostalgia for the Antebellum South. Black people were loveable contented jesters as part of their nature and white people the "adults" who were amused by them.

Minstrelsy was followed by the nonrecognition era (1954–1967) during the rise of the Civil Rights Movement. Because no one could ignore the debasing quality of the minstrelsy era, and TV producers weren't ready to show the radical politics, riots, and empowerment of black people, the networks went silent on the questions of black people. It was impossible to continue with the stereotypes that the NAACP had protested, but there was no replacement vision of black people as yet. When black sitcoms reemerged in the assimilationist era (1968–1971), shows like *Julia* featured a very light-skinned nurse who made little reference to her blackness and had no problems with white people. In *Room 222*, the equally light-skinned protagonist Pete Dixon, a high school teacher, faces so little discrimination that he can make lighthearted jokes about it. Here were soothing portraits of black people who expressed very little difference from white people and had little baggage or resentment toward white people. They were hardworking, heroic, and perfectly blended with their white cast members. Means refers to this as "cultural abandonment" as if black difference or culture had disappeared.

This was followed by a long period of social relevancy and ridiculed black subjectivity (1972–1983). Instead of ignoring blackness, race became the subject of the story and a "black" perspective on the world was explained by mostly black characters. Most of these shows took place in the ghetto and the characters lived in poverty, segregated from white communities. Influenced by Civil Rights, these shows attempted to invoke pity in white people, such as in *Good Times* where the father and mother living in the projects are daily struggling to keep their kids in school and out of trouble. In every episode of *Good Times*, they were beset by problems of surviving: paying the rent, staying out trouble with the police, getting an education. In a study of black sitcoms, consistent patterns in these families could be found such as isolation from white people, homes without fathers, and black mothers dominating the household and making critical decisions.[25]

Like minstrel shows, popular shows like these were sometimes the only way white people in the suburbs "interacted" with black people—they were essential in teaching what blackness meant in a more positive (albeit stereotyped) light: here were wise salt-of-the-earth mothers and determined hard-working but failing fathers who didn't lose their temper as they suffered injustice. However, in *Good Times*, they couldn't resist adding J. J. Walker, a coon stereotype, who ended up dominating the show and spiking ratings. Walker was often found yelling out his catch phrase "Dyn-o-mite!," which was merchandised on coffee mugs and T-shirts and repeated by white and black kids everywhere. *Sanford and Son*, *What's Happening*, *That's My Mama*, *The Jeffersons*—all fell into similar patterns as *Good Times*, reinforcing these stereotypes, and showing viewers a fictional black home (which most of these white producers had never experienced). Characters all spoke and moved alike (jive talkin', high fiving, swag walking, eye rolling, teeth sucking, and raucous laughter), and characters often had a scheme to make a quick buck and were lazy in the coon tradition.

Another popular black family-style show brought cute, wisecracking black ghetto children into the homes of white wealthy families to serve as comedic entertainment or to evoke maudlin sentiment such as in *Webster* and *Diff'rent Strokes*. Their blackness was a plot device and gimmick as in *Diff'rent*

Strokes where Arnold, the adopted child could always be relied upon to look at his brother with wide-eyed distortion and say in Black Voice, "What you talkin' 'bout Willis?"

Finally, the black family and diversity (1984–1989) stage veered away from negative stereotyping and offered successful educated families in shows like *The Cosby Show, A Different World*, and *Frank's Place*. Here black people were no longer segregated and they represented the black middle class who were sophisticated and cultured. These shows allowed for diverse politics and economic status (no longer all in the 'hood)—here they were seen in college, at work, and at home.

The Cosby Show was a radical change in black sitcoms that always placed black people in the ghetto with the same generic lives of struggle or brought ghetto kids into white neighborhoods to laugh at the fish out of water theme. Scholars applauded its freedom from black fetishized images of the past, but criticized it for promoting a version of enlightened racism[26] or the belief that it's not racism that is the problem, but rather lazy black people. If black families like the Cosbys can make it easily to their success, everyone else can too, it suggested. *The Cosby Show* debuted in 1984 and showed an affluent family who ignored race except occasionally to create a showcase for black pride (jazz, the Civil Rights Movement, Black Arts Movement, Harlem Renaissance). These episodes were usually about the mischief of the five Cosby children and the Cosby parents modeling excellent child-rearing practices: patience, firm standards, and loveable kidding around. *New York Magazine* once called it "little more than 'Leave it to Beaver' in blackface."[27]

However, instead of black families relating to this new image, free of ugly stereotypes, many black and white people didn't associate the Cosbys with a black family. In a study done by Sut Jhally and Justin Lewis,[28] although black viewers could connect to the family, these respondents connected to "common family problems," not anything that they felt was decidedly black. *The Cosby Show* was about a "family that happens to be black," and its lack of attention to how this black family actually made it to such success earned it the label colorblind. *The Cosby Show*'s success was made to seem natural and easy without addressing how a black husband and wife could become doctors and lawyers when they were clearly doing this in the 1950s and 1960s, a time of quotas and glass ceilings.

Inspired by these black-produced shows that were finding success for both black and white audiences, Fox entered a new stage of programing. This shifted away from black as object to black as subject. In Kristal Brent Zook's *Color by Fox*, she asserts that this new stage brought with it four key elements of black-produced television: autobiography, meaning a tendency toward collective and individual authorship of black experience; improvisation, the practice of inventing and ad-libbing unscripted dialogue or action; aesthetics, a certain pride in visual signifiers of blackness; and drama, a marked desire for complex characterizations and emotionally challenging subject matter[29] (which she clarified as the ability to "explore painful in group memories and experiences").[30] These are all found in *Black-ish* episodes, which seems a continuation of this black subjectivity genre, but more transparent and self-conscious in its discussion of blackness.

This new class of black families as seen in these shows highlights the importance of displaying wealthy black families on TV to overcome the stereotype that black equals poor. This oversimplification has excluded the voices of wealthy and upper-class and educated black Americans, invalidating their experiences as black people because they aren't close to an economically degraded past or present. Often a black person who moves up from poverty is accused of trying to be white or being an Uncle Tom. Obama often had this accusation hurled at him and when his daughter Malia chose Harvard for college, there was a backlash from some black people who felt the Obamas were "selling out."

Because of this history of wealth being disidentified with blackness, *Black-ish* focuses often on the wealth and success of Dre and his family. *The Cosby Show*, *The Jeffersons*, and *The Fresh Prince of Bel-Air* were other black sitcoms that showed financially successful black characters. In *The Jeffersons*, what is emphasized is George's nouveau riche attitude and his gauche, ghetto way of behaving in contrast to his wealthy white neighbors. *Fresh Prince* in the 1980s was another positive show that began to question assumptions about blackness and poverty by juxtaposing the Fresh Prince (played by Will Smith) who moves from the ghetto to his wealthy Uncle Phil's in the suburbs of Los Angeles.

Zook writes about what these Black Family and Diversity shows did for black people—they opened up possibilities. Shows in the late 1980s, early 1990s "presented the refreshing possibility that racial authenticity could be negotiated rather than assumed—or perhaps done away with altogether."[31] She refers to a "buffer" caste (wealthy educated successful blacks) who, although only a small fraction of the total African American population, "experienced a certain, strange inclusion, one that blurred established notions of race." Unlike the 1960s and before, what counted as black was no longer clear by the 1980s, nor was it clear who now suffered enough to be a legitimate member of the black club.[32]

Whereas in *Black-ish*, the father is trying to hold tight to whatever he has left of his blackness, *Fresh Prince* is the opposite as Uncle Phil and his wife do not like the influence Will is having on their children. For instance, Will teaches the youngest daughter to rap; later, he challenges Carlton, Uncle Phil's preppy black son, to survive in the ghetto. In other words, Will is making them more black. In contrast to Dre, Uncle Phil does not want his children displaying black cultural traits such as slang, cool walk, ghetto-influenced clothing—and so his children dress and speak in ways often associated with white. The show overturns the simplistic assumption that ghetto equals uncultured when Uncle Phil is shocked to find that Will plays classical piano.[33] These shallow assumptions about blackness are also played out when Will, who often disparages his Uncle and Carlton for seeming white, finds out Uncle Phil actually heard Malcolm X speak.[34] He also has to rethink his simple categories when his cousin Carlton finally has enough of the "what color are you" kinds of teasing. Carlton accepts a bet to last seventy-two hours in the ghetto by playing with an alter ego C-note (a do-rag-wearing, slang-talking ghetto tough fully accepted by the crew) as opposed to his usual self who is a member of the glee club. He chastises Will for his constant judgment: "Look, just because I grew up in the best neighborhoods and pronounce my ng's at the end of a sentence doesn't mean I'm any less black than you. You always act like I don't measure up to some ruler of blackness you carry around." Will has also been the victim of the old equation: "You treat me like I'm some kind of idiot because I talk different" . . . "Differently," Carlton adds.[35]

The Cosby Show seemed to be a turning point from the shows that preceded it in that all its characters were intelligent, loving, wise, and successful, but race was rarely discussed. Still it was a radical shift for many people to see this alternative model on television. *Cosby* showed black inflection, through style, voice, body language, clothing, cultural cues, history—it was the best of black culture, but the episode themes were color neutral. If being black has been oversimplified to being poor, then *The Cosby Show*, the first show about a perfect black family, was revolutionary, showing viewers a well-educated and financially secure black family. Although they were excellent models of what heights black people could reach, many black viewers felt the Huxtable family conflicted with popular notions of blackness.

In *Black-ish*, black identities depend on which generations you come from as shown in the three generations of the Johnson family. Dre and his wife Bow are raising their four children in white suburbia with Dre's divorced parents living with them. The parents and grandparents comment constantly on their own racial identity as they negotiate living with children who don't necessarily see themselves as black. Dre straddles his parents' black activist generation and his own children's multi-ethnic, multiracial world where they don't prioritize race and are disinterested in their father's mission to make them black. His urgency and anxiety about how to remain black and keep his children black is the theme of many episodes, which wink at the construction and performance of his blackness and his awareness of its weakening hold on him. At the same time, it highlights the different beliefs/stereotypes about blackness through both its white and black characters for its white and black viewers.

Both parents are highly self-conscious about their blackness; their historical and ongoing inferior status in society makes them scramble to avoid being seen as one of the racial stereotypes. Dre says to his children before they enter the neighborhood pool party, "So no watermelon!"[36] And his mother Ruby talks about the difficulty she has "napping in front of white people," thus showing her fear of being connected to the "lazy coon" stereotype. Three generations of black people weigh in—grandparents who went through the Civil Rights Movement and are still suspicious of white people; husband and wife who are successful and have not encountered much explicit racism, but are well aware of black history; children (Generation Z) who barely know racism exists: "Why are these people so mad?" asks their youngest son Jack when seeing the coverage of a police officer who isn't indicted for shooting a black teenager.[37]

Before turning to the episodes, it's important to look at how each character has a degree of blackness based on his or her age group. Dre Johnson represents the most anguished generation and is the point of view and narrator of the show. He gets angry in almost every episode, often because he imagines racism everywhere and often makes a fool of himself taking a political stand where there is really nothing to protest. Police stop him and are nice; white neighbors don't invite him to their pool party because they think he doesn't like them and not—as he assumes—because they are racist; they can't book the last adjoining rooms in a nice hotel, not because they are black, but because it's already been booked by another black family; the white boyfriend of their daughter Zoey dumps her because he finds her shallow, not because of race. He is hypocritical and confused and often comes off as overly rigid. His own and best black credential is his having been raised in Compton, Los Angeles. However, his wife and mother often point out that he wasn't one of the tough ones in the neighborhood. In fact, he was nicknamed Teapot for his high-pitched wail when threatened.

Dre's anxiety about feeling black is projected onto others in his family (mainly his wife, his eldest son, and his wife's brother). He can't call into question his parents' blackness because both were involved in the Civil Rights Movement—the ultimate black credential. Also, they haven't been financially successful like Dre, so although they live with him, they keep their connection to poverty and struggle intact. His choice of a biracial wife (she has a white father) doesn't help his case and so he often makes fun of what he calls her own lack of blackness. ("Dre: All of this coming from, uh, a biracial or mixed or omni-colored-complexion, whatever-it-is-they're-calling-it-today woman—who technically isn't even really black?").[38] His son Junior who is nerdy and uncool also embarrasses Dre and calls into question Dre's own image of black masculinity as does his yoga-posing vegan, spoken word poet brother-in-law.

Bow Johnson, Dre's biracial wife, is also very conscious of managing people's impressions of her. She seems to believe what her mother-in-law Ruby accuses her of—that she isn't black because of her white father. She gets politically passionate as an activist (burns dolls outside stores because they don't have enough diversity; leads protest for zero tolerance for the word N*gger), but often finds herself finding contradictions in what she is fighting for. She's against using the word N*gger but then backs down when her son Jack uses a variation of it in a school talent show. She feels that a lack of black dolls is deeply affecting her daughter, but then sees it's probably real life models that matter in the end. She is often in the position of having to defend her blackness against her mother-in-law and husband: "Okay, well, if I'm not really black, then could somebody please tell my hair and my ass?"[39]

Andre Junior, the eldest son, is relatively unconscious of color. He does extra credit for school, loves *Lord of the Rings*, and isn't black enough for his father. His lack of awareness of his own nerdiness makes him often the voice of reason and authenticity. He is black, but that is only a minor part of his identity. He can perform blackness, but prefers to be authentic, which for him is uncool, and he doesn't buy into his dad's vision of the world (Junior: "Face it, dad, the world's different from when you were growing up. There's no midday dance shows on, nobody irons their jeans, and some cops are okay").[40] In "The Nod," Dre tries to convince Junior that black is a tribe he is part of. He notices Junior doesn't do the nod of solidarity when walking by other black people. Although his father explains it as "the internationally accepted, yet unspoken, sign of acknowledgment of black folks around the world."[41] Junior does it only with fellow nerds.

The antithesis of Junior is Zoey, the eldest daughter who is effortlessly popular and her father's favorite. She confesses part of that is her blackness, which makes her cool and which explains her father's admiration. She has white friends, but wears her hair in an array of black hairstyles and feels confident in her beauty as a black woman. Her teenage self-absorption makes her completely disinterested in discussions of race.

Jack and Diane, the twins and youngest, don't see the racial divide at all—they are innocent of history, protected, and untouched by racism. In one episode, the twins describe a girl without mentioning she is the only other black child in the class. Jack doesn't know Obama was the first black president and doesn't understand the furor caused by singing a rap song with the word N*gga in it for school. While Jack is innocent, Diane is portrayed as conniving and heartless. She is confident and finds her mother's earnestness about "being whatever she wants" to be unnecessary.

Pops is constantly putting Dre down and making fun of his easy lifestyle. He uses his generation's involvement in the Civil Rights Movement to show his superiority although his true contribution is questionable. Ruby is a born-again Christian after a life of sexual freedom, relentlessly hostile to Bow presumably because she is part white, and often makes fun of her mixed race (Ruby: "Not now, hybrid![42] If I didn't know you were mixed, I'd swear you were Chinese"[43]).

Many compare *Black-ish* to *Cosby* as it is also a large family with two highly successful professional parents who are in love and not struggling daily with racism. However, they differ significantly in the messages they are offering. *The Cosby Show* was at times pedantic. He had after all studied child educa-tion and had Harvard child psychiatrist Dr. Alvin F. Poussaint working with him to make sure the messages were positive. So materialism was frowned upon and anything that smelled of stereotype was carefully avoided. His children were obedient for the most part and dealt with all the standard fare of classic white sitcoms: crushes at school, academic struggles, friendships, work ethic. Interestingly, *Black-ish* despite the one-minute tutorial at the beginning and reflection at the end allows for a wider range of black pos-sibilities than *Cosby*'s careful goodness. Dre, Bow, and the kids are materi-alistic and this is encouraged. The opening shot in the pilot episode shows Dre facing a souped up closet with its own lighting filled with an enormous collection of sneakers. His wife wants to go to a spa instead of a march on Martin Luther King Day. His daughter Zoey is obsessed with clothing and selfies. They get takeout almost every night rather than a home-cooked meal. They aren't that interested in their children's grades in school. There is even an episode about how spoiled the kids are ("Hunger"). They throw their son a showy bro-mitzvah where they all dress like rappers with gold chains— *Cosby* would never hear of it. While *Cosby* emphasized the innocence and goodness of children, Diane, one of the twins in *Black-ish*, is sinister and without values. The family comments often on it as a source of humor rather than real concern. Zoey is shallow and Dre is almost proud of her because of it. Junior is earnest and hardworking, but Dre can't hide his distaste for him.

While *The Cosby Show* carefully avoids stereotypes, *Black-ish* boldly plays with them. *Cosby* tried to be a role model; *Black-ish* just tries to be honest. Work in *Cosby* barely causes a sweat as Cosby works from the house and is appreciated by all his patients, mostly white. There are no office politics or even the troubling issues of colleagues. Cosby seems to simply give check-ups to grateful people, but there is no other aspect of work that distresses him. In contrast, Dre is the token black voice in his office and often put on the spot to explain to his clueless boss and coworkers about the black rules. In *Black-ish*, white people are an important presence, often parodied in their micro-aggressions or political correctness whereas white people aren't set up as different in *Cosby*. Cosby's father is filled with wise advice and clean humor. Dre's father goes to the track, is afraid of the taxman, and is ready to beat his grandchildren at the slightest provocation. Cosby's wife is a successful lawyer and never overworked or overwhelmed; Bow is always stressed and constantly needing reassurance about her mothering skills. The grandfather and father in *Cosby* teach the kids about jazz, while Dre and his father teach Junior how to scan for and appreciate women with big behinds. Cosby's parents reminisce about seeing some of the greatest black jazz musicians, but they do not celebrate other forms of black street culture. *Black-ish* celebrates street culture: Hot sauce, fried chicken, Skittles, grape soda, gold chains, big butts, tough ghetto cousins, rap music.

It's a barrier breaker to have white audiences peer into how black people construct their own blackness and expose for white people that there is no coherent definition of blackness among black people. We see this with Dre's white coworkers mostly seen around the conference table debating and questioning aspects of blackness. They are innocent and careful (politically correct) and at times cloddish ("How would a black man say good morning?" asks Dre's white coworker Josh in the pilot episode[44]), but Dre is the designated spokesperson who is also conscious at times he's making things up as he goes. In one episode he is unaware that he has been favoring lighter-skinned black models in his work in advertising. This is pointed out to him by white coworkers and a fellow black coworker. Dre shows a real confidence in telling white people what black is while he secretly questions it for himself and his family. The show acknowledges black peer pressure to dislike the police, but shows Dre secretly calling them when he hears a noise. This is such a regular occurrence, they have their own key to his house.

Given that black sitcoms in the past were targeted toward white people and often consciously perpetuated stereotypes, this show is not worrying about pleasing or offending white audiences. Anderson, who plays Dre, said that people in their community responded to the episode called "The Nod" with "Yo man you're showing too much."[45] He explained on the *Colbert* show that the show was "giving [white people] a peek into our world, our life and what's going on."[46]

This role of black tutor for white people is shown in an episode that explores who can say N*gga in the episode "The Word." Dre looks at the group of Zoey's friends sitting on the couch and points to each one in turn (three white guys and a racially ambiguous one): "You cannot say it. You definitely can't say it. Hell, you better not even think it. And you I'm gonna need to meet your mom and daddy."[47]

His clarity about being the arbiter of who can utter this word is confused earlier in the episode when they are trying to decide what to teach their son Jack about the word:

Dre: Damn it! It's his birthright! Jewish kids get to go to Israel. Black kids get to say this.

Bow: Dre! That is ridiculous! Nobody should say it. It is an ugly, hateful word with an even uglier and hate-filled history.

Dre: Yeah, of it being said to us, not by us.[48]

This is a conversation white people don't usually have with black people. Because *Black-ish* is a sitcom, not a drama, it takes the sting out of these highly sensitive issues by using irony. Simultaneously the scene is not unintelligible to a white audience, thus *Black-ish* accurately and understandably conveys racial discrimination from a black perspective to white audiences.

Although white people have become more aware of racism, their own privilege, micro-aggressions, and black history, these more subtle intraracial struggles have been hidden. Christine Acham shows how radical this new representation of black family life has opened up possibilities for how blackness is defined. She writes in her book *Revolution Televised:*

Dre's mentality represents "authentic" blackness, and every time his family challenges him or his confidence in stereotypical definitions of blackness falters, the authority of authentic blackness is undermined. Viewers are shown that an African-American family can be successful, and challenged to rethink blackness. By undermining attempts to define blackness, the Johnsons' representation of African-Americans becomes as valid as any other.[49]

In the following discussion, I review five themes I have found from four seasons of *Black-ish* that speak to the softening of the binary and the consciousness of its construction. Each category eviscerates the idea that there is a blackness that can be explained to white people and enforced among black people. By showing characters debating, mistaking, and changing their minds about the rules, it reveals their emptiness. In addition, using the stereotypes and also evading them shows how stereotypes are not related to anything substantial, innate, or natural about blackness. Finally, it looks at racial ambiguity and the lack of clear binary definitions for the next generation. The categories are as follows:

1. Black people using stereotypes to their advantage in front of white people.
2. Black people performing in ways that evade being stereotyped in front of white people.

3. White people performing "I'm cool with blackness" and thus "I'm not a racist."
4. Black people policing authentic blackness.
5. Racial fluidity in Generation Z.

A very big part of performance is how black people on the show consciously play into white expectations of black stereotypes to benefit them somehow or make fun of white people's unwavering faith in these stereotypes. As Michelle Stevens explains:

> The fact that some black comedians forge a connection with the audience through stereotypes of the (black) self is subversive to the degree it allows both black and white audiences to recognize something of themselves—of their own culturally shaped biases—in the performer. This goes beyond some understanding of the black condition and what it is like to be black. The black comedian encourages us to laugh at the absurdity of our stereotypes.[50]

One example of this is when Dre and Bow realize their wedding certificate isn't valid and they immediately play out the stereotypes.

> Dre: I can't believe I'm a baby daddy. Oh My God.
>
> Bow: That means I'm a single mother who's also a successful doctor. I'm a profile in courage. If "Oprah" was still on, she would want to meet me.[51]

In "The Gift of Hunger," Dre says to Zoey who is working in his office, "You've only been at work ten minutes, and you're already on break? Are you trying to perpetuate the stereotypes?"[52]

Bow and Dre get out of going to a white friend's church by using a stereotype of black churchgoers.

> Bow: We'll just play the race card. So, culturally speaking, we just we have, like, a different idea of Sunday church.
>
> Dre: Yeah, culturally speaking, we're looking for something a little more—
>
> Bow: Livelier. Livelier.[53]

These two nonchurch-goers are playing on the stereotype of the black church with singing, dancing, noise, and jubilation and black people as inherently faithful. Zoey's college application doesn't outright lie, but relies on admissions officers to read these things as the black victim:

> Imagine living in a home where your mother can't stop having children, where you are constantly taking in another mouth to feed, a home where grandparents,

uncles, siblings all huddle together in one room, where only the strongest will survive, a home where you'll never know where your next meal is coming from. . . . A home where your mother is in and out of the hospital, where men don't vote, where the man who may or may not be your father often skips work to feed his addictions.

As she goes through the list, each image defies the stereotype. So for example "never know where your next meal is coming from" has the family trying to decide on takeout menus. After she completes reading it, her mother exclaims, "Guess who is going to college?!"[54]

One stereotype that is often used in the show is the excesses of rap culture. In "Gift of Hunger," the family appear all in silver chains and all white (Jack wearing a white fur vest) as they make all the moves of a gansta rap video and throw cash from the roof of an ice cream truck. In "Switch Hitting," Dre dresses in gold chains holding the collar of a pit bull to meet a client who is expecting him to "keep it real." Each time they play a stereotype and acknowledge it, it empties it of its meaning and potency.

Another stereotype is that all black people are political activists or should be. Junior consciously uses stereotypes to get elected at school by dressing like Malcolm X, claiming to be the descendant of a slave and showing KKK images—playing the angry black man stereotype to the hilt.[55] In "Martin Luther Skiing Day," Dre's white colleagues are surprised he's not worshipping Martin Luther King and doesn't feel the need to treat it as a black holiday. Charlie and Dre play with the stereotypes that black people are political activists when their boss implies they should take the day off:

Dre: Uh, what do you mean "feel free to take the day off"? MLK is a national holiday, not a black holiday. Obama's inauguration black holiday. OJ getting off black holiday.

Charlie: Roscoe's chicken and waffles grand opening.[56]

Here the coon stereotype of the lazy fried-chicken-eating coon is revived by Charlie.

The show often acknowledges the politics around black hair. Dre knows that the expectation for being read as blacker includes hairstyle and clothing. Before his white client comes over (who is expecting a black family cliché), Dre says to his wife (who has straightened her hair):

Dre: I need your curls.

Bow: But it took me a month to get this appointment.

Dre: Okay, okay, you know what? Cornrows. I want everybody in cornrows. We're gonna have cornrow line from biggest to smallest. And Junior he can anchor the rear in a do-rag.[57]

Here Dre goes from straight hair to curls to cornrows to a do-rag moving along the black authenticity line till he gets to the ghetto stereotype. Each hairstyle is increasingly associated with getting blacker until it moves to poor and disenfranchised. Dre openly provokes his boss when he is asked to make a video about Los Angeles for "urban" audiences. Like Junior's election campaign, Dre calls in the stereotype repertoire of black images: Malcolm X speaking, cop cars speeding, riots, boxing, O. J. being chased by police, and the sound of prison doors slamming. This in-your-face attempt to make a point about clichés to his boss almost gets him fired.

The show plays with white guilt and uses black stereotyping to seize control and use it to advantage; it also shows the flipside of stereotyping—the experience that every minority group has—the urge to avoid being associated with a stereotype. This often results in overcompensating to avoid seeming like one. It explores the self-consciousness of black people in always seeing themselves in the eyes of white people who might stereotype them. These episodes explore the lengths that black people will undergo to avoid being put in that box. In "Sink or Swim," Dre takes on the stereotype of black people not knowing how to swim, which he explains in his tutorial at the beginning of the episode (segregated swimming pools, separate but not equal places to learn to swim, slaves running away through swamps). However, when he has an exchange with his white neighbor, he goes to ridiculous lengths to hide the fact that he can't swim:

Bow: So, we have to spend our Saturday with people that we don't like so that you can prove to someone whose opinion you don't care about that you can swim? Which, might I remind you, you cannot.

Dre: —For now, all right?—[Sighs] So, shh. I've got to buckle down if I'm gonna learn to swim in a week. I basically got this.[58]

In fact, Dre can't swim and ends up humiliating himself as he shrieks nonstop and almost drowns, which his son films, and it goes viral.

In "Who's Afraid of the Big Black Man," both Charlie and Dre are afraid of being seen as a black predator (Buck) stereotype. A small white girl seems to be lost in the elevator, but both Dre and Charlie avoid trying to help her. All three black male workers (Charlie, Dre, and Curtis) one by one come in visibly shaken by the experience, but their white coworkers (Josh and Stevens) are nonplussed. They try and explain.

Dre: Okay, look, I know it looks bad, but that is a little white girl. And as a black man

Josh: No! No. You do not get to play the race card today. Not with that.

Charlie: Sorry I'm late. There was a little snowflake on the elevator, so I had to take the stairs.

Dre: Me too.

Charlie: Careful, Dre. Someone's out there setting traps.

Stevens: I don't understand. Why are you two so afraid of a baby?

Dre: We don't have the luxury of being helpful because we're instantly seen as threats.

Stevens: Well that's just common sense.

Curtis: Look, I'm sorry I'm late, boss. There's a little white girl in the elevator. Almost had me. I saw my freedom flash right before my eyes.[59]

Here all three black colleagues acknowledge the danger of the stereotype while the white coworkers are skeptical, but Stevens clumsily reveals that he believes the stereotype. (Responding to Dre's "we're instantly seen as threats," Stevens answers, "Well that's just common sense.")

Bow, the mother of the Johnson family, is hypervigilant about not being the stereotype that white people will assume she is. She is very proud that she is a doctor and often lords it over people (old college friends, pool party, retorts to children and husband). This is partly to assert herself as a black professional woman and not be taken for a nanny or servant. In "Hunger," the parents try to teach a lesson and get their kids to earn money. The assumption is immediately made by their clueless neighbor that they are a family with a slew of kids needing charity. Bow goes out of her way to show her wealth and status to overrule that image (dressing in fur and jewelry).

Black-ish has captured a truth about the emptiness of these stereotypes and yet their power to drive behavior in both black and white communities. It's not surprising it feels honest to most viewers as Barris takes 90 percent of it from real life situations. It critiques the overly sensitized dialogue around race that has stunted growth and understanding between races. In fact, showrunner Barris uses the show partly to open up these conversations. He believes "we are a society which talks less about race than ever—at least openly—because of political correctness and this has made the situation worse."[60]

Black-ish often shows how much discomfort white people have not only with black people, but with other white people when it comes to issues of race. Much of the time, they are trying to prove they aren't racist. White people's confusion about what is a sensitive issue and what is okay in terms of cultural fluidity (can they high five; rap; do certain dance steps; question the use of the words negro, colored, black; use black linguistic terms like "my brotha"?). Dre allows his white assistant Kris to be an "honorary brother" whom he greets with a signature handshake. But if Josh, another white coworker, tries to give Dre a nickname, a special handshake, or dance, he is shamed. Dre calls out, "That's inappropriate, highly inappropriate!" These white characters trying to use black vernacular or prove they are "down" with black people in some cases is an attempt to cover their prejudices and misunderstandings about black people.[61] White people in this show are befuddled on how to behave around black people and certain sensitive subjects, so they ask their in-house experts Dre and Charlie to explain the black rules. But the rules are unclear. The inconsistency of the system is mocked when Charlie gives a tutorial on who can say N*gger. The chart reads: "Who can say N word" and in the "No" column is the word "police."

> Jeff: Mexicans can't say the "N" word, but Dominicans are okay?
>
> Charlie: Exactly. Puerto Ricans are cool, too. Unless you're a J-Lo Puerto Rican.
>
> Stevens: As opposed to a?
>
> Charlie and Curtis: Rosie Perez.
>
> Curtis: Look, it's simple. Big pun, fat Joe okay.
>
> Charlie: Mm-hmm. Mark Anthony, Ricky Martin, no bueno.
>
> Charlie: Mnh-mnh. See, basically, the whole terror squad can say it. —But not Menudo.
>
> Curtis: Agreed.
>
> Lucy: Oh, what about that thuggish ruggish bone Don Lemon?
>
> Charlie and Curtis: Hell no!
>
> Curtis: I wish he would.
>
> Charlie: Not even when he's quoting the president.
>
> Curtis: Mm-hmm.
>
> Charlie: And speaking of presidents, Bill Clinton probably shouldn't use it, neither. But I wouldn't be crazy-mad if he did.[62]

Here they are playing with the idea of who is obviously black, which includes Bill Clinton (a reference to Toni Morrison's ironic statement that he is the first black president). Puerto Ricans are included as they are often mistaken for black, but he distinguishes J-Lo Puerto Rican from Rosie Perez, basically pointing out the differences in class. Charlie and Curtis appear perfectly clear on who is in and who is out, but their tutees are baffled at what seems random.

Later Dre is reminded of arbitrariness of the black rules. In one episode, he is uncomfortable with Junior's white friend Kyle stepping into what he sees as black territory. He seems to be more knowledgeable than Dre's family about Martin Luther King.

> Kyle: My family usually teaches literacy at the local prison for MLK day.
>
> Junior: How come we never do anything like that for Martin Luther King Day?
>
> Dre: Uh, because we're black all year long. They're white. They have to do extra credit.[63]

Here Dre shows more of an ownership of Martin Luther King than the white neighbor. White people have to earn a connection to King while he makes it clear to Junior that black people have it automatically.

Black characters often dislike what they see as infringement on their territory, which includes the Civil Rights Movement for Pops. He competes with Bow's white father in a civil rights off.

> Paul: Did you guys see "Selma"? Complete game-changer. So awe-inspiring.
>
> Pops: I saw the original in 1965. Mine was called "Detroit."
>
> Alicia: Paul actually walked across that bridge with the reverend doctor.
>
> Pops: Oh. Good for him. He was still a white man when he got to the other side of the bridge, though, yes? And probably ate at a restaurant. At the counter.[64]

Here Pops refers to the injustices committed in the country's racial past as credentials that give him an excuse to opt out of activism.

When it comes to black authenticity, black people are often the most stringent rule enforcers with each other. One way his parents police Dre's blackness is political activism. What makes someone authentic is having been part of the historic struggle for black rights. Pops lived during the time of the Civil Rights Movement, which he uses often to bludgeon his son, but is often caught in the act of artifice:

> Pops: Oh, why don't y'all go get a room? I can't believe I marched on Washington and fought for my country to watch y'all do that mess.
>
> Dre: You shot yourself in the foot to get out of the army. And you were in D.C. For an Isley Brothers concert.[65]

Here, Dre has a rare moment where he can expose his father's posing as an activist to take down his higher position on the black hierarchy.

Another important and contested area of black authenticity is language. Using standard English is often seen as "white" while slang makes you authentically black. This is often played out in the episodes:

> Bow: There is a rich panoply of different ways to experience blackness.
>
> Dre: None of which include the words "rich panoply."
>
> Pops: Now you're sounding like her.
>
> Bow: What does that mean? Huh? You mean I sound intelligent? Cultured? Educated?—
>
> Dre: Pretentious, bougie, and obnoxious.[66]

Dre mocks himself when he is explaining in the white tutorial how he can code switch, but then trips up as he's doing it: "We have our mainstream selves to be in 'The Man's' world, and we have our down-home selves for the brothers. Some of us handle the switch effortlessly. From now on, I'm keepin' it real, one hundred, damn it, I mean, a hunnit."[67] Here Dre's years away in white neighborhoods make it hard to hold on to accurate street dialect.

Lack of knowledge of black music and musical taste also can expose you as less authentically black. Junior is finishing his school election speech by dancing to the rap song "Panda" when his iPod suddenly starts playing "Ten Million Fireflies" (an electronic top 40 hit) and his black cover is blown. Dre uses people's knowledge of rap music as a way to read where someone is on the black continuum as he does to his wife.

> Dre: Can you believe this, though? This white dude is questioning me about my blackness.
>
> Bow: Huh, I wonder what that's like, somebody constantly questioning your blackness. Just because you misquoted the lyrics to "Ain't No Fun" (a rap song).[68]

Later Pops calls him a sellout partly because his language has changed.

> Pops: Sellout! I remember the day it happened! You stopped saying "nah mean?" And started saying "you know what I mean?" Saddest day of my life.[69]

Food is another way people determine authenticity. Pops complains to Bow about the meal they are eating.

> Pops: Actually, you told me I was coming over to eat fried chicken—I have no idea what the hell this is.
>
> Bow: —It's fried chicken.

Pops: —Really?—

Bow: It's baked fried chicken.

Pops: Oh, so fried fried chicken is too black for you.[70]

Later getting organic hummus and kettle corn from the farmer's market is used as evidence to show a client that Dre is not authentically black while Charlie's combination of goldfish and hot sauce gets him black kudos. In another episode Ruby, who is known to the family as making a great Christmas dinner filled with traditional Southern black food, such as sweet potato pie and ham, gets exposed as having ordered it all from a Puerto Rican woman.[71] The clichés about what black people eat and what white people eat is a strait jacket that none of the characters can abide.

Closeness to Africa is an attempted way to gain authenticity, but it is doomed to failure as many black people have a limited connection. Dre, at times, tries to access Africa as a way to reinvigorate his blackness, but Pops shuts him down.

Dre: So, next Saturday, when you turn 13, you're becoming a man, too a black man, because I'm throwing you an African rites of passage ceremony.

Pops: What is this mess you're doing?

Dre: This ain't no mess, Pops. This is our culture.

Pops: This ain't our culture. We black, not African. Africans don't even like us.

Junior: Dad, can I go?

Dre: No. Stand right there and experience your roots.

Pops: You're better off watching "Roots."[72]

Here Pops reminds Dre that the African connection has been lost when he says "this ain't our culture" when Dre tries to imitate an African coming of age ceremony to replace the Bar Mitzvah his son was hoping for. Dre is making up things as he goes, which further proves the arbitrariness of this ceremony. Junior is completely disengaged and when Dre orders him to "experience your roots," Pops correctly suggests that watching a TV program about slavery would be more engaging than a ceremony connected to a place that they have only a symbolic connection to. "We black, not African," Pops reminds him. "Africans don't even like us." Here he is alluding to the fact that Africans coming to America often don't feel an immediate connection to black Americans although black people at times will assume one.[73]

One aspect of modern blackness that the show takes on is the racial flu-idity of Dre's children's generation. Although Dre's parents keep defining everything in terms of the black/white binary, his kids see and live in a very different world where mixed race, gender fluidity, and self-identification are more the norm. As Charlie says when trying to comfort him for his daughter having a white boyfriend. "Dre, it's 2015. Your kids are gonna date who they're gonna date. Race don't matter. 'Cause in 10 years, we all gonna look Puerto Rican."[74] Junior forces his father to question what "black folks" are as they sieve through Facebook for black friends for Junior. As ethnically ambiguous darker-skinned people walk by, it reveals his father's own lack of understanding of what is black.

Dre: What about him?

Junior: He's Filipino.

Dre: [Chuckles] I'm sure that's what his mother tells him.—Hey, what about that dude?—

Junior: Sri Lankan.

Dre: Not even a real place.—[Gasps] What about him?—

Junior: He's from Malawi.

Dre: Where's that?

Junior: Africa.

Dre: Pass.[75]

In the end, Dre admits to having no connection to Africa and no clear instinct for identifying his own.

Throughout these episodes, Dre's hypocrisy is revealed. There is no one black experience or black rule book. Although he has put himself in the pos-ition of teaching his children and the *Black-ish* audience, he is unsure how to navigate in his current environment. Dre is often portrayed as alternately weepy, emotional, scared, or strident and angry. Battling racism is not what makes his life hard, but rather his own self-consciousness and battles with authenticity.

In Marlon Riggs's 1994 documentary *Black Is . . . Black Ain't*, he applies the metaphor of gumbo to explore the intraracial conflict in determining blackness. He shows the variety of black identity, but also expresses the weight and rigidity of former definitions of blackness that excluded gay people and were suspicious of the educated and non-Christian; it also demanded loyalty to "black" causes. One moment in the film that shows how much things have changed is when Angela Davis, the former Black Panther and activist, declares her right to be any kind of black she wants. The Panthers had a very clear criteria for blackness, strict solidarity, hypermasculinity, and fully joining in one notion of blackness in order to overthrow a system of whiteness. But the older Davis says, "The way I act, the way I talk, the way I think reflects all the places I've been; and I've been a lot of places."[76]

Black-ish points the way to a blackness that is beyond the binary by showing the falseness of the narratives that help sustain it, but also the confusion and lack of consensus among black people about what it means. It shows the constant negotiations white people are making to participate in blackness, but not commit micro-aggressions or be seen as racist. There is no going back to the clear demarcations between black and white, and the scaffolding that has held them up is destabilized. *Black-ish* shows with humor how much work it is to try and keep them in place and the foolishness of anyone thinking they can clearly define something so vast.

NOTES

1. "The Racial Draft."
2. Race percentages here alludes to the "white folklore" that there were pure races.
3. Wade-Currie, Adon, "The Receptivity of Black Audiences to Progressive Black-Television," 7.
4. Blake, Meredith, "President Obama Names His Favorite Show of 2015—And No, It's Not 'Homeland.'"
5. Wetterberg, Lyndsey Lynn, "Deconstructing 'Chappelle's Show': Race, Masculinity, and Comedy as Resistance," 9.
6. Ellison, Ralph, *Invisible Man*, 16.
7. Ellison, "Change the Joke, Slip the Yoke," 53–54.
8. Even the 1977 miniseries about slavery called *Roots*, which was supposed to further the civil rights agenda, continued to "perform" black for white audiences (the men were sexless and patient; the woman sad victims).
9. This term was coined by Dan Matlin, *On the Corner: African American Intellectuals and the Urban Crisis*, for black people who are sought out to explain race to white people.
10. Means Coleman, Robin R., *African American Viewers and the Black Situation Comedy: Situating Racial Humor*; Haggins, Bambi "The Black Situation Comedy"; Zook, Kristal Brent, *Color by Fox: The Fox Network and the Revolution in Black Television*; Greenberg, Bradley S., and Kimberly A. Neuendorf, "Black Family Interactions on Television"; Leonard, David J., and Lisa Guerrero, *African Americans on Television: Race-ing for Ratings*; Bogle, Donald, *Toms, Coons, Mulattoes, Mammies and Bucks: An Interpretive History of Blacks in American Films*.
11. Hunt, Darnell M., *Channeling Blackness: Studies on Television and Race in America*; Dalton, Mary M., and Laura Linder, *The Sitcom Reader: America Viewed*

and Skewed; Leonard and Guerrero, *African Americans on Television: Race-ing for Ratings*.

12. Harper, Lisa Sharon, "Black-Ish: Reimagining Blackness on Television."

13. Wade-Currie, "The Receptivity of Black Audiences to Progressive Black-Television."

14. Harris, Aisha, "How Black-Ish Earned the Right to Call Itself Black-Ish."

15. The Late Show with Stephen Colbert, *Anthony Anderson Explains Black vs. Black-Ish*; The Late Show with Stephen Colbert, *Laurence Fishburne Talks Oscars, Race and "Black-ish"*; The Late Show with Stephen Colbert, *Tracee Ellis Ross: I Believe in a Colorful World*.

16. Barris, Kenya, Njeri Brown, and Devanshi Patel, *Black-ish*, "Pilot."

17. Barris, Brown, and Patel, *Black-ish*, "Pilot."

18. Means Coleman, *African American Viewers and the Black Situation Comedy: Situating Racial Humor*, 159.

19. Barris, Brown, and Patel.

20. Phillips, Tracy, "Anthony Anderson on Throwing Bro Mitzvahs, Being 'Black-ish' and Pushing the Envelope."

21. Isenberg, Liz, "'Black-ish' Cast, Larry Wilmore Talk Breaking Down Barriers and Trevor Noah Controversy."

22. Means Coleman, *African American Viewers and the Black Situation Comedy*, 49.

23. Mammies being played by men were traditional minstrel characters and men were used in *Birth of a Nation* to play the thick, kerchief wearing, sexless bossy women who took care of the house and children of white employers.

24. This extremely helpful breakdown of the phases of black sitcom can be found in Coleman and McIlwain's "The Hidden Truths in Black Sitcoms."

25. Greenberg and Neuendorf, "Black Family Interactions on Television."

26. Inniss, Leslie B., and Joe R. Feagin, "The Cosby Show: The View from the Black Middle Class"; Jhally, Sut and Justin Lewis, *Enlightened Racism: The Cosby Show, Audiences, and the Myth of the American Dream*.

27. Leonard, John, "Leave It to Cosby."

28. Jhally and Lewis, *Enlightened Racism*, 703.

29. Zook, Kristal Brent, *Color by Fox: The Fox Network and the Revolution in Black Television*, 5.

30. Zook, 9.

31. Zook, 2–3.

32. Zook, 3.

33. Borowitz, Andy, and Susan Borowitz, *The Fresh Prince of Bel-Air*, "The Fresh Prince Project."

34. Borowitz and Borowitz.

35. Edwards, Rob, *The Fresh Prince of Bel-Air*, "72 Hours."

36. Lerner, Gail, and Damilare Sonoiki, *Black-ish*, "Sink or Swim."

37. Barris, Kenya, and Damilare Sonoiki, *Black-ish*, "Hope."

38. Barris, Brown, and Patel, *Black-ish*, "Pilot."

39. Barris, Brown, and Patel.

40. Shockley, Lindsey, et al., *Black-ish*, "Martin Luther Skiing Day."

41. Barris, Brown, and Patel, *Black-ish*, "The Nod."

42. Saji, Peter, and Damilare Sonoiki, *Black-ish*, "Twindependence."

43. Lerner, Brown, and Patel, *Black-ish*, "Black Santa/White Christmas."

44. Barris, Brown, and Patel, *Black-ish*, "Pilot."

45. The Late Show with Stephen Colbert, *Anthony Anderson Explains Black vs. Black-ish.*

46. The Late Show with Stephen Colbert.

47. Barris, Kenya, Lisa McQuillan, and Damilare Sonoiki, *Black-ish*, "The Word."

48. Barris, McQuillan, and Sonoiki.

49. Acham, Christine, *Revolution Televised: Prime Time and the Struggle for Black Power.*

50. Stevens, Michelle, "Black Comedians Poke Fun at Racial Stereotypes."

51. Nickerson, Corey et al., *Black-ish*, "Parental Guidance."

52. Saji, Brown, and Patel, *Black-ish*, "The Gift of Hunger."

53. Nickerson, McQuillan and Sonoiki, *Black-ish*, "Churched."

54. Nickerson.

55. Nickerson, *Black-ish*, "40 Acres and a Vote."

56. Shockley et al., *Black-ish*, "Martin Luther Skiing Day."

57. Barris et al., *Black-ish*, "Switch Hitting."

58. Lerner and Sonoiki, *Black-ish*, "Sink or Swim."

59. Saji, *Black-ish*, "Who's Afraid of the Big Black Man?"

60. Khaleeli, Homa, "Obama Loves It, Trump Called It Racist."

61. A good example of this is in the social thriller *Get Out* directed by Jordan Peele when a white liberal father greets his daughter's black boyfriend and says, "Mah Man" and when asking about their relationship, "How long has this 'thang' been happening?"

62. Barris, McQuillan, and Sonoiki, *Black-ish*, "The Word."

63. Shockley et al., *Black-ish*, "Martin Luther Skiing Day."

64. Nickerson et al., *Black-ish*, "Parental Guidance."

65. Barris, Brown, and Patel, *Black-ish*, "Pilot."

66. Nickerson et al.

67. Barris et al., *Black-ish*, "Switch Hitting."

68. Barris et al.

69. Barris et al.

70. Barris, Brown, and Patel, *Black-ish*, "Pilot."

71. Barris, Taylor, and White, *Black-ish*, "Just Christmas, Baby."

72. Barris, Brown, and Patel.

73. See Chimamanda Ngozi Adichie's novel *Americanah* for an exploration of the Black American and African relationship in America.

74. Hemingson, David, Njeri Brown, and Devanshi Patel, *Black-ish*, "Andre from Marseille."

75. Barris, Brown, and Patel, *Black-ish*, "The Nod."

76. Riggs, Marlon, *Black Is . . . Black Ain't.*

Chapter 6

Talking About Race

Black, White, and Mixed-Race Focus Groups

In the previous chapters, I looked at how two public figures revealed to us how the country is thinking about the black/white binary, and how two industries are changing to reflect the new demographic but also the shift in racial thinking. In this chapter, I turn to the words of Americans of different ages and races to elicit patterns in thinking about the binary today. In June 2017, I conducted six focus groups to talk about racial identity, using the controversial "transracial" Dolezal as a catalyst for discussion. I chose New York City because it is extremely diverse and also known for being progressive; here, I thought, I would get a microcosm of the cutting edge of people's attitudes about the black/white binary. I thought these New York focus groups would capture the leading edge of change and give a sense of the direction the country is moving in. However, I found that although these groups recognize intellectually that race is performed rather than biological, they revealed ideas that pointed toward more fixed racial categories. It seems that the changes in demographics as well as the intellectual shifts that have begun to blur boundaries of black and white have provoked anxiety among both black and white people who are defending the color line even as they acknowledge its constructedness.

In both black and white groups, participants showed defensive reactions about letting go of racial categories.[1] In addition, the historical and ongoing trauma of our racial history still affects black and white people today. The white groups revealed a fear of being seen as racist, but also showed variations on racialized thinking such as biological essentialism, experiential essentialism, colorblindness, exoticization, and stereotyping. The mostly homogeneous agreement in the white group that Dolezal could not become black seemed a by-product of their fear of being racist; Dolezal was ignoring the kind of sensitivity about which they felt hypervigilant, appropriating black culture. So although they showed admiration for black culture, they also showed an anxiety about overstepping their racial boundary and committing micro-aggressions.

The black groups also revealed unity in thinking about race, sharing with each other vulnerability and also pride and affection about being black. However, this bond seemed also built on their mistrust of whites (which fell at times into stereotyping and generalization about white people). In addition, they had strong feelings about policing black authenticity even as they acknowledged how much they resented being scrutinized by others on this. Their thinking on Dolezal revealed essentialist notions about black and white people.

The mixed groups, rather than having a more open mind about racial fluidity, divided quite consistently into views that fell either with the white group or the black group. Their joining the side of white or black views fell exactly on the identity they were ascribed by others. So their understanding of their "mixed" race was overruled by their perceived identity by others.[2]

METHODOLOGY

Because they have socioeconomically and racially varied populations, I advertised for the focus groups at public university Hunter College in the City University of New York and Riverside Church, an interdenominational interracial Christian church. These concepts of race as a myth and social construct are commonly understood in certain areas like New York partly because of their diverse, multiracial populations, but also their more liberal bent. Universities like City College in New York have these ideas on their educational agenda with a core curriculum that emphasizes breaking down the constructs of gender and race.

I conducted two groups of black, two groups of white, and two groups of mixed people. I divided participants into black, white, and mixed-race using a demographic form[3] that allowed people to define their racial status themselves including filling in a blank line. I segregated the groups as I assumed being in a group in which you racially identify would make for ease of conversation and honesty. My three co-facilitators matched the racial identification of the group they were co-facilitating. For the mixed group, they were simply people who checked more than one box on the form. I didn't limit it to black and white mixed, but wanted people who had the perspective of living with a "biracial" identity. I asked the five questions below and allowed the conversation to ramble where it would. Occasionally, I asked clarifying questions, but for the most part, my assistant and I were silent and refrained from facial expressions and verbal encouragement. We audio recorded and transcribed the one-hour sessions. The five questions I asked were:

1. When did you first become aware of race?
2. What makes someone black?
3. Does Rachel Dolezal have a right to be black? Why or why not?
4. Why do you think people have reacted so strongly about her "choosing to be black"?
5. Where did you get your ideas about what makes someone authentically black or white?

WHITE GROUPS[4]

"People do think that, white people do think that, each and every one of us thinks that and it's the problem. You can't just fix it overnight or apparently in thirty years."

—White woman, 20b (after hearing another focus group member say that black, for many white people, means ghetto and criminal)

Overview

The majority of white participants under thirty grew up in white neighborhoods with a homogeneous population. They became aware of race when they encountered their first racial "other" in elementary school. At that point, they didn't make negative associations, only remarked that there was a difference. For many of them, college at Hunter was the first time they began interacting with people of different races and at the same time taking classes about race where they studied British colonialism, Japanese internment in the United States, and Transatlantic slavery. Three of Hunter's eight categories for required courses are about understanding the perspective of others such as US Experience in Its Diversity, World Cultures and Global Issues, and Individual and Society. These classes gave them an awareness of their privilege and the structure of white supremacy, but also a tension about their racial position.

The overall feeling with the under thirties in the white group was self-consciousness. This came out in a lot of hedging language, careful phrasing, apologies, overpoliteness with fellow participants (you go, sorry for interrupting, no you finish, I'm finished), and a fear of sounding racist or treading into the minefields of micro-aggressions and racial definition. They seemed for the most part uncomfortable talking about these things explicitly and often stumbled, backtracked, and rephrased what they meant. One participant swiveled uncomfortably in her chair for the hour, looking at the map on the wall; another spoke in a very measured voice quoting much of the material from her courses, but not giving much away personally. Two of the men looked strained and upset throughout. Many demonstrated a pride in their understanding of race as a construct and how it operates as well as being more "woke" than their racist parents and friends. When they spoke of these "understandings" of race, they felt proud and congratulated others who demonstrated this awareness. There was often uncomfortable laughter at the mention of stereotyping.

The older participants were much less self-conscious and lived during the Civil Rights Movement or the aftermath. They spoke openly and honestly about the language of racist parents and teachers, seemingly unembarrassed, but clear to mention that they were different by their disapproval. These over-thirty white participants grew up without those courses on race, but lived in a context where there were more overt expressions of racism. They referred to racism around them more as a fact of life and didn't show the same outrage. One man admitted to his family's racism against the Chinese (thinking the drycleaners was called "the Chinks") and how he took this as truth. Another talked about other people's response to her white son marrying a black woman. One 81-year-old woman mentioned how she wouldn't let her kids play in a segregated playground in the South, and a 20-year-old woman said "good for you" while the 55-year-old woman responded "that's so cool." Another 55-year-old woman spoke proudly about how in her Greenwich Village neighborhood she dated everyone and didn't make an issue out of racial difference. The older group also seemed to enjoy the discussion more. At the end, three participants weighed in:

> White man, 59: I want another hour.
>
> White woman, 55: This was like therapy. I loved it.
>
> White woman, 81: I enjoyed that.
>
> White man, 59: I feel a little better now, you know.

Fear of Being Racist

One of the most prevalent messages from the younger group was "I'm not racist." This took the form of many self-protective measures to avoid being put in the racist category. In response to the Dolezal question, the examples below show how labeling others as racist makes them feel safe from being called racist.

White man, 26: Yeah, I think it's pretty BS too, just because again, I feel like she's (Dolezal) being stereotypical. What makes her feel African American? The fact that she has an afro? That's racist.

(Three women laugh)

Two white women at once: Yeah, that's racist.

White woman, 20b: I don't want to be judged by saying it, but I think it's wrong. Obviously she can say she is black, but she's not. Like, she's not black.

One woman found the notion of even identifying traits of blackness as Dolezal did was racist stereotyping:

White woman, 20a: Whatever you feel, is something internal and to say that you feel black, what does that mean? Does that mean that . . . that's stereotyping in itself, if you say, "Oh, I like basketball and I like to eat watermelon. I like fried chicken." That's being stereotypical and being racist.

White woman, 23: I like it too.

White woman, 20a: You can't, yeah I love them but does that say, "Hey, I'm black now because I love me some fried chicken"? Like what?

In her response to the question "what is blackness?" another participant shows a fear of answering by deflecting onto the facilitator the label of a slightly racist study or question:

White woman, 20b: Can I be honest? I personally think that these questions are just very subjectory[5] toward black people. You wouldn't sit in a group and talk about white people like this. You know what I mean? I'm not saying that this is like a bad group or anything. I'm just saying that these questions are really hard to answer, well obviously, especially because anything that you say will sound racist. There will be controversy over anything, because these questions aren't going to be asked toward a group of black people about how white people are. That's our society. That's the society that we live in. What's the question again?

Facilitator: What is black? What does that mean?

White woman, 20b: I can't answer that. I don't like that question.

In response to the "What is black" question, many were afraid to answer outright:

White woman, 20c: It's interesting, because when you ask that, do you mean physically the look of it or a stereotypical construct that society made of the definition of black?

Facilitator: I'm saying what do you think it means?

White woman, 20c: In my personal opinion? I think it can mean two different things. I think it's also a stereotype. There's stereotyped behaviors attributed to each race, which I'm not a fan of, but that's what exists. It has influenced our criminal justice system a lot, I think, especially in the law in convicting people. A lot more African Americans are in prison, and that's why they are associated with crime because of those race . . . because of the unjust criminal justice system that we have that favors upper class and the fact that classes are stereotypically involved with certain races. It's another stereotyped part of it, but I don't think that tells the difference between who's white or black.

After clarifying if her answer is to be personal, she gives a rather generic description of the criminal justice system.

Part of the fear of being racist shows in their pride of being distinct from racist neighbors and parents. A 20-year-old woman answering the question of "where do you get your ideas of black and white" told about her parents' response to her moving to Harlem:

White woman, 20d: "Oh, I'm moving to Harlem," and they said, "Oh, you better be careful out there." I was like, "Really? That's what you're going to say to me? Really?"

In the older group although many admitted to hearing racist things from their families, they declared that they themselves were not racist. A 55-year-old woman claimed to not be racist herself, but declared both her husbands and her sister-in-law to clearly be racists.

Except for one 26-year-old man, the fear of committing micro-aggressions was evident in all white participants. In discussion about how to tell what someone is when they are racially ambiguous and if you would ask them outright, they were all careful with their answers:

White woman, 20b: Honestly, I would probably just assume that they're mixed. But maybe certain traits about their hair, because African Americans tend to have curlier hair, and there's a certain structure with that. And maybe just certain. . . . No. I think . . . not facial features . . . but probably hair would be a big teller for me.

White woman, 55: Generally, I'd just look at somebody's skin color . . . but if it's hard to tell, I also would probably look at the texture of their hair.

White woman, 81: How they present themselves.

Facilitator: What does that mean.

White woman, 55: Oh, That's not fair.

White woman, 81: Some people want you to know that they are how they present themselves. They act in a certain way, so that you won't misinterpret what they are.

(She explains that her white nephew who has a black mother and white father has attitudes that are completely white, including racist attitudes about blacks [he uses phrases like "if blacks want to succeed . . . "].)

The 55-year-old white woman who said, "That's not fair," assumes, like the earlier 20-year-old white woman, that the facilitator was setting traps to catch the racists:

White woman, 20a: I'm not trying to be like the PC police, but it's just a very touchy thing to ask people, "What are you?" I ask anyone, like, "Oh, where are you from?" You could ask about someone's culture without being offensive. It's not something you need to dance around as much as what people think. Definitely pick and choose your words.

There was an exchange with several participants when one 26-year-old man said he would ask people directly what they are, which showed their vigilance about committing micro-aggressions:

White woman, 20b: I don't think there's anything wrong with asking. I'm not saying that you did anything wrong. I just think that . . .

White man, 26: You're afraid of offending them by asking them, why would that be offensive?

White woman, 20b: No, I don't think it's offensive.

White woman, 23: I don't think about offending them. I think it's just, me personally, that's not the first thing that's on my mind. Once I get to know someone based on their interests or whatever, then I'm like, "Oh, where are you from, ethnicity?" or like, "Where's your family from?"

White woman, 20b: Yeah, exactly.

Sometimes they admitted to their frustration with how careful they have to be:

White woman, 55: But you still have to watch your vocabulary or you get in trouble like Bill Maher did.

White man, 59: That's another thing. I don't understand it either. Certain groups, certain color skin people can say certain words, and others can't.

White woman, 20a: We take over a lot of stuff and we have a lot of privilege. It's like, if you say something, then you're being too aggressive and complaining too much, whereas if you don't say anything . . . you're damned if you do, damned if you don't.

Another white man, 21, synthesized well what was going on in this group and in the culture outside: "That's what's wrong with society. People are a little too sensitive and they can't have these types of conversations."

Sometimes they softened the blow of being associated with racism by blaming their white privilege, something the younger participants were aware was a direct result of this idea being integrated into their college curriculum. Many referred to these classes at Hunter as the moment they woke up to their position.

White woman, 23: Personally, to be honest, when I'm in a room full of people, I guess in my brain, I do say like, "We're all white." In my brain, I do have a race thing where I'm just like . . . I don't know how to put this in words. That's my brain. I'm like, okay . . .

White woman, 20b: You're not being racist.

Often their guilt was assuaged by the understanding that these cultural biases were in the air and not something they did wrong.

White woman, 20c: But if you're walking down the street, and you see a black guy with chains versus a white guy with chains, you're going to be more scared of the black guy with chains.

White woman, 55: The media did that to us.

White woman, 81: We've been conditioned.

White woman, 55: We're conditioned. Exactly.

The fear of being associated with racism dominated the discussion on race and at times it felt as though they didn't feel free to give completely honest answers because of their anxiety of how they would be perceived.

As the conversation unfolded many of them contradicted themselves. Although the majority spoke about the falseness and construct of race and a claim that they were not racist, some made statements that slipped into biological essentialism, experiential essentialism, colorblindness, exoticization, or stereotyping (that whiteness equals educated). One outlier was a 26-year-old white man who had grown up socializing primarily with black and Mexican kids, and he kept setting off the rest by his unself-conscious descriptions of his friends and their difference that shocked the other participants.

> White man 26: Black culture is different from Hispanic culture, which is different from white culture. You go hang out with your Mexican friends or your black friends. You're not going to be doing the same thing with every single people. I go hang out with my Mexican friends and we're eating tacos and chimichurris and steaks, watching soccer. With my black friends we're probably going to watch basketball and big group gatherings, everyone going around talking to each other. White people are kind of boring.

Later he admitted, "I think that the stereotype about that is, more black is going to be more ghetto, criminal, whereas if someone acts like a white person, like he was saying, that means they're less black. There's black people that are like, 'Oh, he's black, but he's white.'"

Biological Essentialism

Some of the younger white participants revealed a belief in the pseudoscience of biological race that claims black and white people have different blood when answering the Rachel Dolezal question.

> White woman, 20b: I think again it brings me back to the whole point of that's biologically not her genetic race. She can identify with the culture, but not the physical . . . I don't know how to explain it.
>
> White woman, 20d: *Race is biological* and ethnicity is cultural.
>
> White woman, 20a: I think it's complete bullshit. Also, there's so much history that goes along with being black and all the roots from that. Just to say that because you have cultural simil . . . not similarities, you have cultural interests that you like that are black, that doesn't mean that *the blood in your veins . . .* I just don't, I think that's really dumb for someone to say. I have a ton of black friends, but I'm not going to say because I enjoy hanging out with them that means I'm black. (laughter) That's a part of someone that's . . . I don't know, maybe I'm acting a little bit outlandish.

Another, 20b, showed that she treated black people like one group, one voice, one body when she was referring to Dolezal's choosing to be black, but also falls into racial science again:

> White woman, 20b: To be honest, yeah, I want to hear their (black people's) opinion. I think that they would be really insulted just like how we are. It's not right. *God created you for a reason. God gave you your body, your facial*

structures, everything for a reason. I think, personally, she's just saying, "*F my genetics.* F my family. F how God put me on this planet for."

White woman, 20b: *It's genetics. It's science.* You can't screw with science. It doesn't make sense. I don't know. That's ridiculous.

White woman, 55: I'm not a scientist or anything. I think that's what you are talking about ethnicity *based on blood or whatever, science, real science.* But culturally we change how we behave.

Experiential Essentialism

At one point, a woman became aware that the group was all-white discussing black people and expressed curiosity on what the "black perspective" would be:

White woman, 20a: I'm not black, so I can't say this. I wish someone in the room could represent and say . . . I would love to hear their insight on this. Just another perspective.

Facilitator: Insight on what?

White woman, 20a: On being black. What would their answers be in what we're discussing right now. Would they be different? Would they be more educated? I could take millions of courses, but I don't care about that. I'm not black. I can't feel what they feel. I can only sympathize for them.

Another white man, 21, generalized about black people being fighters:

I was going to say, I think it shows a lot of great persistence to how they got to this country and what they've been able to do, to fight for their freedom, to finally have a black president. I think that was a great milestone in African American . . . that's what I associate black with, African American. I think, if you look over time, just they're fighters.

A white woman, 20b, agreed:

I think that being black is powerful because they work so hard to get to where they are. It's not easy. It's not a cakewalk. Of course there could be different situations for different things, but it's just an easier . . . we have such an advantage for careers, for connections, for everything. I think just the fact that when they're successful, it's something to really be proud of.

This was seconded by white woman 20a, who proclaimed black people to be trying to present themselves as powerful:

I think power is really important within the African American race just because they feel as if they aren't powerful. That's why they portray themselves as being powerful, strong people. They are. There's no dig there, but I definitely think that they try and push that aspect of themselves out to eventually or essentially let people know that they are powerful.

Colorblindness

Some of them fell into the easy answer of colorblindness, claiming there was no difference at all:

White man, 21: With me, I don't separate. I don't say, "Oh, I have a black friend." I just say, "Denzel is my favorite actor," or, "Everton is my friend." Or whatever like, I don't know, sometimes I feel like definitely where I grew up, we still separate the two. I just feel like there's no real point. I'm the same as a black person with everything besides the color of my skin.

White woman, 20b: I totally agree with that. I know a lot of people at home that are like, "Oh, my black friend." It's like, why do you even have to say that? They're still a friend. It doesn't matter.

White woman, 20d: I think that the labeling that they're both suggesting is because, well not because, but I think it was definitely like fed off for the fact when Obama was president. Everyone was like, "Oh, he was the first black president," instead of just being, "Oh, he is our president."

White woman, 81: We should all be colorblind, but it's not there.

White woman, 55: We should be, and they should . . .

White woman, 81: I kept thinking the more intermarriage there was, the more people there would be, but it just keeps dividing itself. It doesn't ever become one complete . . .

White woman, 55: Because we have so many racist people in this country.

White man, 21: Just to go off of that, I forget what interview it was, but Morgan Freeman said it the best. He doesn't want an African American history month. His history, his race is American history. Why does it have to be African American history? There's no white history month. If we just got rid of the labels, if people stopped on both sides just trying to make it more than it really is, I think the race divide would ease up.

White man, 59: Really no difference but the color of your skin, everything is all mixed now.

Exoticization

Another common occurrence was to express admiration and idealization of black celebrities:

> White man, 21: There just seems to be something about the black culture that they have fun with their passion about everything that they do. Again, not going back to stereotypes, but even with sports, African Americans seem more celebratory than white people ever are. I just feel like they're a passionate culture.

> White woman, 20a: Think of, okay I'm the biggest Beyoncé fan, but think of one of the most talented women I know. She's black, even though people sometimes don't notice her race that much. She is black. Jay-Z and a lot of them are musicians and a lot of them are athletes, but you know what? I think, well there's this whole, I always see it on Facebook. There's Black Magic Club, Black Magic and all this stuff that are saying to empower black people. It shouldn't, it is what it is, but it shouldn't be that it's a negative connotation, just because of the color of your skin. I was in this class called Representation of Race in Film and Media and a lot of our stereotypes that we use today are because of Hollywood and what they portray in their movies. Finally, there actually is becoming a law in Hollywood that you have to go through this process of making sure every movie now is diverse, racially.

> White woman, 23: I grew up in the dance world and I studied at Alvin Ailey for a very long time where I was actually the only white person. Everyone around me was African American. I just idolize them. I just think that black in general, I think that symbolizes power and strength.

Stereotyping

Many expressed a belief that whiteness is associated for them with educated and well spoken:

> White woman, 55: But they'll also . . . white people . . . will be the first to say how a black person is trying to act white.

> White woman, 81: Right. They were an Uncle Tom era. They're an Oreo cookie—black on the outside, white on the inside.

> White woman, 55: They're not happy with anything, then, that they do.

> White man, 26: The more blacker, the stereotype is more black more ghetto. If someone acts like a white person, they are less black.

> Facilitator: So, act like a white person. Can you say a little more about that?

> White man, 26: Professional. Talks normal.

> Facilitator: Okay, normal meaning?

White man, 26: I guess white. I guess white is the normal.

Facilitator: Okay, anyone else?

White man, 21: But that's the problem, though.

White man, 26: Exactly. We said that stereotypes still exist. That is the problem.

White man, 21: But again, there are plenty of white people who . . .

White man, 26: That are trash, yeah.

White man, 21: Yeah, but I wouldn't say that they're black.

White man, 26: Of course.

One white woman, 55, find herself annoyed by Oprah's code switching, but by the end reveals she's also perplexed by the rigidness of "acting black" or "acting white."

White woman, 55: I used to watch Oprah. She bothered me sometimes, because she would conduct herself in a . . . I shouldn't even use this term. . . . She conducted herself in a very white way when she was interviewing and she was doing things. Then certain subject matters would come up, and she would change her whole tone. She would say it in a way that maybe a kid on the street in a black neighborhood would. I always was like, "What is she trying to prove? Just be who you are and say it the way you say it. You don't need to change your accent and your verbiage."

White woman, 81: That's a very common thing now.

White woman, 55: Yeah. We see it sometimes even . . . not that he really does, but Steve Harvey will do the same kind of thing, where he'll go off and act what he considers more black than . . .

White woman, 81: He makes himself that. I see it with him all the time.

White woman, 55: But why should that be blackness? Why does it have to be that way? Why? Why can't everybody just behave the way they want to? Maybe you get a white person who wants to be hip-hop . . .

Response to Dolezal

In response to Dolezal, the under-thirty white participants saw her as doing something that goes against everything they have been taught in terms of political correctness. While they feel very self-conscious about sounding racist, being accused of cultural appropriation or micro-aggressions, Dolezal crossed the line boldly and without apology. Their admiration for black culture but their inability to be black made them hostile to her, perhaps because she got away with something they can't—to cross over into black culture and community and be part of it. Most white participants made positive assumptions about black people while also admitting they had certain negative associations that wouldn't easily go away. The white group also showed an intellectual awareness of race as a social construct and were trained to tread carefully on issues of race so as not to appear racist. However, many of the older ideas about race were revealed over time in this group. Many showed an awareness of privilege and regret about past ways of thinking. As one 36-year-old white woman put it referring to the O. J. Simpson trial:

> I look back very stereotypical white and that we didn't have race and we were neutral and a-political and if other people just weren't so into race then everything would be fine. And, so, for me being raised white was, sort of, being raised to believe I was a-racial. That if race was ever an issue it's because someone else was making it so.

BLACK GROUPS

"She can't be black and I can't be white, period. No way, nothing she can do is going to make her black in the sense that I understand. Just like there's nothing that I can do that's going to make me white."

—Black man, 68

Overview

In contrast to the white groups who mostly became aware of their whiteness in college, most of the people in the black groups said that they became aware of their blackness early on (one peeing next to someone in elementary school, another going to a predominantly white school and seeing mostly financial differences, which she later identified as race). One man said he was aware of his race from birth because he had a parent of each color. This differed from the white groups who became aware of racial "others" in elementary school, but not their own privilege until later. Another key difference is that older and younger black participants weren't clearly demarcated in their views the way the white participants under thirty were from the participants over thirty.

Overall the black groups seemed to enjoy the discussion like a social gathering. They did not seem on trial in the way that characterized the feel of the white group, and many showed vulnerability in the stories they shared. There was also a noticeable bond that formed during the hour. The session was marked by laughter, cross-talk, and a lot of nodding of heads, echoing language, and "mm hmmms." Several times, they united over discussions of police brutality and racism. The tone was a weary acceptance about black arrests and police suspicion. When one 30-year-old black man told a story about seeing a drunken white man at a Mets game talking rudely to the police without any retaliation, he joked, "It must be nice." The other people in the group laughed in solidarity and one 46-year-old black man replied, "You'd be in jail."

Another noticeable feature about the black groups were that they seemed marked by reflective honesty. They were much more personal than the white groups that often spoke in more abstract terms. Many leaned in to the table, used emotive hand gestures, and had voices that went from soft and barely audible to one woman who spoke loudly and even did a little dance to illustrate her happiness at finding the church. Many black participants told deeply personal stories and didn't veer away from emotionally tense topics. One 72-year-old black woman who was a teacher admitted to racializing some of her students as "from the hood" although she self-corrected and also said (while laughing) that black teachers don't admit that to white teachers, but they too can be racist. Another 30-year-old black man recounted not being "trusted" as black by the black community in college because of his white mother and his participation on the swim team. Later when he joined a black fraternity, he was accepted, but was baffled as to why they wouldn't accept him before. Another 68-year-old black man shared a memory of being assumed white when in an all-black Boy Scout troop by a blind Japanese boy. A woman talked about getting beaten up for "talking white," and another man told about the experience of seeing white people cheer the night Martin Luther King was shot.

Everyone was aware of the social construction of blackness and the lack of scientific validity behind the concept of race, but they all had rules about who could or could not be black that the majority agreed on. There was much discussion of both black and white people policing black authenticity (particularly in the accusation/label of "acting white"), which they all resented. However, many of them during the discussion seemed comfortable being the arbiters of who could and could not be black.

Mistrust of White People

Whereas the white group barely mentioned the fact that Dolezal could have been perceived as being dishonest, the black group were particularly bothered by what they saw as her lying. There was much talk about her not only deceiving people, but gaining something she didn't necessarily earn. Her accessing insider status by having black people take her in as black was seen as a kind of false pretense. Because there is a fundamental wariness about white people in much of the black community and expectations of not getting treated fairly, trust was a word that came up a lot. Just as "racist" was the most repeated word in the white focus groups, words like "dishonesty," "trust," "suspect," and "lie" dominated the discussion in the black groups. So although the white group did not see Dolezal as being deceptive or focus on her wearing her hair differently as a conscious choice to mislead, the black group's key reason for rejecting her was this deception. Some felt it was intentional duplicity, presenting herself as something she was not or masquerading as a black person. Many felt she came into her leadership role in the NAACP through dishonest means, which destroyed her credibility. One woman thought she was lying in order to be able to get certain advantages, and that even her book was a way to make money and exploit black people. One man referred to her culturally appropriating as part of a long pattern of white people dismissing the voices of black people. He talked about the common occurrence of white people "appropriating, taking on and then speaking for as opposed to with [black people]. And, even when there is cell-phone footage, Eric Garner being choked. . . . You have the head of the police here in New York saying, "He wasn't choked." And, you're like, "Are you kidding me?" Here he emphasized the expectation that white voices will be valid over black ones and connected this to Dolezal leading the NAACP, a black organization. What made Dolezal's choice particularly egregious for many is that she came from a privileged position as white and was "tricking" black people. Black man, 68:

> But, there's something fundamentally wrong with. . . . This is a white woman, who's exercising a privilege to assume this identity which is not authentic to her. That's fundamentally troubling. . . . So, while I think she might vote the right way in the issues that I care about, and Ben Carson wouldn't, that still doesn't win my trust because I think there's *something fundamentally wrong with her* and I think she's engaging in this profound deception and dishonesty and exercising a privilege which no black person has.

A black woman, 37, was particularly bothered by what she saw as Dolezal lying when she showed a picture of her adopted father:

> I don't think it would have been as problematic if she didn't really lie about it. I don't think there's a problem with trying to be an ally to a group. Bringing it all and saying, "I identify with your struggle and I want to help that." But, she lied and showed pictures of her with an old black man and said, "This is my father," who clearly was not her father. So, I think that deception kind of hurt her case. *I don't understand the need to deny yourself of who you are* to that extent to where you would lie to the masses.

Interestingly, when she talks about Dolezal's choice to become black, she refers to it as "deny yourself of who you are" rather than the opposite, which is what Dolezal claimed to be doing—allowing herself to be her true self.

Many were bothered by her accessing the black community's intimacy as unethical. One referred to her as an interloper:

> Black man, 46: I don't buy it. I don't accept it. I understand she has a desire to identify with the African American community, for some reason, but I don't understand her naming herself, or claiming/presenting herself, as a black woman.

The consensus that Dolezal was lying to the black community about her race fell often into notions of essentialism: "There is a black experience and it's not one she could ever have." But in addition, there were strict parameters about her being unequivocally white and her denying her true race by identifying as black.

Black Bond

This mistrust of Dolezal was deepened by a feeling of solidarity and community that comes as a result of that shared history that they strongly felt cannot be experienced by an outsider. There was a sense of respect for the trials that black people and their ancestors had gone through that Dolezal could never have. Her stepping in midway, so to speak, was seen as disrespectful as well as dishonest. Black participants had a nuanced understanding of their experience of racism. This was a key factor in rejecting Dolezal as black. Because Dolezal did not have the social construct of blackness put upon her early on in her life, she was able to evade all the burden that goes with that: biased treatment by police, media, teachers, employers, and so on. The bond that resulted from this burden was another reason Dolezal was rejected as a false member of the group. The sharing of that experience of daily injustices they admitted created a bond:

> Black man, 68: I will say that, this isn't just about being back, if a person identifies as a person of color I'd probably have a different affinity with them than if I just knew them to identify as being white.
>
> Black man, 46: You get there quicker?
>
> Black man, 68: Mm-hmm. Yeah.

The insider status that many participants felt they had with other black people and was evident in the group bonding that took place over the hour was something Dolezal couldn't know. Dolezal was accessing an intimacy that had been earned through hardship. One man emphasized the bond when answering how to define blackness: "Both these brothers are black," he smiled and pointed to the two men next to him. Another talked about the difference between being able to call someone "Ma N*gga" or be called that by someone else as his sign of closeness versus mistrust.

One black woman, 37, spoke about the unnamable bond between black people that is beyond the physical:

> Black people have had to re-embrace their culture. Because, a lot of it has been taken away from them through the trans-Atlantic slave trade and just white-washing and American pop culture and all these things have kind of diluted their original identities. So, now it's to the point where you have to make an effort to teach your children about ancestry. *So, it's more than just the physical, it's absolutely more than that . . .*

One 46-year-old black man referred to how his father was the one who gave him a positive sense of his black identity and feeling of community by his phrase "Remember to act like somebody."

> Black man, 46: It often felt like a punitive statement like, "Don't go off and embarrass us." But, I think also what he instilled in me was a sense of "You belong." As much as you can shape their identity about you or what they think of you, present yourself as being good and acceptable. . . . Whether it's predominantly white or black or whatever, there's a sense of knowing me and valuing my experience of blackness as being good and okay.

Everyday Racism

One of the other key differences between the black and white group was the black group shared an understanding that rigid racial categories aren't changing much and that race and gender are very different constructs (this in response to parallels being suggested between Dolezal and transgender Caitlyn Jenner). There was a strictness to the categories of black and white when seen from a position of justice and power. In referring to the Philando Castile shooting:

> Black man, 30: But, no I mean, you cry together about these things and you are angry about these things, you're shocked, you're dismayed but I think there is a general consensus, at least among my black friends. My black friends and black family like, "Same shit, different day."

Another man emphasized the lack of choice to disengage from the news:

Black man, 30: Or, at least some folks . . . can literally turn that off social issues and just be stuck in their own bubble or whatever they. . . . For me this is my life. Understanding and experiencing being harassed by police. Like, I've literally gotten pulled over for going 60 in a 65.

One 68-year-old black man responded jokingly when asked what institutions made him understand his blackness. He answered, "I can't just say the United States of America?" The group laughed.

Talking White

The consensus in the group was that questions of black authenticity were offensive. They were taken from patterns on the plantation when lighter-skinned black people and darker-skinned black people were set against each other by white people giving them separate privileges. Black people questioning your blackness was just as offensive as white people questioning your blackness. Many in the group had the experience when they showed their education or spoke standard English that their blackness was challenged and they were accused of acting white. They were constantly reminded to show their black side more or be taken for imposters mimicking white people, or worse, being more white than black.

One black man, 46, expressed his resentment about questions of black authenticity,

> I don't know what that means, it feels to me like the comparisons of who's black enough, who's good enough to be, either in or outside the group. And, historically I feel like that's a tool of white supremacy and oppression. . . . So, I think that's dangerous. . . . It's a dangerous question to pose.

One woman, 21, talked about her blackness being questioned because she didn't present as black. She seemed to self-monitor, believing she wasn't really black because she didn't present that way:

> Black woman, 21: You look at me and aesthetically I look like a little Indian girl. So, that happens a lot, it happened to a point where I started to question myself and I was like, "What am I? How am I? I don't know where I come from." But, my family are Afro-Caribbean and also Indo-Caribbean so I identify with both races. But, I think that people who look more authentically black, than I do, often find it problematic that I identify as black because I don't have the same outside features. So, again when it comes to society, and when they look at me, they don't have the same preconceived notions and stigmas when they look at me as opposed to when they look at someone else who does look more authentically black. And, a lot of people think that's not fair and that's probably true.

Everyone in the group shared a pride in being black and they equally shared a resentment of having their blackness questioned because of the way they spoke or dressed.

Just as the white groups were very uncomfortable with defining blackness but did talk about when black people "acted white," the black group showed resentment toward questions of black authenticity, but at the same time monitored the color line uncompromisingly. They were all indignant at the claims that they were less black or "acting white" when they spoke proper English. One woman was called an Oreo for talking white—others were accused of being disingenuous by white people when they were observed to code switch in different contexts. The freedom to express different sides of themselves fully through their behavior often met with accusations by both black and white people of being Oreos, Toms, or acting white. The right to move beyond a narrow definition of black was a common frustration.

A black woman, 72, emphasized the risk in talking white: "Some of the time when I was a child I talked too proper. I used to get beat up on that basis, bullies go directly for me because I talk proper. They want to beat somebody up. . . . Because talking white it gets you in trouble, you know?" Another woman in a different group expressed the same opinion:

Black woman, 21: I think from a very generic and societal perspective, it has a lot to do, it has super-jaded, with behavior and the culture that you engage in. So, for example I guess, when I was in middle school I listened to a lot of rock music and everyone was like, "Wow, you're so Oreo!" And, I was like, "What's an Oreo?" And, they were like, "It means you're white on the inside." And, I was like, "What?" And, again, it goes back to the dialect and I have a lot of friends who go to Ivy League schools and their peers will tell them, "Oh, but you're not like really black because you don't act like your friends who live in the Bronx; you're different because you're proper." Or, whatever. Yeah, I think it has a lot to do with behavior. I think there is just this general view and stigma around blackness being some rowdy kid from the south Bronx.

Another woman emphasized how the black community will even refer to a "white voice," which she describes as a sort of performance just as her blackness is.

Black woman, 37: Even though the joke in the black community is when you go to work you turn on your white voice and all these things. I never really bought into that because I didn't see a need to. I am who I am and I was brought up to be confident in who I am and that I shouldn't cower behind my skin color or my culture and be proud of it. But, it happens, it does happen, where people do put on that performance and say, "Well, I'm going into this room full of white people I need to put on my white voice. I need to dress a certain way. I need to

. . . " Or, you have those that are defiant and say, "Okay, well I'm going to be extra black. I'm going to put my headband on, my African kente cloth headband, when everybody is in a suit and tie."

A 68-year-old black man explained the expansiveness of his true identity and his basic right to express all sides of himself: "I appropriate more of myself. I am lots of things and I can sit in the seminar, in the classroom, and I can be on the corner in a black community and talk, and relate, in a very different way. But, I am all of those things, it's not being dishonest or more authentic it's shifting kind of." A 46-year-old black man agreed: "Yeah, there's cultural context for how you show up in different places."

A black man, 46, talked about the flack he gets from other people when he adapts to his environment:

> But, later in life, having in white friends and then being in settings where I'm around the larger black community, they're like, "Oh, you said different things there. What does that mean?" I don't know, there was a critique of my authenticity as a person I was like, "No, I'm just in a different place where I get to express different sides of who I am." But, it felt like it was a barrier to them like, "Oh, my gosh. You're doing this different thing, we don't know what you are anymore. You don't fit into our box."

One woman only felt truly free to express her whole self (without limiting racial definitions) in the church.

> Black woman, 72: My experience that way was so different was going from the school environment to the church. The church I felt accepted me, regardless. So, you're in a culture where it's okay to get happy and do your dance to the music and stuff. And, everybody is doing it. But, if you're out there, no doubt, they would reject that as well as it didn't matter in church whether you talked. . . . Your lingo just started blending in with the rest of the people so you become bicultural by dialect and everything else. So, that was for me, I was living in several different worlds.

Policing Black Authenticity

Despite the long detailed discussion about how offensive it is to have your blackness questioned by white or black people, or being accused of acting white if you expressed anything beyond black slang, the black group did a lot of policing of blackness themselves with Dolezal, but also with hypothetical others.

One black man, 46, reiterated the idea of constructed blackness. He explained that even if the person doesn't identity as black, if they are read that way, that's enough. He told two stories of him assuming two different Dominican men were black and having them both deny their blackness. One of these men was being confused with him at work, so the 46-year-old man reminded him, "If they are confusing you and me, you black!" A 37-year-old black woman weighed in on the immutability of skin color and thus Dolezal is reduced for her as passing rather than transraciality: "When you put this thing on like a costume and parade around and claim that you identify with these struggles, there's no way that you can because you did not live that experience."

A black woman, 72, referred to a black activist James Coen who says that you are black if you identify with the cause of the oppressed:

> So, I don't know whether he would say they are absolutely black, in a racial sense, but they inherit a certain amount of it by stepping into the cause of the oppressed. But, that's as far as I can go. I don't know.

She also referred to being in a relationship with a black man as partially making you black. A 32-year-old black man vehemently disagreed with this. He argued that being in a relationship with someone who is black might make you understand more, but it doesn't make you black. He referred to his white mother who was married to his black father, but definitely was not black. When a 30-year-old man said that Dolezal isn't black, he thought, "She has the right to *say* that she is black."

Others responded emphatically:

> Black man, 68: Except she's not black.

> Black man, 46: She's not black.

> Black man, 68: She is not black. Her mommy and daddy are not black.

One man added that you can get close and be an ally, but no further.

> Black man, 30: I think those folks can be allies. I think there's a trait that one can take on as an ally and that brings a whole different set of experiences, right? To be stared at in an interracial relationship is, I think, also uniquely different than being a black person stared at. So, being a white person in that interracial relationship I think that brings a set of experiences and I think being a black person brings the different experiences.

Later the same black man, 30, spoke about not trusting black people who don't support black causes and also implied they were less black:

> I'm looking at you with the side eye. So, there are different things but I don't come into it, and I meet a person of color or a black person, and I have this list

of twenty questions that I need to ask them first. But, you're black until proven otherwise by your own admission based on your own potential political, social allegiances. And, again, that doesn't take away that they haven't experienced racism but if we go back that there's also a cultural reference, *to what blackness means in America*, then yeah I would say that there is, or at least there are, folks that I would be like, "Nah, I can't talk to you about this anymore."

A black woman, 72, disagreed and mainly defined blackness as others constructing you that way, not by your allegiance to black causes.

I think there's a range of different characteristics within the black community and there are fewer and fewer essentialist definitions that people can be black but not loyal to black people or black causes. But, just because, in their mind, they are in denial or they have some kind of ideology that separates them from the best interests of black people does not mean they are not black. They are a type of person that has always existed. When they were getting ready to have the slave riots there was always one that ran back and told the master because they could get certain benefits by doing that. They were black, they were in the field, they were just doing something different and they had a different political orientation. So, I don't think they're not black because society is what socially constructs them as black. Trump sees Carson as black, even if Carson doesn't see himself as black. And, he's treated a certain way, he's not put in certain positions within Trump's administration because he's black regardless of what he says. So, yeah, I think the system defines you as being in a group because of social construction.

In the black group, there was a lot of talk about loyalty and trustworthiness, which were key factors in their identity as black people. So if you weren't defending the black cause, you could have your black credentials removed:

Black man, 30: Ben Carson, Omarosa[6] they've lost their cultural black card, you know what I mean? Like, the black community doesn't trust them. I'm not saying we trust Rachel Dolezal either but if I had to choose, and they were the last two to be chosen for the basketball team, I'm going with Rachel, personally, over Uncle Ben.

One black man, 68, went further and felt legitimacy relied on historic enslavement:

In this culture of racists, as it is, if you're a person of color though not African American you may be treated as a black person. But, I identify with folks from diaspora, who experienced and grow out of the experience of slavery here and who have a drop of black blood in them. If my sister walked in this room now you would not pick her as my sister, you might think she was her cousin, she looks like you [pointing to white facilitator] much more than she looks like me.

Here, his sister who is not read as black, was unequivocally black to him, but others who are not read as black are not black. People didn't agree on what made you black, but each person had a definition for themselves that had a clear division with little room for flexibility.

Response to Dolezal

When it came to Rachel Dolezal, there was real agreement. She was indisputably rejected primarily because of the missing history of burden, ancestry, and her freedom of choice. She wasn't marked from birth as black and had not had that reflected back at her daily, which is the experience of most black people. She can have compassion for black people, admire their culture and history, but the immutability of having black skin, and the burden and lack of respect and justice that comes with it, could not be hers.

> Black woman, 21: As much as you internalize that when someone looks at you they don't see the same thing, and they don't think the same thing, that thing they think when they look at someone who is actually black. And, you can also be like Rachel, and do the aesthetics, and come off as black but if you ever change your mind then you can just wash all that away and you can go back to your white privilege.
>
> Facilitator: So, it's mainly about the choice for you?
>
> Black woman, 37: Yeah, absolutely.
>
> Black woman, 21: Yeah, they can't decide that one day they want to be white then make that happen.
>
> Black woman, 37: There are literally thousands of people, around the world, that are physically removing the melanin from their skin. Trying to be white, and as soon as they stop using the creams that black comes back.

Overall the black groups believed in the immutability of blackness. As one man said, "She can't be black and I can't be white—period." Although Dolezal was read as black for eight years, she was not black. White people couldn't be black because they were never racially constructed that way and they were on the privileged side of the racial construct. However, many left the door open for other groups who didn't necessarily see themselves as black. If they were read as black, that was enough for membership. The group was unanimous in believing Dominicans were black. Indians were racialized differently (more positively) so couldn't be black in the same way. Overall, the black groups showed a resistance to anyone being black who lacked the burden of being racially constructed that way (who would not be read as black).

Black woman, 72: I think race is a social construction in that, I think, it doesn't have any scientific validity. But, I think, in my opinion I go with the one principle that any time that you are black, and visibly so, then there's some aspect of your being that's going to be socially constructed. And, so I think that defines you as black. The fact that the culture socially constructs your being, your body, but it has no scientific validity. And, most scientist have rejected it as an actual reality.

All group members agreed with her, but over the course of the discussion they all had criteria for group membership that were very specific: community activism and self-identification were not included; ancestry, history, experience of daily racism since birth were.

MIXED-RACE GROUPS

Overview

I assumed the mixed-race groups would have a more open attitude toward Dolezal's transracialism because they had had the experience of belonging to two groups or the feeling of being in between groups. However the mixed groups broke down very clearly in sounding either like the white or the black group depending on how they were read racially. Therefore, a Puerto Rican man, an African American/Latino woman, and an African American/white mixed woman (their own identifiers in the demographic form) who all were read as black had identical attitudes to the black group patterns (belief that being read and treated as black makes you black). However, the mixed people who could be read as white had similar opinions to the white group (fear of sounding racist, uncomfortable answering questions and revealing attitudes of bioracism, essentialism, and colorblindness). These included a Jewish mixed man, a Spanish mixed man, a Pacific Islander/Muslim woman and a mixed race Muslim man (their own identifiers in the demographic form).

The Muslim man was only taken for Muslim when dressed a certain way (when on his way to prayer); otherwise he was read as white. The Spanish man was told "but you are white" by the Puerto Rican man. Later the Puerto Rican man admitted to being devastated when he came to the United States and started being treated as black: "When I lived in Puerto Rico, I was a human being, but when I came to New York I became something else." Although these participants identified themselves as mixed race on the demographic form, in fact, during the focus groups they were identified by other group members and referred to their experience in the outside community as being on the black/white binary. The limits of this study prevented me from having racially ambiguous participants who might have had different answers and experiences from the phenotypically black or white participants who identified themselves as "mixed." If they are not put in the binary themselves and escape the burden/bond of the black construct or have the privilege of the white construct, it might change their attitudes about fluidity.

Overall, the groups made clear that for white people, although they change how they talk about race, they still hold fast to certain racialized ways of thinking. For black people, the burden they have endured and the community they have created through being black makes them hold on to what they have earned and feel possessive of the experience. The similar reactions from people within racial groups shows just how much the experience of the history and the binary have traumatized people in different ways, but both have been left with a kind of PTSD, which was clearly operating in all the groups. Race is highly charged for white people and their guilt and fear of contributing in any way to the history of that system makes them contort their logic in ways that attempt to point to them not being racist. Black people are territorial about their experience of being black, partly out of pride and partly out of having endured so much. They want blackness to be less restrictive and encompass all sides of themselves, but feel possessive of the community and history enough to not want anyone to feel they can join without having gone through the trials they have.

People's intensity about these issues is coming from the ongoing traumatizing effects of race in the United States and because US identity was constructed on the notion of strict racial boundaries. Although these boundaries caused pain and suffering, they also created a bond that is rich and valued. The black groups seemed unwilling to let go of that while the white groups seemed to keep the line partly out of unconscious bias that they revealed over the hour, but also out of respect for the history (or a fear of offending). Despite the damage caused by the binary and people's awareness of this damage, both groups are holding on out of long, deeply held patterns about identity and a fear of losing their centers of self that were created through the binary.

NOTES

1. Two groups that are particularly aggressive in recent years are white nationalists who have been encouraged by Trump and social justice warriors who have been empowered by new narratives in college curricula. They are equally aggressive in asserting the identity of other races (although often taking opposite positions). In reinvigorating these essentialist notions of race, they seek to deny the rights and dignity of others. While they would be very interesting to run focus groups on, they are outside the scope of this study.

2. I was aware that sometimes groups will speak in unison because of peer pressure.

3. See appendix 1.

4. The limits of this study didn't allow for a set of groups of white populations in Southern states or in more conservative areas where there is a prevalence of more outright racism.

5. She meant to say subjective.

6. Actor Omarosa Manigault.

Coda

A canvasser for Obama in his first run as president told me a story that perfectly encapsulates the paradox of our times as we move forward in our racial thinking but also cling to the binary. She rang the bell and asked the woman at the door where she expected to cast her ballot. The woman yelled to her husband in the back of the house, "Who are we voting for?" He called back, "We're voting for the N*gger."

We are making progress in some ways, enough to elect a black president for two terms, but the way we think about race is still mired in the language and ideology of white supremacy that have been implanted in our minds for generations. As I have shown in chapters 2 and 3, Obama and Dolezal made their idiosyncratic racial choices, which they laid bare in their autobiographies, and showed with precision just how identity can be personal, malleable, and at times, outside of society's rigid structures.

The intricacy of how racial identity is formed, but also interpreted, as illustrated in Hank Willis Thomas's 2012 piece *Baron at the Crossroads* (see figure 7.1).

This work shows a man split down the middle with both his face painted and his body dressed in half white and half black. He is costumed from the minstrel shows of the past in top hat and tails. But unlike these minstrel performers, he is not doing a routine of any kind or engaging with the viewer. In fact, he is lost in thought and reflection, the opposite of the unthinking minstrel. He has his privacy and dignity and reminds us of the man beneath the denigrating caricature. But Willis Thomas goes further by covering this photograph with a film called Lumisty, which is applied to the plexi of the frame and creates a blurred perspective when viewed directly on. To see this image clearly, you must walk back and forth in front of it to catch a moment of visual precision and really see him. In this work of art, the viewers

Figure 7.1 *Baron at the Crossroads* (2012), by Hank Willis Thomas. Unique hand-painted chromogenic print with mixed media.
Source: Hank Willis Thomas (artist) in collaboration with Sanford Biggers, from the series Wayfarer; Publisher: Jack Shainman Gallery, New York.

participate in creating identity by the choices they make in where they look and move. We, the viewers, are always complicit in creating race.

There is no one reading of race, there are no clear rules, there is no one experience, and the binary is a fiction that should be retired like Willis Thomas's tap dancing minstrel who is no longer acting, but seated and human. If we can walk by each other and see that identity is complex and shifts with our perspective, we have a chance to pull aside the curtain of the binary and see each other as fully human.

Appendix 1

Demographic Information Form

Instructions: Please provide a response for each of the following:

1. What is your age? _____
2. What is your sex?
   Female ☐   Male ☐   Trans ☐ _____ ☐
3. What is your marital status?
   Single ☐   Married ☐   Separated ☐   Divorced ☐   Widowed ☐
4. What is your annual income (or combined annual income if you have a spouse)?
   Less than $60,000 ☐ $60,001 to $70,000 ☐ $70,001 to $80,000 ☐
   $80,001 to $90,000 ☐ $90,001 to $100,000 ☐   Greater than $100,000 ☐
5. With which racial or ethnic category do you identify?
   Mixed Race ☐   African American ☐   Asian/Pacific Islander ☐   Caucasian ☐   Latino ☐
   _____
6. With what denomination or faith tradition do you most closely identify_____
7. What time of the day works best for you to attend the focus group? (You will need to come in one day between June 19 and June 23 for approximately one hour.)

   Morning ☐   Afternoon ☐   Early Evening ☐

Appendix 2

Flyer for Focus Groups

PARTICIPANTS NEEDED FOR FOCUS GROUPS TO

Discuss Racial Identity and Fluidity

Dr. Lisa Kingstone, Teaching Fellow on Race and Identity in the Department of International Development at King's College London

Dr. Lisa Kingstone is researching a book on changing ideas about racial identity in American culture drawing upon recent events such as what happened in the case of Rachel Dolezal. Rachel Dolezal was president of the Spokane NAACP and accepted as a black woman until she was outed by her white parents. Some people believe it was her right to "become black" or claim to be transracial. Others felt it was race fraud. Through exploring the recent media controversy over Dolezal, we would love to hear how you determine someone's race and where you draw the boundaries.

To participate in one of our groups, please email _____ at _____
Groups will be held between June 19 and June 23; times TBD
Refreshments will be served

Bibliography

1W Focus Group. Interview by Lisa Kingstone. In person. Hunter College, 2017.

2B Focus Group. Interview by Lisa Kingstone. In person. Riverside Church, NYC, 2017.

2W Focus Group. Interview by Lisa Kingstone. In person. Hunter College, 2017.

3B Focus Group. Interview by Lisa Kingstone. In person. Hunter College, 2017.

3M Focus Group. Interview by Lisa Kingstone. In person. Hunter College, 2017.

3M Focus Group. Interview by Lisa Kingstone. In person. Hunter College, 2017.

ABC News. *"Black-ish": Is a Sitcom Mixing Comedy with Controversy.* Video, 2016. https://www.youtube.com/watch?v=GCeAuO8njJI.

ABC News. *Philando Castile Shooting.* Livestream Video, 2016. https://www.youtube.com/watch?v=p5Pt1nkw3Mk.

Acham, Christine. *Revolution Televised: Prime Time and the Struggle for Black Power.* Minneapolis, MN: University of Minnesota Press, 2005.

Adichie, Chimamanda Ngozi. *Americanah.* New York: Anchor, 2014.

Allen, Theodore W. *The Invention of the White Race: The Origin of Racial Oppression in Anglo-America.* London: Verso, 1997.

Alonso, Mauricio Trujillo. *President Obama Campaign Event at the Apollo Theatre.* Video, 2012. https://www.youtube.com/watch?v=oImKXcEyBfc.

American Anthropological Association. "AAA Statement on Race." May 17, 1998. http://www.americananthro.org/ConnectwithAAA/Content.aspx?ItemNumber=2583.

Ammons, Elizabeth. *Harriet Beecher Stowe's "Uncle Tom's Cabin": A Casebook.* Oxford: Oxford University Press, 2007.

Anderson, Elijah. *The Cosmopolitan Canopy: Race and Civility in Everyday Life.* New York: W. W. Norton, 2011.

Aspinall, P. J, and Miri Song. *Mixed Race Identities.* New York: Palgrave Macmillan, 2013.

Avlon, John. "Scary New GOP Poll." *The Daily Beast*, 2010. http://www.thedailybeast.com/scary-new-gop-poll.

Baker, Houston A. *Blues, Ideology, and Afro-American Literature: A Vernacular Theory*. Chicago: University of Chicago Press, 1984.

Baker, Katie J. M. "A Much-Needed Primer on Cultural Appropriation." *Jezebel. com*, 2018. https://jezebel.com/5959698/a-much-needed-primer-on-cultural-appropriation.

Baldwin, James. *The Fire Next Time*. New York: Dial Press, 1963.

Baldwin, James. "On Being 'White' . . . and Other Lies." In *Black on White: Black Writers on What It Means to Be White*, ed. David R. Roediger, 177–180. New York: Schocken Books, 1998.

Ball, Donald W. "Toward a Sociology of toys: Inanimate Objects, Socialization, and the Demography of the Doll World." *The Sociological Quarterly* 8, no. 4 (1967): 447–458. doi:10.1111/j.1533-8525.1967.tb01081.x.

"Barack Obama and the Myth of a Post-Racial America." *Choice Reviews Online* 51, no. 11 (2014).

Barack Obama Real Cool. Video, 2009. https://www.youtube.com/watch?v=30-1 YueJivk.

"Barbie Launch First Black Doll That Is NOT Just a Painted Version of White Doll." *Mail Online*, 2009. http://www.dailymail.co.uk/news/article-1219257/Barbie-launch-black-doll-look-like-real-people-having-fuller-features.

Barbie the Icon. http://www.mudec.it/eng/barbie. Mudec, 2016.

"Barbie's Makeover: Now Can We Stop Talking About My Body?" *Thenational. Ae*, 2016. http://www.thenational.ae/world/americas/barbies-makeover-now-can-we-stop-talking-about-my-body.

Barreto, Amílcar Antonio, and Richard L O'Bryant. *American Identity in the Age of Obama*. New York: Routledge, 2014.

Barris, Kenya, Njeri Brown, and Devanshi Patel. "The Nod." *Black-ish*, season 1, episode 3, directed by James Griffiths, aired on October 8, 2014 (Burbank, CA: ABC).

Barris, Kenya, Njeri Brown, and Devanshi Patel. "Pilot." *Black-ish*, season 1, episode 1, directed by James Griffiths, aired on September 24, 2014 (Burbank, CA: ABC).

Barris, Kenya, et al. "Switch Hitting." *Black-ish*, season 1, episode 20, directed by Ken Whittingham, aired on April 22, 2015 (Burbank, CA: ABC).

Barris, Kenya, Lisa McQuillan, and Damilare Sonoiki. "The Word." *Black-ish*, season 2, episode 1, directed by Matt Sohn, aired on September 23, 2015 (Burbank, CA: ABC).

Barris, Kenya, and Damilare Sonoiki. "Hope." *Black-ish*, season 2, episode 16, directed by Beth McCarthy-Miller, aired on February 24, 2016 (Burbank, CA: ABC).

Barris, Kenya, Yamara Taylor, and Steven White. "Just Christmas, Baby." *Black-ish*, season 3, episode 10, directed by John Fortenberry, aired on December 14, 2016 (Burbank, CA: ABC).

Barris, Kenya, and Larry Wilmore. "Liberal Arts." *Black-ish*, season 3, episode 23, directed by James Griffiths, aired on May 3, 2017 (Burbank, CA: ABC).

Bastién, Angelica. "Claiming the Future of Black TV." *The Atlantic*, 2017. https://www.theatlantic.com/entertainment/archive/2017/01/claiming-the-future-of-black-tv/514562/.

Becker, Howard S. *Outsiders: Studies in the Sociology of Deviance.* New York: Free Press, 1963.

Beinart, Peter. "Why White People Like Barack Obama." CBS News, 2007. http://www.cbsnews.com/news/why-white-people-like-barack-obama/.

Bernstein, Robin. "Children's Books, Dolls, and the Performance of Race: Or, the Possibility of Children's Literature." *PMLA* 126, no. 1 (2011): 160–169.

Bernstein, Robin. *Racial innocence: Performing American Childhood from Slavery to Civil Rights.* New York: New York University Press, 2012.

Best, Robert, and Marissa Beck. Interview by Lisa Kingstone. Phone, 2017.

Bindman, David, and Henry Louis Gates. *The Image of the Black in Western Art* (series). Cambridge, MA: Harvard University Press, 2011.

Black Demographics. "The African American Middle Class." http://blackdemographics.com/households/middle-class/.

"Black Doll Collecting." Blackdollcollecting.Blogspot.Co.Uk, 2017. http://blackdollcollecting.blogspot.co.uk/.

"Black-ish Will Never Be the Cosby Show . . . and That's Perfect." Truly Tafakari (Blog), 2015. http://www.trulytafakari.com/black-ish-will-never-cosby-show-thats-ok/.

Blake, Meredith. "President Obama Names His Favorite Show of 2015—and No, It's Not 'Homeland.'" *Los Angeles Times*, December 9, 2015. http://www.latimes.com/entertainment/la-et-st-president-obama-favorite-tv-show-the-knick-20151209-story.html.

Bobo, Jacqueline, Cynthia Hudley, and Claudine Michel. *The Black Studies Reader.* New York: Routledge, 2004.

Bogle, Donald. *Toms, Coons, Mulattoes, Mammies and Bucks: An Interpretive History of Blacks in American Films.* 4th ed. New York: Bloomsbury, 2001.

Boone, Jamal. *Barack Obama Michelle Malia Sasha Family Full Interview.* Video, 2008. https://www.youtube.com/watch?v=NLWkPGJmZtA.

Borowitz, Andy, and Borowitz, Susan. "The Fresh Prince Project." *The Fresh Prince of Bel-Air*, season 1, episode 1, directed by Debbie Allen, aired on September 10, 1990 (Los Angeles, CA: NBC).

Boyd, Todd, ed. *African Americans and Popular Culture.* Volume 1: *Theatre, Film and Television.* New York: Praeger, 2010.

Bright, Sheila Pree. "Plastic Bodies." Sheilapreebright. http://www.sheilapreebright.com/gallery.

Brook, Tom. "When White Actors Play Other Races." BBC, 2015. http://www.bbc.co.uk/culture/story/20151006-when-white-actors-play-other-races.

Brooks, David. "Thinking About Obama." *New York Times*, October 17, 2008. http://www.nytimes.com/2008/10/17/opinion/17brooks.html?mcubz=0.

Brownson, Laura. *The Racial Divide.* Video. United States: Netflix, 2018.

Broyard, Bliss. *One Drop: My Father's Hidden Life—A Story of Race and Family Secrets.* New York: Little, Brown, 2007.

Brubaker, Rogers. *Trans: Gender and Race in an Age of Unsettled Identities.* Princeton, NJ: Princeton University Press, 2016.

Brumfield, Ben. "Race of Rachel Dolezal, Head of Spokane NAACP, Comes Under Question." *Edition.Cnn.Com*, 2016. http://edition.cnn.com/2015/06/12/us/washington-spokane-naacp-rachel-dolezal-identity/.

Bunche Center for African American Studies at UCLA. *2015 Hollywood Diversity Report: Flipping the Script*. Los Angeles, 2015.

Calderone, Michael. "Matthews: 'I Forgot He Was Black Tonight for an Hour.'" Politico (Blog), 2010. http://www.politico.com/blogs/michaelcalderone/0110/Matthews_I_forgot_he_was_black_tonight_for_an_hour.html.

Campbell, Alexia Fernández. "Census Was Wrong: 7 Percent of Americans Are Multiracial, Not 2 Percent." *The Atlantic*, June 18, 2015. https://www.theatlantic.com/politics/archive/2015/06/census-was-wrong-7-percent-of-americans-are-multiracial-not-2-percent/432159/.

Capehart, Jonathan. "The Damage Rachel Dolezal Has Done." *Washington Post*, June 12, 2015. https://www.washingtonpost.com/blogs/post-partisan/wp/2015/06/12/the-damage-rachel-dolezal-has-done/.

Carvajal, Doreen. "With Museum Shows in Europe, Barbie Gets Her Moment with the Masters." *New York Times*, March 11, 2016. https://www.nytimes.com/2016/03/11/arts/design/with-museum-shows-in-europe-barbie-gets-her-moment-with-the-masters.html?_r=0.

CBS News, Associated Press. "Mattel Introduces Black Barbies." 2009. https://www.cbsnews.com/news/mattel-introduces-black-barbies/.

CBSN. *2007: Barack Obama*. Video, 2012. http://www.cbsnews.com/videos/2007-barack-obama/.

Chastain, Mary Ann. "Barack, Michelle and Oprah Winfrey, 2008." *New York Daily News*. http://www.nydailynews.com/life-style/relationship-michelle-barack-obama-years-gallery-1.2815893?pmSlide=1.2815881.

Chin, Elizabeth. "Ethnically Correct Dolls: Toying with the Race Industry." *American Anthropologist* 101, no. 2 (1999): 305–321. doi:10.1525/aa.1999.101.2.305.

Chin, Elizabeth. *Purchasing Power: Black Kids and American Consumer Culture*. Minneapolis: University of Minnesota Press, 2001.

Clair, Matthew. "Black Intellectuals and White Audiences." *Public Books*, 2016. http://www.publicbooks.org/black-intellectuals-and-white-audiences/.

Clark, Kenneth B., and Mamie P. Clark. "Emotional Factors in Racial Identification and Preference in Negro Children." *The Journal of Negro Education* 19, no. 3 (1950): 341. doi:10.2307/2966491.

Clark, Kenneth B., and Mamie P. Clark. "Racial Identification Preference in Negro Children." In *Readings in Social Psychology*. New York: Holt, 1947.

CNN. "Obama: Police Who Arrested Professor 'Acted Stupidly.'" July 22, 2009. http://edition.cnn.com/2009/US/07/22/harvard.gates.interview/#cnnSTCText.

Coates, Ta-Nehisi. *Between the World and Me*. New York: Spiegel and Grau, 2015.

Coates, Ta-Nehisi. "Donald Trump Is the First White President." *The Atlantic*, October 2017. https://www.theatlantic.com/magazine/archive/2017/10/the-first-white-president-ta-nehisi-coates/537909/.

Cohn, D'Vera. "It's Official: Minority Babies Are the Majority among the Nation's Infants, but Only Just." Pew Research Center (Blog), June 23, 2016.

Cone, James H. *Black Theology and Black Power*. New York: The Seabury Press, 1969.

Craft, William, and Ellen Craft. *Running a Thousand Miles for Freedom: Or, the Escape of William and Ellen Craft from Slavery*. Cambridge: Cambridge University Press, 2013.

Crow, Charles L. *History of the Gothic: American Gothic*. Cardiff, Wales: University of Wales Press, 2009.

Crowley Coker, Hillary. "When Rachel Dolezal Attended Howard University, She Was Still White." Jezebel.Com, 2015. http://jezebel.com/when-rachel-dolezal-attended-howard-university-she-was-1710941472.

C-SPAN. *Barack Obama Speech at 2004 DNC Convention*. Video, 2008. https://www.youtube.com/watch?v=eWynt87PaJ0.

C-SPAN. *President Obama at 2013 White House Correspondents' Dinner*. Video, 2013. https://www.youtube.com/watch?v=ON2XWvyePH8.

Cuvier, Georges. *The Animal Kingdom Arranged in Conformity with Its Organization*. Translated from French by H. M. Murtrie. New York: G. & C. & H. Carvill, 1831.

The Daily Mail. "Barbie Launch First Black Doll That Is Not Just a Painted Version of a White Doll." 2009. http://www.dailymail.co.uk/news/article-1219257/Barbie-launch-black-doll-look-like-real-people-having-fuller-features.html.

Dalton, Mary M., and Laura R. Linder. *The Sitcom Reader: America Viewed and Skewed*. Albany: State University of New York Press, 2005.

Daniel, G. Reginald. *More Than Black? Multiracial Identity and the New Racial Order*. Philadelphia: Temple University Press, 2002.

Daniel, Reginald G., and Hettie V. Williams. *Race and the Obama Phenomenon: The Vision of a More Perfect Multiracial Union*. Minneapolis: University Press of Mississippi, 2014.

Daniels, Jessie. "Race and Racism in Internet Studies: A Review and Critique." *New Media & Society* 15, no. 5 (August 1, 2013): 695–719. https://doi.org/10.1177/1461444812462849.

Dates, Jannette L., and William Barlow. *Split Image: African Americans in the Mass Media*. Washington, DC: Howard University Press, 1990.

Davis, F. James. *Who Is Black? One Nation's Definition*. University Park: Pennsylvania State University Press, 1991.

Davis, Norma S. *A Lark Ascends: Florence Kate Upton, Artist and Illustrator*. Metuchen, NJ: Scarecrow Press, 1992.

Dawkins, Marcia Alesan. *Clearly Invisible: Racial Passing and the Color of Cultural Identity*. Waco, TX: Baylor University Press, 2012.

de Crèvecoeur Hector, J St. John . *Letters from an American Farmer*. http://xroads.virginia.edu/~hyper/crev/home.html.

Dichter, Ernest. *Ernest Dichter Papers*. Accession 2407. Wilmington, DE: Hagley Museum and Library. Accessed 13 July 2017. http://findingaids.hagley.org/xtf/view?docId=ead/2407.xml.

Dickerson, Debra J. "Colorblind." *Salon*, January 22, 2007. http://www.salon.com/2007/01/22/obama_161/.

Dickerson, Debra J. *The End of Blackness: Returning the Souls of Black Folk to Their Rightful Owners*. New York: Pantheon Books, 2004.

Dolezal, Joshua. *Down from the Mountaintop: From Belief to Belonging*. Iowa City: University of Iowa Press, 2014.

Dolezal, Rachel. *Ebony Tresses*, n.d.

Dolezal, Rachel. Interview by Lisa Kingstone. Skype, June 1, 2017.

Dolezal, Rachel. *Rachel Dolezal, MFA*. 2016. http://racheldolezal.blogspot.co.uk.

Dolezal, Rachel, and Storms Reback. *In Full Color: Finding My Place in a Black and White World*. Dallas, TX: BenBella Books, 2017.

"Doll for Negro Children: New Toy Which Is Anthropologically Correct Fills an Old Need." *Life Magazine*, 1951.

"The Doll Test for Racial Self-Hate: Did It Ever Make Sense?" Theroot.com, 2014. http://www.theroot.com/the-doll-test-for-racial-self-hate-did-it-ever-make-se-1790875716.

Douglass, Frederick. "Mr. Douglass Interviewed." *Washington Post*, January 26, 1884.

Dovidio, John F., and Samuel L. Gaertner. "Aversive Racism." *Advances in Experimental Social Psychology*, 36: 1–52. Academic Press, 2004.

Dreisinger, Baz. *Near Black: White-to-Black Passing in American Culture*. Amherst: University of Massachusetts Press, 2008.

Du Bois, W. E. B. *The Souls of Black Folk*. New York: Pocket Books, 2005.

DuCille, Ann. *Skin Trade*. Cambridge, MA: Harvard University Press, 1996.

Dyson, Michael Eric. *I May Not Get There with You: The True Martin Luther King, Jr*. New York: Free Press, 2000.

Edwards, Erica R. "The Black President Hokum." *American Quarterly* 63, no. 1 (2011): 33–59. doi:10.1353/aq.2011.0013.

Edwards, Rob. "72 Hours." *The Fresh Prince of Bel-Air*, season 1, episode 23, directed by Rae Kraus, aired on March 11, 1991 (Los Angeles, CA: NBC).

Ehrenstein, David. "Obama the 'Magic Negro.'" *Los Angeles Times*, 2007. http://www.latimes.com/la-oe-ehrenstein19mar19-story.html.

Ellis, Trey. "The New Black Aesthetic." *Callaloo* 38 (1989): 233–243.

Ellison, Ralph. "Change the Joke, Slip the Yoke." *American Studies 2001: Introduction to American Studies*. http://amst2001.neatline-uva.org/items/show/1220.

Ellison, Ralph. *Invisible Man*. 2nd ed. New York: Vintage Books, 1995.

Ellison, Ralph. "What America Would Be Like without Blacks." *Time*, 1970. http://teachingamericanhistory.org/library/document/what-america-would-be-like-without-blacks/.

Ellison, Ralph, and John F Callahan. *The Collected Essays of Ralph Ellison*. New York: Modern Library, 1995.

Esrada, Sheryl. "Rachel Dolezal's Replacement Naima Quarles-Burnley Speaks Out." *Diversityinc*, 2015. http://www.diversityinc.com/news/rachel-dolezals-replacement-naima-quarles-burnley-speaks-out/.

Fanon, Frantz. *Black Skin, White Masks*. London: Grove Press, 2008.

Favor, J. Martin. *Authentic Blackness: The Folk in the New Negro Renaissance*. Durham, NC: Duke University Press, 1999.

Fiedler, Leslie A. *Waiting for the End: The American Literary Scene from Hemingway to Baldwin*. London: Jonathan Cape, 1965.

Fields, Karen Elise, and Barbara Jeanne Fields. *Racecraft: The Soul of Inequality in American Life*. New York: Verso, 2012.

Fieldstadt, Elisha, and Lamarre Giselle. "NAACP Chapter President Rachel Dolezal Plans to Address Race Controversy Monday." NBCnews.com, 2015. http://www.nbcnews.com/news/us-news/embattled-naacp-president-rachel-dolezal-will-address-race-controversy-monday-n374986.

Fikes, Robert. "The Passing of Passing: A Peculiarly American Racial Tradition Approaches Irrelevance." Blackpast.Org, 2016. http://www.blackpast.org/perspectives/passing-passing-peculiarly-american-racial-tradition-approaches-irrelevance.

Fisher, Lauren. "A Look Back at Barbie's Evolving Outfits and Professions over the Years." *Harper's Bazaar*, 2017. http://www.harpersbazaar.com/culture/features/g6966/barbie-exhibit-les-arts-decoratifs.

Foeman, Anita. Interview by Lisa Kingstone. Phone, June 20, 2017.

Forbes, Kenyatta. Interview by Lisa Kingstone. Phone, July 24, 2017.

Forman-Brunell, Miriam. "Interrogating the Meanings of Dolls: New Directions in Doll Studies." *Girlhood Studies* 5, no. 1 (2012). doi:10.3167/ghs.2012.050102.

Fredrickson, George M. *White Supremacy: A Comparative Study of American and South African History*. New York: Oxford University Press, 1981.

President Obama and Anger Translator Luther. Video, 2016. https://www.youtube.com/watch?v=EnLyUHexQHQ.

"Gabriela/Girl of the Year/American Girl." Americangirl.com, 2017. http://www.americangirl.com/shop/girl-of-the-year-gabriela/gabriela-ffj89.

Gajanan, Mahita. "Zoe Saldana Faces Criticism over Dark Makeup in Nina Simone Film Trailer." *The Guardian*, 2016. https://www.theguardian.com/music/2016/mar/02/zoe-saldana-nina-simone-black-makeup-film-trailer.

Garber, Megan. "Barbie's Hips Don't Lie." *The Atlantic*, 2016. https://www.theatlantic.com/entertainment/archive/2016/01/barbies-hips-dont-lie/432741/.

Gardner, Lyn. "Colour-Blind Casting: How Far Have We Really Come?" *The Guardian*, 2016. https://www.theguardian.com/stage/theatreblog/2016/jan/13/colour-blind-casting.

Garner, Steve. *Whiteness: An Introduction*. London: Routledge, 2007.

Garrett, Debbie. "Lecture and Sara Lee Doll." November 6, 2017.

Garvey, Amy Jacques. *Garvey and Garveyism*. London: Collier Macmillan, 1970.

Gates, Henry Louis. *The Signifying Monkey*. Oxford: Oxford University Press, 2014.

Gates, Henry Louis, Jr. "TV's Black World Turns—But Stays Unreal." *New York Times*, November 12, 1989. http://www.nytimes.com/1989/11/12/arts/tv-s-black-world-turns-but-stays-unreal.html?pagewanted=all.

Ghartey-Tagoe Kootin, Amma Y. "Lessons in Blackbody Minstrelsy: Old Plantation and the Manufacture of Black Authenticity." *The Drama Review* 57, no. 2 (2013): 102–122.

Ginsberg, Elaine K. *Passing and the Fictions of Identity*. Durham, NC: Duke University Press, 1996.

Givhan, Robin. "First Lady Michelle Obama Serves as Fashion Icon." *Washington Post*, January 21, 2013. https://www.washingtonpost.com/lifestyle/style/first-lady-michelle-obama-serves-as-fashion-icon/2013/01/21/655215dc-6413-11e2-85f5-a8a9228e55e7_story.html?utm_term=.87baa2c7ee68.

Goff, Phillip Atiba, Jennifer L. Eberhardt, Melissa J. Williams, and Matthew Christian Jackson. "Not Yet Human: Implicit Knowledge, Historical Dehumanization, and Contemporary Consequences." *Journal of Personality and Social Psychology* 94, no. 2 (February 2008): 292–306. https://doi.org/10.1037/0022-3514.94.2.292.

Golden, Thelma, and Hamza Walker. *Freestyle*. New York: Studio Museum in Harlem, 2001.

Gordon, Milton M. *Assimilation in American Life: The Role of Race, Religion and National Origins*. New York: Oxford University Press, 1964.

Gossett, Thomas F. *Race: The History of an Idea*. New York: Oxford University Press, 1997.

Gossett, Thomas F. *Uncle Tom's Cabin and American Culture*. Dallas, TX: Southern Methodist University Press, 1985.

Grant, Madison. *The Passing of the Great Race: Or, the Racial Basis of European History*. New York; C. Scribner's Sons, 1922.

Gray, Herman. *Watching Race: Television and the Struggle for Blackness*. Minneapolis: University of Minnesota Press, 2004.

Greenberg, Bradley S., and Kimberly A. Neuendorf. "Black Family Interactions on Television." In *Life on Television: Content Analysis of U.S. TV Drama*, ed. Bradley S. Greenberg, 173–181. Norwood, NJ: ABLEX, 1980.

Griffin, John Howard. *Black Like Me*. San Antonio, TX: Wings Press, 2011.

Griffiths, James. "Liberal Arts." *Black-ish*. ABC, May 3, 2017.

Gross, Ariela J. "Litigating Whiteness: Trials of Racial Determination in the Nineteenth-Century South." *The Yale Law Journal* 108, no. 1 (1998): 109. doi:10.2307/797472.

The Guardian. *Teary Barack Obama Thanks Michelle in Farewell Speech*. Video, 2017. https://www.theguardian.com/us-news/video/2017/jan/11/teary-barack-obama-thanks-michelle-in-farewell-speech-video.

Gubar, Susan. *Racechanges: White Skin, Black Face in American Culture*. New York: Oxford University Press, 1997.

Guerrero, Lisa. "Can the Subaltern Shop? The Commodification of Difference in the Bratz Dolls." *Cultural Studies ↔ Critical Methodologies* 9, no. 2 (2008): 186–196. doi:10.1177/1532708608325939.

Haggins, Bambi. "The Black Situation Comedy." In *African Americans and Popular Culture*. Volume 1: *Theater, Film, and Television*, ed. Todd Boyd, 217–244. Westport, CT: Praeger, 2008.

Hains, Rebecca C. "An Afternoon of Productive Play with Problematic Dolls: The Importance of Foregrounding Children's Voices in Research." *Girlhood Studies* 5, no. 1 (2012). doi:10.3167/ghs.2012.050108.

Hall, Granville Stanley, and Alexander Caswell Ellis. *A Study of Dolls*. New York & Chicago: E.L. Kellogg & Co., 1897. https://catalog.hathitrust.org/Record/006908160.

Hall, Stuart. "What Is This 'Black' in Black Popular Culture?" In *Black Popular Culture*, ed. Gina Dent, Michele Wallace, and Dia Center for the Arts, 21–33. Seattle: Bay Press, 1992.

Hall, Stuart, Jessica Evans, and Sean Nixon. *Representation: Cultural Representations and Signifying Practices*. 2nd ed. London: Sage, 2013.

Harden, Jacalyn Denise. *Double Cross: Japanese Americans in Black and White Chicago*. Minneapolis: University of Minnesota Press, 2003.

Harper, Lisa Sharon. "Black-ish: Reimagining Blackness on Television." *Huffpost*, 2014. http://www.huffingtonpost.com/lisa-sharon-harper/blackish-reimagining-blac_b_6071128.html-please.

Harris, Aisha. "How Black-ish Earned the Right to Call Itself Black-ish." *Slate*, 2015. http://www.slate.com/articles/arts/television/2015/04/black_ish_finale_the_show_s_title_may_be_provocative_but_it_s_not_offensive.html.

Harris, Heather E., Kimberly R. Moffitt, and Catherine R. Squires. *The Obama Effect: Multidisciplinary Renderings of the 2008 Campaign*. Albany: State University of New York Press, 2010.

Hegel, G. W. F. *Phenomenology of Spirit*. Translated by A. V. Miller. Oxford: Oxford University Press, 2013.

Hemingson, David, Njeri Brown, and Devanshi Patel. "Andre from Marseille." *Black-ish*, season 1, episode 14, directed by Phil Traill, aired on February 18, 2015 (Burbank, CA: ABC).

Hendon, Rickey. *Black Enough/White Enough: The Obama Dilemma*. Chicago: Third World Press, 2009.

Henry, Charles P., Robert L. Allen, and Robert Chrisman. *The Obama Phenomenon: Toward a Multiracial Democracy*. Urbana: University of Illinois Press, 2011.

Herrera, Brian. *Latin Numbers: Playing Latino in 20th Century US Popular Performance*. Michigan: University of Michigan Press, 2015.

Herrnstein, Richard J., and Charles A. Murray. *The Bell Curve*. New York: Simon & Schuster, 1996.

Highfield, Roger. "DNA Survey Finds All Humans Are 99.9Pc the Same." *The Telegraph*, 2016. http://www.telegraph.co.uk/news/worldnews/northamerica/usa/1416706/DNA-survey-finds-all-humans-are-99.9pc-the-same.html.

Hill, George H. *Ebony Images: Black Americans and Television*. Carson, CA: Daystar, 1986.

Hix, Lisa. "Black Is Beautiful: Why Black Dolls Matter." *Collectors Weekly*, 2013. http://www.collectorsweekly.com/articles/black-is-beautiful-why-black-dolls-matter/.

Hobbs, Allyson Vanessa. *A Chosen Exile: A History of Racial Passing in American Life*. Cambridge: Harvard University Press, 2014.

Hobson, Laura Z. *Gentleman's Agreement*. New York: Simon & Schuster, 1947.

Hollinger, David A. *Postethnic America: Beyond Multiculturalism*. New York: Basic Books, 1995.

hooks, bell. *Ain't I a Woman: Black Women and Feminism*. 2nd ed. New York: Routledge, 2014.

Hopson, Darlene Powell, and Derek S. Hopson. *Different and Wonderful: Raising Black Children in a Race-Conscious Society*. New York: Prentice Hall Press, 1990.

Horsley, Scott. "Obama Gets in Touch with His Irish Roots." NPR.org, May 23, 2011. https://www.npr.org/2011/05/23/136580099/obama-gets-in-touch-with-his-irish-roots.

Hsu, Hua. "The End of White America?" *The Atlantic*, February 2009. https://www.theatlantic.com/magazine/archive/2009/01/the-end-of-white-america/307208/.

Hunt, Darnell M. *Channeling Blackness: Studies on Television and Race in America*. New York: Oxford University Press, 2005.

Ifill, Gwen. *The Breakthrough: Politics and Race in the Age of Obama*. New York: Doubleday, 2009.

Inniss, Leslie B., and Joe R. Feagin. "The Cosby Show: The View from the Black Middle Class." *Journal of Black Studies* 25, no. 6 (1995): 692–711.

Interview with Dr. Kenneth Clark. Interview by Blackside inc. Radio. Washington University Libraries, Film and Media Archive, Henry Hampton Collection., 1985.

Isenberg, Liz. "'Black-ish' Cast, Larry Wilmore Talk Breaking Down Barriers and Trevor Noah Controversy." *The Hollywood Reporter*, 2015. http://www.hollywoodreporter.com/live-feed/black-ish-cast-larry-wilmore-789922.

Jackson, Kathy Merlock. *Rituals and Patterns in Children's Lives*. Madison: University of Wisconsin Press/Popular Press, 2005.

Japtok, Martin, and Jerry Rafiki Jenkins. *Authentic Blackness "Real" Blackness: Essays on the Meaning of Blackness in Literature and Culture*. New York: Peter Lang, 2011.

Jeff, Selle, and Maureen Dolan. "Black Like Me." Cdapress.com, 2015. http://www.cdapress.com/news/local_news/article_385adfeb-76f3-5050-98b4-d4bf021c423f.html.

Jefferson, Thomas. *Notes on the State of Virginia*. Annotated edition. New York: Penguin Classics, 1998.

Jeffries, Michael P. *Paint the White House Black: Barack Obama and the Meaning of Race in America*. Stanford, CA: Stanford University Press, 2013.

Jhally, Sut, and Justin Lewis. *Enlightened Racism: The Cosby Show, Audiences, and the Myth of the American Dream*. Boulder, CO: Westview Press, 1992.

Johnson, E. Patrick. *Appropriating Blackness: Performance and the Politics of Authenticity*. Durham, NC: Duke University Press, 2003.

Johnson, James Weldon. *The Autobiography of an Ex-Coloured Man*. Mineola, NY: Dover Publications, 1995.

Johnson, Mat, and Warren Pleece. *Incognegro*. London: Titan, 2009.

Jolivette, Andrew J. *Obama and the Biracial Factor: The Battle for a New American Majority*. Bristol, UK: Policy Press, 2012.

Jones, Charisse, and Kumea Shorter-Gooden. *Shifting: The Double Lives of Black Women in America*. HarperCollins e-books, 2009.

Jones, David. "1 Million Strong Against ABC's New Sitcom 'Black-ish.'" Change.org, 2015. https://www.change.org/p/abc-1-million-strong-against-abc-s-new-sitcom-black-ish.

Jones, Lisa. *Bulletproof Diva: Tales of Race, Sex, and Hair*. New York: Anchor Books, 1995.

Jones, Robert P. *The End of White Christian America*. New York: Simon & Schuster, 2016.

Jordan, Winthrop D. *White over Black: American Attitudes Toward the Negro, 1550–1812*. 2nd ed. Chapel Hill: University of North Carolina Press, 2012.

Joyce, Kathryn. "The Homeschool Apostates." *American Prospect Longform*, 2014. http://prospect.org/article/homeschool-apostates.

Julious, Britt. "Hollywood 'Race Casting': What the Industry Is Getting Wrong About Diversity." *The Guardian*, 2015. https://www.theguardian.com/tv-and-radio/tvandradioblog/2015/mar/25/deadlines-race-casting-article-tvs-diversity-wrong.

Keneally, Meghan. "A Timeline of Dolezal's Transition from White to "Black."" ABC News, 2016. http://abcnews.go.com/US/rachel-dolezal-timeline-naacp-leaders-transition-white-black/story?id=31801772.

Kennedy, Randall. *Nigger: The Strange Career of a Troublesome Word*. New York: First Vintage Books, 2002.

Kennedy, Randall. "Racial Passing." *Ohio State Law Journal* 62, no. 1145 (2001).

Kennedy, Randy. "White Artist's Painting of Emmett Till at Whitney Biennial Draws Protests." *New York Times*, March 21, 2017, sec. Art & Design. https://www.nytimes.com/2017/03/21/arts/design/painting-of-emmett-till-at-whitney-biennial-draws-protests.html.

Khaleeli, Homa. "Obama Loves It, Trump Called It Racist: Why Black-ish Is TV's Most Divisive Show." *The Guardian*, February 25, 2017, sec. Television & Radio. http://www.theguardian.com/tv-and-radio/2017/feb/25/series-creator-kenya-barris-on-abc-sitcom-black-ish.

Kim, Eunsun, and Sebastien Falletti. *A Thousand Miles to Freedom: My Escape from North Korea*. New York: St. Martin's Press, 2015.

Kincheloe, Joe L. *White Reign: Deploying Whiteness in America*. New York: St. Martin's Press, 2000.

King, Martin Luther, Jr. "Sermon at Temple Israel of Hollywood." Accessed December 12, 2017.

King, Martin Luther, Jr. *Why We Can't Wait*. New York: Signet, 2000.

King, Richard H. "Becoming Black, Becoming President." *Patterns of Prejudice* 45, nos. 1–2 (2011): 62–85.

Knowles, Samantha M. *Why Do You Have Black Dolls*. DVD, 2012.

Knox, Robert. *The Races of Men: A Fragment*. London: H. Renshaw, 1850.

Koerner, Claudia. "Student Who Posted Rachel Dolezal Interview Wanted Public to See Her 'Be Herself.'" *Buzzfeednews*, 2016. https://www.buzzfeed.com/claudiakoerner/rachel-dolezal-describes-struggles-of-life-as-a-black-woman?utm_term=.wmMW7GYMY#.guy5z7oyo.

Kroeger, Brooke. *Passing: When People Can't Be Who They Are*. New York: PublicAffairs, 2004.

KXLY. *Raw Interview with Rachel Dolezal*. Video, 2015. http://www.kxly.com/news/local-news/spokane/raw-interview-with-rachel-dolezal/164143437.

Larsen, Nella. *Passing*. New York: Penguin Books, 1997.

The Late Show with Stephen Colbert. *Anthony Anderson Explains Black vs. Black-ish*. Video, 2016. https://www.youtube.com/watch?v=2ZdivKBpMqY.

The Late Show with Stephen Colbert. *Laurence Fishburne Talks Oscars, Race & "Black-ish."* Video, 2016. https://www.youtube.com/watch?v=XR4ND0Nu0TA.

The Late Show with Stephen Colbert. *Tracee Ellis Ross: I Believe in a Colorful World*. Video, 2016. https://www.youtube.com/watch?v=e1_x1GV5HSg.

Lazarus, Emma. "The New Colossus." National Park Service, November 2, 1883. https://www.nps.gov/stli/learn/historyculture/colossus.htm.

Leary, Joy DeGruy. *Post Traumatic Slave Syndrome: America's Legacy of Enduring Injury and Healing*. Portland, OR: Uptone Press, 2005.

Lee, Youyoung. "A History of Blackface in Films, in All Its Incarnations." *The Huffington Post*, 2013. http://www.huffingtonpost.com/2013/11/01/history-of-blackface_n_4175051.html.

Leonard, David J., and Lisa Guerrero. *African Americans in Television: Race-ing for Ratings*. Santa Barbara, CA: Praeger, 2013.

Leonard, John. "Leave It to Cosby." *New York Magazine*, 1984.

LeRoy, Justin. *Chasing Daybreak: A Film About Mixed Race in America*. DVD. Mavin Foundation, 2005.

Lerner, Gail, Njeri Brown, and Devanshi Patel. "Black Santa/White Christmas." *Black-ish*, season 1, episode 10, directed by Elliot Hegarty, aired on December 10, 2014 (Burbank, CA: ABC).

Lerner, Gail, and Damilare Sonoiki. "Sink or Swim." *Black-ish*, season 2, episode 14, directed by Michael Schultz, aired on February 10, 2016 (Burbank, CA: ABC).

Lesavage, Halie. "The First-Ever Hijab-Wearing Barbie Is Here, and Ibtihaj Muhammad Is Beyond Excited." *Glamour*, November 13, 2017. https://www.glamour.com/story/first-ever-hijab-wearing-barbie-ibtihaj-muhammad.

Leslie, Mitchell. "The History of Everyone and Everything." Stanford Alumni, 1999. https://alumni.stanford.edu/get/page/magazine/article/?article_id=40759.

Lewis, George. "Barack Hussein Obama: The Use of History in the Creation of an 'American' President." *Patterns of Prejudice* 45, nos. 1–2 (2011): 43–61.

Lilly, Courtney. "The Name Game." *Black-ish*, season 3, episode 14, directed by Gail Lerner, aired on February 8, 2017 (Burbank, CA: ABC).

Linnaeus, Caroli. *Systema Naturae: Sive Regna Tria Naturæ Systematice Proposita Per Classes, Ordines, Genera, & Species*. Leiden: Theodorum Haak, 1735.

Lord, M. G. *Forever Barbie*. New York: Morrow and Co., 1994.

Lott, Eric. *Love and Theft: Blackface Minstrelsy and the American Working Class*. 2nd ed. New York: Oxford University Press, 2013.

Lueger, Michael. "'You Don't Read Latino': Discussing the History of Latinx Casting with Brian Eugenio Herrera." Podcast. *Howlround*, 2016. http://howlround.com/theatre-history-podcast-11-you-don-t-read-latino-discussing-the-history-of-latinx-casting-with-brian.

Lupack, Barbara Tepa. *Literary Adaptations in Black American Cinema*. Rochester, NY: University of Rochester Press, 2010.

Malcolm X, and Alex Haley. *The Autobiography of Malcolm X*. New York: Ballantine Books, 1992.

MacDonald, J. Fred. *Blacks and White TV: African Americans in Television Since 1948*. 2nd ed. Chicago: Nelson-Hall Publishers, 1992.

Mailer, Norman. *The White Negro*. San Francisco: City Lights Books, 1957.

Mathis-Lilley, Ben. "Dolezal Says She's Felt Black from Early Age, Evades Tougher Credibility Questions on Today." *Slate*, 2015. http://www.slate.com/blogs/the_slatest/2015/06/16/rachel_dolezal_today_show_interview_says_she_s_long_felt_black_defends_actions.html.

Matlin, Daniel. *On the Corner: African American Intellectuals and the Urban Crisis*. Cambridge, MA: Harvard University Press, 2013.

Mazama, Ama, and Molefi Kete Asante. *Barack Obama: Political Frontiers and Racial Agency*. Thousand Oaks, CA: CQ Press/SAGE, 2012.

McBride-Irby, Stacey. Interview by Lisa Kingstone. Facebook, June 26, 2017.

McIntosh, Peggy. "White Privilege: Unpacking the Invisible Knapsack." *Peace and Freedom Magazine*, 1989.

Means Coleman, Robin R. *African American Viewers and the Black Situation Comedy: Situating Racial Humor*. New York: Garland, 1998.

Means Coleman, Robin R., and Charlton D. McIlwain. "The Hidden Truths in Black Sitcoms." In *The Sitcom Reader: America Viewed and Skewed*, 2nd edition. New York: SUNY Press, 125–138.

Meiners, Christoph. *Grundriß Der Geschichte Der Menschheit*. Lemgo: Im Verlage der Meyerschen Buchhandlung, 1785.

Merritt, Bishetta, and Carolyn A. Stroman. "Black Family Imagery and Interactions on Television." *Journal of Black Studies* 23, no. 4 (1993): 492–499. doi:10.1177/002193479302300404.

Metzler, Christopher J. "Barack Obama's Faustian Bargain and the Fight for America's Racial Soul." In *Barack Obama: Political Frontiers and Racial Agency*, ed. Ama Mazama and Molefi Kete Asante, 153–166. Thousand Oaks, CA: CQ Press/SAGE, 2012.

Metzler, Christopher J. *The Construction and Rearticulation of Race in a Post-Racial America*. Bloomington, IN: AuthorHouse, 2008.

Metzler, Christopher J. "The Myth of a 'Post-Racial' America: A Global Perspective." Blog. *Diverse: Issues in Higher Education*, 2008. http://diverseeducation.com/article/31083/.

Metzler, Christopher J. "Why Obama Has Not Yet Given Us a 'Post-Racial' America." Your Black Scholar (Blog), 2009. http://yourblackscholar.blogspot.co.uk/2009/05/why-obama-has-not-yet-given-us-post.html?showComment=1355920123124.

"MIBDH: Early Ideal Dolls." Blackdollcollecting.Blogspot.co.uk, 2017. http://blackdollcollecting.blogspot.co.uk/2010/02/mibdh-early-ideal-dolls.html.

Michaels, Walter Benn. "Autobiography of an Ex-White Man." *Transition*, no. 73 (1997): 122. doi:10.2307/2935449.

Mitchell-Kernan, Claudia. "Signifying, Loud-Talking and Marking." In *Signifyin(g), Sanctifyin', and Slam Dunking: A Reader in African American Expressive Culture*, ed. Gena Dagel Caponi, 309–330. Amherst: University of Massachusetts Press, 1999.

"Moments in Black Doll History—Garvey's UNIA Doll Factory." Black Doll Collecting (Blog), 2010. http://blackdollcollecting.blogspot.co.uk/2010/02/moments-in-black-doll-history-garveys.html.

Morrison, Toni. "On the First Black President." *The New Yorker*, October 5, 1998. http://www.newyorker.com/magazine/1998/10/05/comment-6543.

Morrison, Toni. *Playing in the Dark: Whiteness and the Literary Imagination.* Cambridge, MA: Harvard University Press, 2015.

MSNBC. *Rachel Dolezal on Her Connection with the Black Experience.* Video, 2015. http://www.msnbc.com/melissa-harris-perry/watch/rachel-dolezal-on-the-black-experience-465316419576.

Murdoch, Cassie. "It Looks Like Girls Is Going to Have a Black Character After All." Jezebel.com, 2012. http://jezebel.com/5905583/it-looks-like-girls-is-going-to-have-a-black-character-after-all.

Myrdal, Gunnar. *An American Dilemma.* Volume 1: *The Negro Problem and Modern Democracy.* New Brunswick, NJ: Transaction Publishers, 1996.

NBC. *Maya Rudolph Rachel Dolezal Impression. Late Night with Seth Meyers.* Video, 2015. https://www.youtube.com/watch?v=ieowIzQwYvs.

NBC. *Rachel Dolezal: "Nothing About Being White Describes Who I Am."* Video, 2015. http://www.nbcnews.com/video/nightly-news/57506309#57506309.

NBC. *Rachel Dolezal Breaks Her Silence: "I Identify as Black."* Video, 2015. https://www.youtube.com/watch?v=lG9Q2_Hv83k.

Nerad, Julie Cary. *Passing Interest: Racial Passing in US Novels, Memoirs, Television, and Film, 1990–2010.* Albany: State University of New York Press, 2014.

"New Boom in Ethnic Toys." *Ebony*, 1993.

The New York Times. "The Delusions of Rachel Dolezal." 2016. http://www.nytimes.com/2015/06/18/opinion/charles-blow-the-delusions-of-dolezal.html.

The New York Times. "Obama's Father's Day Remarks (Transcript)." 2008. http://www.nytimes.com/2008/06/15/us/politics/15text-obama.html?mcubz=0.

The New York Times. *Obama Inauguration 2013/Barack Obama's Complete 2013 Inauguration Speech. New York Times.* Video, 2013. https://www.youtube.com/watch?v=zncqb-n3zMo.

Newman-Carrasco, Rochelle. Interview by Lisa Kingstone. In person, 2017.

Nguyen, Jenny, and Amanda Koontz Anthony. "Black Authenticity: Defining the Ideals and Expectations in the Construction of 'Real' Blackness." *Sociology Compass* 8, no. 6 (2014): 770–779. doi:10.1111/soc4.12171.

Nickerson, Corey. "40 Acres and a Vote." *Black-ish*, season 3, episode 3, directed by Ken Whittingham, aired on October 5, 2016 (Burbank, CA: ABC).

Nickerson, Corey, Lisa McQuillan, and Damilare Sonoiki. "Churched." *Black-ish*, season 2, episode 5, directed by Victor Nelli Jr., aired on October 21, 2015 (Burbank, CA: ABC).

Nickerson, Corey, et al. "Parental Guidance." *Black-ish*, season 1, episode 16, directed by Michael Schultz, aired on March 4, 2015 (Burbank, CA: ABC).

Nittle, Nadra Kareem. "Donald Trump Has Long History of Racist Remarks and Behavior." ThoughtCo, October 3, 2017. https://www.thoughtco.com/trump-long-history-racist-remarksbehavior-2834550.

Nobles, Melissa. *Shades of Citizenship: Race and the Census in Modern Politics.* Stanford, CA: Stanford University Press, 2000.

North, Michael. *The Dialect of Modernism: Race, Language, and Twentieth-Century Literature.* New York: Oxford University Press, 1994.

NPR. "WATCH: In Interview, Rachel Dolezal Admits She Was Born White." Image, 2015. http://www.npr.org/sections/thetwo-way/2015/11/03/454318619/watch-in-interview-rachel-dolezal-admits-she-was-born-white.

Nussbaum, Emily. "'Black-ish' Transforms the Family Sitcom." *The New Yorker*, 2016. http://www.newyorker.com/magazine/2016/04/25/black-ish-transforms-the-family-sitcom.

Nussbaum, Emily. "In Living Color: With 'Black-ish,' Kenya Barris Rethinks the Family Sitcom." *The New Yorker*, 2016. http://www.newyorker.com/magazine/2016/04/25/black-ish-transforms-the-family-sitcom.

Obama, Barack. *The Audacity of Hope: Thoughts on Reclaiming the American Dream.* New York: Crown Publishers, 2006.

Obama, Barack. *Dreams from My Father: A Story of Race and Inheritance.* Edinburgh: Canongate, 2009.

O'Connor, Flannery. *A Good Man Is Hard to Find and Other Stories.* New York: Harcourt Brace Jovanovich, 1977.

Omi, Michael, and Howard Winant. *Racial Formation in the United States: From the 1960s to the 1990s.* New York: Routledge, 1994.

Orbe, Mark P. *Communication Realities in a "Post-Racial" Society: What the U.S. Public Really Thinks About Barack Obama.* Lanham, MD: Lexington Books, 2011.

Painter, Nell Irvin. *Southern History Across the Color Line.* Chapel Hill: The University of North Carolina Press, 2013.

Painter, Nell Irvin. "What Is Whiteness?" *New York Times*, June 20, 2015, sec. Opinion. https://www.nytimes.com/2015/06/21/opinion/sunday/what-is-whiteness.html.

Pao, Angela Chia-yi. *No Safe Spaces: Re-Casting Race, Ethnicity, and Nationality in American Theater.* Ann Arbor: University of Michigan Press, 2010.

"Parents: Rachel Dolezal Being Dishonest, Deceptive." *Edition.Cnn*, 2015. http://edition.cnn.com/videos/us/2015/06/12/naacp-rachel-dolezal-race-parents-full-intvu-ath.cnn/video/playlists/naacp-rachel-dolezal-race-controversy/.

Pauker, Kristen. "Intergroup Social Perception Lab." http://manoa.hawaii.edu/isplab/.

Peck, Raoul. *I Am Not Your Negro.* DVD. Velvet Film, 2017.

Phillips, Tracy. "Anthony Anderson on Throwing Bro Mitzvahs, Being "Black-ish" & Pushing the Envelope." *Biography*, 2014. https://www.biography.com/news/black-ish-anthony-anderson-interview.

"Play Stuff Blog: The Other Sara Lee: A Doll Story." Museumofplay.org, 2017. http://www.museumofplay.org/blog/play-stuff/2013/04/the-other-sara-lee-a-doll-story/.

Porter, Judith D. R. *Black Child, White Child: The Development of Racial Attitudes.* Cambridge, MA: Harvard University Press, 1971.

Powers, Kelly. "Data for Barbie Chapter." Email, 2017.

Preston, Mark. "Reid Apologizes for Racial Remarks About Obama During Campaign." CNN, 2010. http://edition.cnn.com/2010/POLITICS/01/09/obama.reid/index.html.

Rachel Dolezal Isn't the Only One Doing Black Face. Video, 2015. https://www.youtube.com/watch?v=b-rVbRefE8U.

"The Racial Draft." Chappelle's Show, 2004. https://vimeo.com/61499874.

Rand, Erica. *Barbie's Queer Accessories.* Durham, NC: Duke University Press, 1995.

Rankine, Claudia. *Citizen: An American Lyric.* Minneapolis, MN: Graywolf Press, 2014.

Raskin, Donna. "The Michelle Obama Arm Workout." https://www.fitnessmagazine.com/workout/arms/exercises/how-to-get-michelle-obamas-arms-the-workout-plan/.

Rastogi, Nina. "'Please Submit All Ethnicities': The Tricky Business of Writing Casting Notices." *Slate Magazine*, 2012. http://www.slate.com/articles/arts/culturebox/2012/07/casting_and_race_the_tricky_business_of_writing_casting_notices.html.

Raynor, Sharon. "My First Black Barbie: Transforming the Image." Journals.Sagepub.Com, 2008. http://journals.sagepub.com/doi/abs/10.1177/1532708608326607.

Redcay, Anna. "Dependent States: The Child's Part in Nineteenth-Century American Culture by Karen Sánchez-Eppler." *Critical Quarterly* 51, no. 1 (2009): 139–146. doi:10.1111/j.1467-8705.2009.01841.x.

Reed, Ishmael. *Barack Obama and the Jim Crow Media: The Return of the Nigger Breakers.* Montreal: Baraka Books, 2010.

Reifowitz, Ian. *Obama's America: A Transformative Vision of Our National Identity.* Washington, DC: Potomac Books, 2012.

Remnick, David. *The Bridge: The Life and Rise of Barack Obama.* New York: Alfred A. Knopf, 2010.

"Response Re: Rachel Dolezal.'" Spokanenaacp.com, 2015. http://spokanenaacp.com/crisis-communication/.

Reynolds, David S. *Mightier than the Sword: Uncle Tom's Cabin and the Battle for America.* W. W. Norton, 2011.

Riggs, Marlon. *Black Is . . . Black Ain't.* DVD. Independent Television Service, 1994.

Robinson, Amy. "To Pass in Drag: Strategies of Entrance into the Visible." PhD diss., University of Pennsylvania, 1993.

Robinson, Eugene. *Disintegration: The Splintering of Black America.* New York: Doubleday, 2010.

Rockquemore, Kerry, and David L Brunsma. *Beyond Black: Biracial Identity in America.* Thousand Oaks, CA: Sage, 2002.

Roediger, David R. *Black on White: Black Writers on What It Means to Be White.* New York: Schocken Books, 1998.

Roediger, David R. *The Wages of Whiteness: Race and the Making of the American Working Class.* London: Verso, 1991.

Rogers, Mary F. *Barbie Culture.* London: Sage, 1998.

Rogin, Michael. *Blackface, White Noise: Jewish Immigrants in the Hollywood Melting Pot.* Berkeley: University of California Press, 1996.

Rosenblatt, Roger. "A Nation of Pained Hearts." *Time*, 1995. http://content.time.com/time/subscriber/article/0,33009,983568,00.html.

Ross, India. "TV in Black and White." *The Financial Times*, 2015. https://www.ft.com/content/1c29db44-e4e8-11e4-bb4b-00144feab7de.

Rothenberg, Paula S. *Race, Class, and Gender in the United States*. New York: St. Martin's Press, 1998.

Saji, Peter. "Who's Afraid of the Big Black Man?" *Black-ish*, season 3, episode 4, directed by Matt Sohn, aired on October 12, 2016 (Burbank, CA: ABC).

Saji, Peter, Njeri Brown, and Devanshi Patel. "The Gift of Hunger." *Black-ish*, season 1, episode 7, directed by Victor Neill Jr., aired on November 12, 2014 (Burbank, CA: ABC).

Saji, Peter, and Damilare Sonoiki. "Twindependence." *Black-ish*, season 2, episode 15, directed by Michael Spiller, aired on February 17, 2016 (Burbank, CA: ABC).

Samuels, Allison. "Rachel Dolezal's True Lies." *Vanity Fair*, 2015. http://www.vanityfair.com/news/2015/07/rachel-dolezal-new-interview-pictures-exclusive.

Sánchez, María Carla, and Linda Schlossberg. *Passing: Identity and Interpretation in Sexuality, Race, and Religion*. New York: New York University Press, 2001.

Sanchez, Raf, and Peter Foster. "'You Rape Our Women and Are Taking over Our Country.'" Charleston Church Gunman told Black Victims, 2016. http://www.telegraph.co.uk/news/worldnews/northamerica/usa/11684957/You-rape-our-women-and-are-taking-over-our-country-Charleston-church-gunman-told-black-victims.html.

Scafidi, Susan. *Who Owns Culture? Appropriation and Authenticity in American Law*. New Brunswick, NJ: Rutgers University Press, 2005.

Schorn, Daniel. "Transcript Excerpt: Sen. Barack Obama. Read a Transcript Excerpt of Steve Kroft's Interview with Sen. Obama." CBS News, 2007. http://www.cbsnews.com/news/transcript-excerpt-sen-barack-obama/5/.

Scott, Daryl Michael. *Contempt and Pity: Social Policy and the Image of the Damaged Black Psyche, 1880–1996*. Chapel Hill: University of North Carolina Press, 1997.

Scott, Janny. "In 2000, Streetwise Veteran Schooled a Bold Young Obama." *New York Times*, 2007. http://www.nytimes.com/2007/09/09/us/politics/09obama.html.

Selle, Jeff, and Maureen Dolan. "'Black Like Me.'" Cdapress.com, 2015. http://www.cdapress.com/news/local_news/article_385adfeb-76f3-5050-98b4-d4bf021c423f.htm.

Senna, Danzy. *Caucasia*. New York: Riverhead Books, 1998.

Shepard, Devon. "Blood Is Thicker than Mud." *The Fresh Prince of Bel-Air*, season 4, episode 8, directed by Chuck Vinson, aired on November 1, 1993 (Burbank, CA: NBC).

Shockley, Lindsey, et al. "Martin Luther Skiing Day." *Black-ish*, season 1, episode 12, directed by Stuart McDonald, aired on January 14, 2015 (Burbank, CA: ABC).

Shriver, Lionel. "Lionel Shriver's Full Speech: 'I Hope the Concept of Cultural Appropriation Is a Passing Fad.'" *The Guardian*, 2016. https://www.theguardian.com/commentisfree/2016/sep/13/lionel-shrivers-full-speech-i-hope-the-concept-of-cultural-appropriation-is-a-passing-fad.

Smith Bryant, June. "More Dolls of Color." *Black Enterprise*, 1991.

Smith, Zadie. "Speaking in Tongues." *The New York Review of Books*, 2009. http://www.nybooks.com/articles/2009/02/26/speaking-in-tongues-2/.

Sollors, Werner. *The Invention of Ethnicity*. New York: Oxford University Press, 1989.

Sollors, Werner. *Neither Black nor White Yet Both: Thematic Explorations of Interracial Literature*. Oxford: Oxford University Press, 1997.

"Speaking of People: Kitty Black Perkins." *Ebony*, 1992.

Squires, Catherine R. *African Americans and the Media*. Cambridge, UK: Polity, 2009.

Steele, Shelby. *A Bound Man: Why We Are Excited About Obama and Why He Can't Win*. New York: Free Press, 2008.

Stephens, Gregory. *On Racial Frontiers: The New Culture of Frederick Douglass, Ralph Ellison, and Bob Marley*. Cambridge: Cambridge University Press, 1999.

Stevens, Michelle. "Black Comedians Poke Fun at Racial Stereotypes." *Psychology Today*, 2015. https://www.psychologytoday.com/blog/contemporary-psychoanalysis-in-action/201505/black-comedians-poke-fun-racial-stereotypes.

Stoddard, Lothrop, *The Rising Tide of Color Against White World Supremacy*. New York: Charles Scribner's Sons, 1921.

Stowe, Harriet Beecher. *Uncle Tom's Cabin*. New York: W. W. Norton, 1994.

"Study: White and Black Children Biased Toward Lighter Skin—CNN.com." Edition.Cnn.Com, 2010. http://edition.cnn.com/2010/US/05/13/doll.study/.

Sundquist, Eric J. *New Essays on Uncle Tom's Cabin*. Cambridge: ProQuest Information and Learning, 2000.

Sykes, Bryan. *The Seven Daughters of Eve: The Science That Reveals Our Genetic Ancestry*. Reprint edition. New York: W. W. Norton, 2002.

Talbot, Margaret. "Little Hotties." *The New Yorker*, 2006. http://www.newyorker.com/magazine/2006/12/04/little-hotties.

TEDx Talks. *Using Ancestry DNA to Explore Our Humanness: Anita Foeman at TEDxWestChester*. Video, 2014. https://www.youtube.com/watch?v=5HRTZVVyJC8.

Tesler, Michael, and David O Sears. *Obama's Race: The 2008 Election and the Dream of a Post-Racial America*. Chicago: University of Chicago Press, 2010.

Thai, Xuan, and Ted Barrett. "Biden's Description of Obama Draws Scrutiny." CNN, 2007. http://edition.cnn.com/2007/POLITICS/01/31/biden.obama/.

Thomas, Sabrina Lynette. "Sara Lee: The Rise and Fall of the Ultimate Negro Doll." *Transforming Anthropology* 15, no. 1 (2007): 38–49. doi:10.1525/tran.2007.15.1.38.

Thompson, Krissah. "Michelle Obama's Posterior Again the Subject of a Public Rant." *Washington Post*, February 4, 2013, sec. Style. https://www.washingtonpost.com/lifestyle/style/michelle-obamas-posterior-again-the-subject-of-a-public-rant/2013/02/04/c119c9a8-6efb-11e2-aa58-243de81040ba_story.html.

Thomson, Helen. "Study of Holocaust Survivors Finds Trauma Passed on to Children's Genes." *The Guardian*, August 21, 2015, sec. Science. http://www.theguardian.com/science/2015/aug/21/study-of-holocaust-survivors-finds-trauma-passed-on-to-childrens-genes.

Thorp, Brandon K. "What Does the Academy Value in a Black Performance?" 2016. http://www.nytimes.com/2016/02/21/movies/what-does-the-academy-value-in-a-black-performance.html?em_pos=large&emc=edit_nn_20160223&nl=morning-briefing&nlid=71521150&_r=0.

"Topsy-Turvy A.K.A. Topsy-Turvey, Double Doll, Two-Sided Doll." Black Doll Collecting (blog), 2013. http://blackdollcollecting.blogspot.co.uk/2013/04/topsy-turvy-aka-topsy-turvey-double.html.

Touré. *Who's Afraid of Post-Blackness?: What It Means to Be Black Now*. New York: Free Press, 2011.

TPM. *Obama: "If I Had a Son, He Would Look Like Trayvon."* Video, 2012. https://www.youtube.com/watch?v=wAPtUfOs7Gs.

Tucker, William H. *The Science and Politics of Racial Research*. Urbana: University of Illinois Press, 1994.

Tuvel, Rebecca. "In Defense of Transracialism." *Hypatia* 32, no. 2 (2017): 263–278. doi:10.1111/hypa.12327.

Twain, Mark. *The Tragedy of Pudd'nhead Wilson: And, the Comedy, Those Extraordinary Twins*. New York: Oxford University Press, 1996.

US Census Bureau. "Race." 2013. http://www.census.gov/topics/population/race/about.html.

Using Ancestry DNA to Explore Our Humanness: Anita Foeman at TEDxWestChester. https://www.youtube.com/watch?v=5HRTZVVyJC8.

Van Vechten, Carl. *Nigger Heaven*. Urbana: University of Illinois Press, 2000.

Velasquez-Manoff, Moises. "What Biracial People Know." *New York Times*, 2017. https://www.nytimes.com/2017/03/04/opinion/sunday/what-biracial-people-know.html?rref=collection%2Fcolumn%2Fmoises-velasquez-manoff&action=click&contentCollection=opinion&region=stream&module=stream_unit&version=latest&contentPlacement=4&pgtype=collection.

von Coudenhove-Kalergi, Richard. *Practical Idealism*. Vienna, 1925.

Wade, Lisa. "Ann Ducille on 'Ethnic' Barbies—Sociological Images." Thesocietypages.org, 2008. https://thesocietypages.org/socimages/2008/10/27/ann-ducille-on-ethnic-barbies/.

Wade-Currie, Adon. "The Receptivity of Black Audiences to Progressive Black-Television." *Dean James E. McLeod Freshman Writing Prize*, 2016. http://openscholarship.wustl.edu/mcleod/2/

Wald, Gayle. *Crossing the Line: Racial Passing in Twentieth-Century U.S. Literature and Culture*. Durham, NC: Duke University Press, 2000.

Ware, Diedre A. "How My Dolls Helped Me Understand Segregation." *The Huffington Post*, 2013. http://www.huffingtonpost.com/diedre-a-ware/black-dolls_b_2741845.html?utm_hp_ref=tw.

Ware, Diedre A. "Treasured Memories: My Childhood Bond with Dolls." *The Huffington Post*, 2013. http://www.huffingtonpost.com/diedre-a-ware/black-dolls_b_2741845.html.

Warner, Kristen Jamaya. "Colorblind TV: Primetime Politics of Race in Television Casting." University of Texas Press at Austin, 2010. https://repositories.lib.utexas.edu/handle/2152/ETD-UT-2010-08-1687.

Warner, Kristen J. *The Cultural Politics of Colorblind TV Casting.* New York: Routledge, 2015.

West, Cornel. *Race Matters.* Boston: Beacon Press, 2001.

Wetterberg, Lyndsey Lynn. "Deconstructing 'Chappelle's Show': Race, Masculinity, and Comedy as Resistance." MA thesis, Minnesota State University, 2012.

Whitaker, Mark. "Blackness, 'Black-ish' and 'The Cosby Show': How Cliff Huxtable Changed American Culture." *Time*, 2014. http://time.com/3388134/black-ish-cosby-show-cliff-huxtable-american-culture/.

Wilkinson, Doris Y. "The Doll Exhibit: A Psycho-Cultural Analysis of Black Female Role Stereotypes." *The Journal of Popular Culture* 21, no. 2 (1987): 19–30. doi:10.1111/j.0022-3840.1987.2102_19.x.

Wilkinson, Doris Y. "Racial Socialization Through Children's Toys: A Sociohistorical Examination." *Journal of Black Studies* 5 (1974): 96–109.

Williams, Brennan. "'Black-ish' Creator Kenya Barris Defines New Show and Responds to Critics." *The Huffington Post*, 2014. http://www.huffingtonpost.com/2014/08/29/black-ish-kenya-barris-critics-_n_5737966.html.

Williams, Juan. "Black Voters Aren't Fully Sold on Obama." NPR, 2007. http://www.npr.org/templates/story/story.php?storyId=7299432.

Williams, Linda. *Playing the Race Card: Melodramas of Black and White from Uncle Tom to O.J. Simpson.* Princeton, NJ: Princeton University Press, 2001.

Wilson, David C., and Matthew O. Hunt. "The First Black President?: Cross-Racial Perceptions of Barack Obama's Race." In *American Identity in the Age of Obama*, ed. Amílcar Antonio Barreto and Richard L. O'Bryant, 222–244. New York: Routledge, 2014.

Wilson, John K. *Barack Obama: This Improbable Quest.* Boulder, CO: Paradigm, 2009.

Winfrey Harris, Tamara. "Black Like Who? Rachel Dolezal's Harmful Masquerade." *New York Times*, 2016. http://www.nytimes.com/2015/06/16/opinion/rachel-dolezals-harmful-masquerade.html?_r=0.

Wingfield, Adia Harvey, and Joe R. Feagin. *Yes We Can?: White Racial Framing and the Obama Presidency.* 2nd ed. London: Routledge, 2013.

Winsor, Morgan. "'Is Rachel Dolezal White or Black? Africana Studies Colleague, NAACP Respond to Controversy.'" Ibtimes.com, 2015. http://www.ibtimes.com/rachel-dolezal-white-or-black-africana-studies-colleague-naacp-respond-controversy-1964994.

Wright, Richard. *Black Boy: A Record of Childhood and Youth.* New York: Harper & Bros., 1945.

Wyche, Steve. "Colin Kaepernick Explains Why He Sat During National Anthem." NFL.com, August 27, 2016. http://www.nfl.com/news/story/0ap3000000691077/article/colin-kaepernick-explains-why-he-sat-during-national-anthem.

Yancy, George, and Feagin, Joe. "American Racism in the 'White Frame.'" *New York Times*, July 27, 2015. //opinionator.blogs.nytimes.com/2015/07/27/american-racism-in-the-white-frame/.

Yang, Jeff. "ASIAN POP/Could Obama Be the First Asian American President?" *San Francisco Chronicle*, 2008. http://www.sfgate.com/entertainment/article/ASIAN-POP-Could-Obama-be-the-first-Asian-2481103.php.

Yoshinaga, Kendra. "Babies of Color Are Now the Majority, Census Says." NPR, 2016. http://www.npr.org/sections/ed/2016/07/01/484325664/babies-of-color-are-now-the-majority-census-says.

Zangwill, Israel. *The Melting Pot Drama in Four Acts*. Whitefish, MT: Kessinger Publishing, 2010.

Zeldis McDonough, Yona, ed. *The Barbie Chronicles: A Living Doll Turns Forty*. New York: Simon & Schuster, 1999.

Zimmer, Carl. "Black? White? A Murky Distinction Grows Still Murkier." 2014. http://www.nytimes.com/2014/12/25/science/23andme-genetic-ethnicity-study.html?_r=1.

Zook, Kristal Brent. *Color by Fox: The Fox Network and the Revolution in Black Television*. New York: Oxford University Press, 1999.

Index

About the Author

Lisa Simone Kingstone is Senior Teaching Fellow in the Department of International Development at King's College London. She has a BA from Barnard College, an MA from Columbia University, and a PhD from the University of Massachusetts at Amherst in English Literature. Before coming to King's, she taught English Literature at the University of Connecticiut and worked as a professional journalist. Her work has appeared in a variety of publications.